W9-BAI-252

Date: 2/4/13

973.923 PAT
Patterson, James T.
The eve of destruction : how
1965 transformed America /

PALM BEACH COUNTY
LIBRARY SYSTEM
3650 SUMMIT BLVD.
WEST PALM BEACH, FL 33406

MORE ADVANCE PRAISE FOR

THE EVE OF DESTRUCTION

"Smart, thoughtful, fast-paced, engaging, and insightful—these are just a few of the adjectives that describe James T. Patterson's masterful new book, *The Eve of Destruction*. Patterson makes a convincing case that you cannot understand America today without coming to terms with this eventful, and in some cases, tragic, year."

—STEVEN M. GILLON, Scholar-in-Residence,
The History Channel

"Based on rich learning and resonant with thoughtful interpretations, this incisive and lucid book does more than identify a point of inflection. Its fascinating chronicle captures and explains how a configuration of racial and social change, popular culture, robust legislative action, and a fierce and often brutal war as well as unrest at home decisively altered the vectors of American life in ways that simply had not been anticipated just before 1965."

—IRA KATZNELSON, Ruggles Professor of
Political Science and History, Columbia University

"While in many respects 1965 was a very good year—the Voting Rights Act, Head Start, and Medicare come quickly to mind—trouble lay ahead. The civil rights coalition was starting to unravel just as the specter of Vietnam loomed large on the horizon. In this illuminating, absorbing, page-turner of a book, James T. Patterson makes the case that 'After 1965, for better and for worse, . . . the United States would never be the same again.'"

—John Dittmer, author of *Local People:
The Struggle for Civil Rights in Mississippi*

THE EVE OF DESTRUCTION

Also by James T. Patterson

Freedom Is Not Enough: The Moynihan Report and America's Struggle over Black Family Life from LBJ to Obama

Restless Giant: The United States from Watergate to Bush v. Gore

Brown v. Board of Education

Grand Expectations: The United States, 1945–1974

America's Struggle Against Poverty in the Twentieth Century

The Dread Disease: Cancer and Modern American Culture

The
EVE *of*

DESTRUCTION

How 1965 Transformed America

JAMES T. PATTERSON

BASIC BOOKS
A MEMBER OF THE PERSEUS BOOKS GROUP
NEW YORK

Copyright © 2012 by James T. Patterson

Published by Basic Books, A Member of the Perseus Books Group

All rights reserved. Printed in the United States of America. No part of
this book may be reproduced in any manner whatsoever without written
permission except in the case of brief quotations embodied in critical articles
and reviews. For information, address Basic Books, 250 West 57th Street,
New York, NY 10107.

Books published by Basic Books are available at special discounts for bulk
purchases in the United States by corporations, institutions, and other
organizations. For more information, please contact the Special Markets
Department at the Perseus Books Group, 2300 Chestnut Street, Suite 200,
Philadelphia, PA 19103, or call (800) 810-4145, ext. 5000, or e-mail
special.markets@perseusbooks.com.

Designed by Linda Mark

Library of Congress Cataloging-in-Publication Data
    Patterson, James T.
    The eve of destruction : how 1965 transformed America / James T. Patterson.
        p. cm.
    Includes index.
    ISBN 978-0-465-01358-6 (hardcover : alk. paper)—ISBN 978-0-465-03348-5
(e-book) 1. United States—History—1961–1969. 2. United States—Politics and
government—1963–1969. 3. United States—Social conditions—1960–1980.
4. Vietnam War, 1961–1975—United States. I. Title.

E846.P37 2012
973.923—dc23
                                                              2012033786

10 9 8 7 6 5 4 3 2 1

*To Luther Spoehr, Tom Roberts, and David Hilliard—
good friends whose comments and criticisms of earlier
drafts greatly improved this book*

CONTENTS

PREFACE

1965: Hinge for the Sixties

WHEN PRESIDENT LYNDON B. JOHNSON TURNED ON THE LIGHTS of the National Christmas Tree on the evening of December 18, 1964, he had reason to be concerned about the state of the nation. The assassination of President John F. Kennedy thirteen months earlier still haunted the country. Troubles were mounting in Vietnam. But LBJ was optimistic about the future and understandably so. In June he had signed the historic Civil Rights Act, which guaranteed a bundle of rights, notably equal access to public accommodations, that would end legal segregation in America. In November he had trounced Barry Goldwater to win a full term as president. The economy was booming as never before. With his wife, Lady Bird, his daughters, Luci and Lynda, Vice President–elect Hubert Humphrey, and various ambassadors at his side, Johnson pressed a button to illuminate five thousand red bulbs on the seventy-two-foot tree.

"These are the most hopeful times in all the years since Christ was born in Bethlehem," he exclaimed. He added, "Today—as never before—man has in his possession the capacities to end war and preserve peace, to eradicate poverty and share abundance, to overcome the diseases that have afflicted the human race and permit all mankind to enjoy their promise in life on this earth."[1]

Many contemporary observers, caught up in the triumphalism of the time, echoed Johnson's confidence about America's prospects and the likelihood of enacting a socially progressive agenda. The political scientist James MacGregor Burns declared, "this is as surely a liberal epoch as the late 19th Century was a conservative one." James Reston, chief political columnist for the *New York Times*, wrote on January 1 that the nation was entering an "Era of Good Feelings." *Time* magazine gushed a month later that America was "On the Fringe of a Golden Era."[2]

Responding to such aspirations, Congress in 1965 would approve an avalanche of Johnson's proposals for a "Great Society"—among them a path-breaking Elementary and Secondary Education Act, Medicare and Medicaid, a powerful Voting Rights Act, and long overdue immigration reform. Meanwhile, the economy continued to flourish. Crime rates and unemployment remained low, marriage rates and male labor force participation high. Detroit-made automobiles ruled the world. By early August, when most of Johnson's Great Society laws had been signed, American liberalism was riding at an all-time high tide—a crest that has not been equaled since that time.

By mid-summer, however, the pervasive optimism of late 1964 and early 1965 was already ebbing. Starting in January, divisions among civil rights advocates widened during angry demonstrations in Selma, Alabama. In early February, LBJ responded to a bloody Vietcong attack on American soldiers at Pleiku by ordering the bombing of North Vietnam. A month later, combat marines splashed ashore at Danang. By late April, antiwar activists, blaming a less than forthright LBJ for opening up a "credibility gap," were staging widely noted protests.

On July 28, Johnson announced another, far larger escalation of the war. A little later, five days after passage of the Voting Rights Act, angry blacks erupted violently in the Watts region of Los Angeles. By October, small but rising numbers of opponents of the Vietnam War were burning draft cards, enraging prowar advocates, and causing confrontations and standoffs. By autumn, rock musicians—one, Barry McGuire, sang "Eve of Destruction," a top hit—were bewailing the materialism, militarism, and racism of American society, even as Republicans, having recovered from the debacle of the 1964 election, were girding up for what they expected would be political triumphs in 1966.

Many Americans, stunned by these pivotal events, have subsequently identified 1965—the year of military escalation, of Watts, of the splintering of the civil rights movement, and of mounting cultural change and polarization—as the time when America's social cohesion began to unravel and when the turbulent phenomenon that would be called "the Sixties" broke into view. They were right to see 1965 as a year of exceptionally rapid and widespread change, though by no means was all of it for the worse. The tumultuous times that erupted in 1965 and that lasted into the early 1970s differed greatly from the early 1960s, which, for the most part, were years of political and social consensus that resembled the 1950s.

A number of writers since that time have also identified 1965 as a pivotal year in American life, the year that the 1960s became the Sixties. Richard Goodwin, who was LBJ's chief speechwriter in 1965, reflected in 1988, "In the single year of 1965—100 years after Appomattox—Lyndon Johnson reached the height of his leadership and set in motion the process of decline." Nicholas Lemann, a prominent journalist, observed in 1991 that "the 1960s turned as if on a hinge" in the summer of 1965. The columnist George Will, writing in 1995, commented, "rarely has there been a year eventful in the way 1965 was." He, too, liked the "hinge" metaphor. "That year," he concluded, "was the hinge of our postwar history."[3] Luc Sante, a writer and cultural critic, added in 2006, "I think Western culture, in the broadest sense of that term, hit some sort of peak around 1965, '66, lost it soon thereafter and has not re-attained that level since."[4]

Sante and others are correct to recognize that battles for reforms and entitlements—racial equality, a wide range of personal choices, freedoms, and rights—intensified considerably in 1965 and led to large and lasting changes. The Sixties that ensued by no means demolished all the liberal advances of 1965—many of them driven into legislation by President Johnson, a masterful congressional manager who is the commanding figure in this book. But the unrest besetting the nation as of late 1965 unnerved many people who lived through it and who have viewed it in hindsight as a pivotal time. Conservatives, shaken by the pace of change, sensed that an inexorably expanding rights-consciousness—a "rights revolution"—was undermining a durable and long-cherished culture of rules and responsibilities, and they were quick—even in 1965—to voice their fears. One such anguished observer was former president Dwight Eisenhower, who wrote a friend in October, "Lack of respect for law, laxness in dress, appearance and thinking, in conduct and in manner, as well as student and other riots with civil disobedience all spring from a common source: a lack of concern for the ancient virtues of decency, respect for law and elders, and old-fashioned patriotism."[5]

Other conservatives have subsequently expressed even greater alarm. House speaker Newt Gingrich, bewailing the disappearance in 1965—as he saw it—of America's pioneer values, lamented in 1995: "From the arrival of English-speaking colonists in 1607 until 1965, there was one continuous civilization built around a set of commonly accepted legal and cultural principles. . . . Since 1965, however, there has been a calculated effort by cultural elites to discredit this civilization and replace it with a culture of irresponsibility that is incompatible with American freedoms as we have known them."[6]

I TURNED THIRTY IN EARLY 1965, AT WHICH TIME I WAS A FIRST-YEAR assistant professor of US history at Indiana University in Bloomington. I had become a father for the first time in December. Finding my way in the Midwest (I was an easterner), I was absorbed in work and family life and was slow, like most Americans in 1965, to recognize that the nation's military involvement in the Vietnam War would turn out to be a disastrous mistake. By late 1965, however, campus-wide "teach-ins" and protests against the war, along with rising racial tensions, were signaling that both the universities and the country at large were being transformed. The triumphalism that had prevailed earlier in the year had come under siege.[7]

To be sure, not everything was changing at the time. Many important manifestations of American culture—movies and television, for instance—did not shake loose from their familiar moorings in 1965.

Organized feminism and environmentalism had yet to surge to the fore. But powerful currents of change, though churning in different directions in the latter half of the year (politics to the Right, aspects of popular culture to the Left), were sweeping aside many of the old ways. Transformative developments in politics, race relations, foreign policies, and (to an extent) popular music form a major part of the story I tell in this book.

In focusing on 1965, I recognize that among the mountains of books on the "long 1960s" (some historians date these as extending from 1958 to 1974), several volumes identify other years as key turning points.[8] Their titles are dramatic and fetching: *The Year Everything Changed* (for 1959); *The Last Innocent Year* (1964); and (what, again?) *The Year Everything Changed* (1969). Many writers seize on 1968, annus horribilis, as the decisive year—after all, it featured the Tet Offensive in Vietnam, the assassinations of Martin Luther King Jr. and Robert Kennedy, and the election of Richard Nixon. These writers, too, employ eye-catching titles (*The Year That Rocked the World, The Year the Dream Died*).[9] But I believe that the major events of 1968, awesome though they were, mainly exacerbated shifts of mood—and of politics, culture, and foreign policies—that first became significant during 1965.[10]

It is also obvious that historical transformation does not arise out of nowhere on January 1 or end on December 31. Developments in the early 1960s, a time of vibrant economic growth that bolstered high expectations and a keen consciousness about individual and group rights, set the stage for many of the epochal events of 1965. In 1960, hormonal birth control (also known as the Pill) became available, making contraception much more accessible to women, and John F. Kennedy was elected president, enlarging a popular sense of possibility for change. In 1961, Freedom Riders, savaged by racists, struggled to desegregate interstate bus terminals in the South. In 1962, Michael Harrington's *The Other America* appeared, laying out a dark vision of national poverty, along with Rachel Carson's *Silent Spring*, which awakened readers to the environmental peril of pesticides. In 1963, Betty Friedan published *The Feminine Mystique*. Martin Luther King led civil rights demonstrations in Birmingham that met with violent resistance, and that August he delivered the speech about his Dream.

In November 1963, the assassination of President Kennedy staggered millions of people. Some believed that American civilization itself, having allowed such a tragedy to happen, must somehow be to blame for his death and that a magical era had passed. Jackie, his widow, intoned after his murder, "There will be great presidents again, but there will never be another Camelot again."[11]

In early 1964, 73 million people watched the Beatles on television's *The Ed Sullivan Show*, galvanizing a "British invasion"—that same year, the Dave Clark Five, the Animals, and the Rolling Stones also toured the country—and reinvigorating rock music in America. Bob Dylan, playing acoustic guitar, released "The Times They Are A-Changin'." Later that year, civil rights activists organized Mississippi's Freedom Summer in a heroic quest for racial justice—and were bloodied in the process. In August 1964, LBJ and his advisers used alleged North Vietnamese attacks on American destroyers in the Gulf of Tonkin as the pretext for military retaliation. The unusually nasty election campaign of that fall presaged the political polarization of the later 1960s.

These and other events have led me to devote the first two chapters of this book to an account of various aspects of American life in late 1964. Though a number of developments in those months roiled the societal calm and foreshadowed the unrest that surged in 1965, I remain struck by how buoyant and confident most white Americans were in late 1964 in contrast to their attitudes at the end of 1965. The full force of the Sixties was yet to arrive in late 1964.

That arrival did occur during the very different year of 1965. When we try to imagine LBJ standing before the National Christmas Tree in December 1965, a far more rancorous time, and proclaiming as he had the year before—that these were "the most hopeful times in all the years since Christ was born in Bethlehem"—we may appreciate how dramatically the United States changed during those consequential twelve months.[12]

1

HIGH EXPECTATIONS

America in Late 1964

LATE 1964 WAS A BUOYANT TIME FOR THE MAJORITY OF AMERICANS: a prosperous year that promoted extraordinarily high expectations about the future. As in the previous twenty years, large numbers of people were flocking to buy houses in the suburbs and climbing into the middle classes. In late July, *Ranger 7* radioed to earth four thousand close-up photos of the moon that indicated the terrain would be safe for a spaceship landing. In early September, Congress approved the Wilderness Act, setting aside some 9.14 million acres as pristine public land, all of it in national forests.

If there could have been a nationwide soundtrack for late 1964, it would have been especially upbeat, featuring hit songs by the Supremes ("Baby Love," "Come See About Me"), the Beatles ("A Hard Day's Night," "I Feel Fine"), and the Beach Boys ("I Get Around"). In movie theaters, Julie Andrews was giving her youthful charges a spoonful of sugar in *Mary Poppins*, and in *My Fair Lady* Audrey Hepburn was proving herself socially mobile under the tutelage of Rex Harrison. Millions of Americans lavished attention, as usual, on the national pastime: the New York Yankees captured their fifth straight American League pennant in late September, only to lose a seven-game World Series to a St. Louis Cardinals team that had snatched the National League title on the frantic final day of an exciting season.

John F. Kennedy's eloquent calls for a New Frontier had raised expectations his death could not dim. Liberals, led by President Johnson, redoubled their efforts for reform. In May, speaking before some eighty thousand enthusiastic listeners (including Republican governor George Romney) at the University of Michigan's football stadium, LBJ had called for congressional approval of a Great Society—a hugely ambitious set of domestic reforms and programs. That August, Congress appropriated $1 billion to support the Economic Opportunity Act, which promised to wage a "War against Poverty." By then, many Americans were confident that LBJ, a masterful leader of Congress, would succeed in securing the enactment of his huge agenda. After his landslide election to a full term, *Time* anointed him "Man of the Year," placing him on the pedestal most recently occupied by Martin Luther King Jr., Pope John XXIII, and JFK.[1]

TO BE SURE, SOME DEVELOPMENTS DISTURBED THIS PREDOMINANTLY positive atmosphere. What happened at the Berkeley campus of the University of California that fall was especially newsworthy. Thanks in part to the arrival on campus of the earliest baby boomers—the large generation of children born between 1946 and 1964, the last year of the boom—Berkeley served more than twenty-five thousand students. (In 1964, California passed New York to become the most populous state.) But a range of issues was sharpening friction between students and Berkeley's administration. At the start of the fall semester, the university prevented students from soliciting support on campus for outside social and political causes, notably racial justice. Angry activists launched what would be called the Free Speech Movement (FSM), which rallied a substantial number of students across the political spectrum on behalf of First Amendment rights. One protestor, Jack Weinberg, memorably exclaimed, "Never trust anyone over thirty," in what would become a persistent and contentious refrain of the Sixties.

Rising discontent at Berkeley over the next three months unleashed marches and demonstrations, conflicts with police, and in early December a thousand-student-strong sit-in and takeover of the university administration building. "Berkeley students," *Time* reported, "have blown off the lid." At three AM on December 3, Governor Edmund "Pat" Brown, a liberal Democrat, authorized some six hundred police to clear students from the building. Over the course of the next twelve hours, they arrested nearly eight hundred protestors, which led many thousands of students to stage a strike that all but paralyzed the university. Mario Savio, an eloquent student leader who had previously that year joined Freedom Summer volunteers for civil rights in Mississippi, arose at a rally to explain that a "time" had come. This, he said, was "when the operation of the machine becomes so odious, makes you so sick at heart, that you can't take part; you can't even passively take part, and you've got to put your bodies upon the gears and upon the wheels, upon the levers, upon all the apparatus and you've got to make it stop. And you've got to indicate to the people who run it, to the people that own it, that unless you're free, the machines will be prevented from working at all."[2]

With Berkeley in turmoil, faculty members rushed to raise bail money and endorse the FSM's essential demands; the university's regents, who had the ultimate authority, agreed to support freedom of speech on campus. Some students continued to demonstrate, but the FSM had triumphed, and the tempest quieted down as of early 1965.[3]

Though few people fully recognized it at the time, the confrontation at Berkeley was a fire bell in the night. Some people later referred to it as the "Fort Sumter of campus unrest from 1964 on."[4] The solidarity of the protestors in December, evident in coverage that aired on national TV, later helped inspire restive young people to rally in large-scale demonstrations that—thanks mainly to the escalation of the Vietnam War—arose on college campuses in 1965 and beyond.[5]

But no social issues in 1964 were more divisive than those involving race and civil rights. These revealed the power of rights consciousness, the most important force behind the turbulent changes in the years that followed. Generated by the extraordinary affluence of the early 1960s and by the soaring rhetoric of Kennedy's New Frontier, this new awareness greatly heightened the expectations of millions of Americans, especially the young, whose increasingly urgent quests for rights, freedoms, and entitlements set off innumerable conflicts and confrontations in 1965 and thereafter.

Though direct-action protest on behalf of civil rights for American Negroes (as African Americans were called in 1964) had a long history, it increased dramatically in the early 1960s. Militant young people in organizations such as the Congress of Racial Equality (CORE) and the Student Nonviolent Coordinating Committee (SNCC) spearheaded protests, mainly in the racially segregated South. In 1964, ten years after the Supreme Court had ruled against state-mandated segregation in the public schools in *Brown v. Board of Education*, only 1 percent of black elementary and secondary school students in the Deep South attended schools with whites. All eleven Southern states (along with seven others) enforced laws banning interracial marriage. Very few Deep South blacks had been allowed to register to vote. From housing to schools to health care to public accommodations, segregation, and discrimination, especially strong in Dixie, were rigidly maintained, often through violence.

In 1964, militant protests against racist practices shook Mississippi, where some one thousand activists, many of them whites of college age, traveled in support of an interracial organizing effort called Freedom Summer. They focused on establishing what they called Freedom Schools for black children and on registering disfranchised black voters. Challenging the all-white Democratic Party, which had long dominated state politics, they also helped local people to create a racially integrated Mississippi Freedom Democratic Party (MFDP) and elected delegates to the Democratic national nominating convention that was to meet in late August.[6] White racists, including law enforcement officers, reacted with violence. They murdered three young activists (two white, one black) in Philadelphia, Mississippi, in June. Later that summer they killed three more activists, shot at thirty-five others (wounding three), beat another eighty, and arrested roughly a thousand. Whites also burned down thirty black churches and bombed thirty homes and other buildings. The scale of white violence in Mississippi that summer, which received considerable coverage in the media, was unprecedented in the recent history of the civil rights movement.[7]

Racial tensions also escalated that summer in Northern cities, where millions of Southern black Americans had been flocking since the 1940s. Some of these migrants managed to find blue-collar work that paid a living wage, and a few others rose into the middle classes, but most learned they had not arrived in a Promised Land. De facto racial segregation and discrimination continued to flourish in the North. A stunning 48 percent of black Americans in 1964 lived in poverty, as compared to 14 percent of whites.

Some of these tensions sparked large-scale racial unrest. After an off-duty white policeman shot and killed a fifteen-year-old black boy on Manhattan's Upper East Side in mid-July, some four thousand blacks erupted in protest in Harlem and Brooklyn. Their revolt, which included looting and burning buildings, lasted five days and nights and left 1 person dead and some 500 injured. More than 450 people were arrested.[8] Racial confrontations then rattled Philadelphia, Chicago, and several other Northern cities.

These racial disturbances, the most significant since World War II, demonstrated that the rage of black Americans, already ascendant in 1964, knew no geographical boundaries. Given such anger, it was hardly surprising that thirty-nine-year-old Malcolm X, who had split from the Nation of Islam in June, converted to orthodox Islam, and established his Organization of Afro-American Unity, was emerging as a magnetic black orator and organizer. Throughout late 1964 and into early 1965, his forceful speeches—not only to inner-city black people but also to students on university campuses—called for pan-Africanism and for black people to stand up for themselves and their families. In his spiritual quest for racial justice he seemed to be slowly gravitating toward support of interracial civil rights initiatives against state-mandated segregation. At the same time he stressed the need for black nationalism because, he argued, whites could not be trusted. By late 1964, he was attracting considerable attention, especially in the ghettos of the North and Midwest.[9]

Many whites, to be sure, supported civil rights causes. Like the activists of Freedom Summer, some of them courageously faced the wrathful violence of white racists. President Johnson, who emerged in 1964 as a determined spokesman against racial injustice, worked effectively to secure the passage in June of the Civil Rights Act. This historic measure, one of the most important laws of the twentieth century, banned racial discrimination in public accommodations, provided for the establishment of an equal employment opportunity commission, and stipulated that public institutions (notably schools and hospitals) found to be discriminating might lose federal funding.

But many Northern white Americans in 1964 continued to oppose major changes in race relations. Governor George Wallace of Alabama, a demagogic segregationist (LBJ once called him a "runty little bastard and just about the most dangerous person around"), drew between 30 and 45 percent of the vote in Democratic presidential primaries that spring in Indiana, Maryland, and Wisconsin.[10] Many of his supporters were blue-collar whites, part of what would be famously termed a civil rights "backlash" growing in the North and thriving on fears that blacks would overrun white schools and neighborhoods.

The anger and violence of that tumultuous summer also helped to radicalize a number of black civil rights leaders, even as the Civil Rights Act promised to provide fundamental change in the construction of American society and government. Many of these leaders especially resented LBJ's treatment of Mississippi Freedom Democratic Party delegates during the Democratic National Convention in Atlantic City. The most divisive issue concerned the seating of delegates from the state: Would they be the white supremacist Democratic Party regulars, who opposed the Civil Rights Act and the party's liberal platform concerning civil rights, or the rival MFDP contingent, most of whom were black? The head of the official delegation was well known as a racist who had branded the NAACP civil rights group as an organization of "Niggers, Alligators, Apes, Coons, and Possums."[11]

Johnson, determined to avoid an open and divisive confrontation, had the FBI wire Martin Luther King's hotel room and the meetings of militant civil rights organizations such as CORE and SNCC. Some thirty FBI agents provided the president with up-to-the-minute accounts of the MFDP delegates' plans. Though the information he acquired was not of much use, he managed to orchestrate a behind-the-scenes deal that among other things would have allowed the seating at-large of two MFDP delegates, who would have full voting rights at the convention but would not sit with the party regulars or formally represent the state.

This modest concession to the MFDP infuriated Mississippi's thirty-four regulars, all but four of whom packed their bags and went home. But the compromise failed to satisfy most of the MFDP members. Having labored democratically to elect delegates, they now discovered that the president was resisting their claims. One of the MFDP's most eloquent spokespersons, Fannie Lou Hamer, the twentieth child of impoverished sharecroppers and a voting rights advocate, had told the credentials committee in a nationally televised speech how she had been thrown into a cell the previous year by white highway patrolmen, who then ordered black prisoners to beat her with blackjacks. She declared, "We want to register, to become first-class citizens, and if the Freedom Democratic Party is not seated now, I question America." Joining other MFDP delegates to reject LBJ's compromise, she proclaimed, "We didn't come all this way for no two seats."[12]

This conflict at the convention marked a turning point for many black Americans waging the freedom struggle. "Never again were we lulled into believing that our task was exposing injustices so that the 'good' people of America could eliminate them," SNCC member Cleveland Sellers would later say. "We left Atlantic City with the knowledge that the movement had turned into something else. After Atlantic City, our struggle was not for civil rights, but for liberation."[13]

—

IT IS CLEAR IN RETROSPECT THAT TWO PHENOMENA—THE SHARPENING of racial tensions and the demographic change that allowed a large wave of young adult baby boomers to define themselves as a specific generation—contributed to the rising rights consciousness and incipient polarization of the mid and late 1960s. But this emerging conflict, which was soon to set off a struggle over values and power, was not so obvious at the time. Most young Americans in 1964 did not yet see themselves as belonging to a distinctive or self-conscious generation. Having grown up in an affluent culture, many were developing higher expectations than their parents had, but there was relatively little media discussion in early 1965 about righteously assertive or rebellious youth. *Time* went so far as to conclude, "The classic conflict between parents and children is letting up."[14]

Time had good reason to make such a generalization. While Tom Wolfe was writing provocatively in 1964 about teenage "culture-makers"—jeans-and-T-shirt-clad boys building hot rods, dance-crazy girls wearing stretch pants—the majority of young Americans as of the end of 1964 did not appear to be turning against their parents. And the older generation, perhaps influenced by Dr. Benjamin Spock's best-selling *Baby and Child Care,* were raising their children with a lighter touch than that taken by their own parents.[15] Any ramifications from Dr. Spock's approach did not arouse much concern in 1964. It was only later, in 1965 and thereafter, when considerably larger numbers of young people were crowding the colleges, that these expectations combined with opposition to the war in Vietnam to energize a rising boomer self-awareness as well as widespread student activism. Then, not in 1964, conservatives would loudly lament the "permissiveness" of parents and the antics of what Richard Nixon and his vice president, Spiro Agnew, were to call the "Spock-marked generation."

High school and college students in 1964 even physically resembled their 1950s counterparts. Some, caught up in Beatlemania, had mop tops. But very few young men sported beards or long hair. You looked cool if you had just had a haircut. Mario Savio of the FSM was among the many male activists at Berkeley who donned ties while protesting. Many college men had crew cuts, and they wore chinos, not jeans. Afros were exceedingly rare. Most women of high school and college age also wore their hair short and dressed conservatively, often with matching sweaters and skirts, and sported kneesocks and loafers. (*Seventeen,* "America's Teen-Age Magazine," still airbrushed navels out of their photographs.[16]) Miniskirts, which would first appear in London in 1965, were unseen at the time. Though a few young people were experimenting with LSD, which was legal in California until 1966, the psychedelic drug culture widely associated with the Sixties had not yet arrived.

In what was still a rules-based—not a rights-based—American culture, school authorities enforced codes of dress and comportment at every level of education. Many schools at the time circulated detailed handbooks to make certain that students obeyed dictates regarding clothes and behavior. One such publication, from North Hills High

School just outside Pittsburgh, ran to 103 pages, decreeing shorts, slacks, "after 5-style dresses," or "similar outer garments" were unacceptable wear during the school day. "V-neck sweaters, if low cut, must be worn with a blouse or a scarf." Skirts had to be "loose enough to allow one handful of material to be held at the side" and "no shorter than the middle of the knee, both sitting and standing." Girls were not allowed to use "heavy makeup," "evening shades of lipstick," eyeliners, or eye shadow. Boys had to wear shirts with collars—no T-shirts—and "only the top button may be left unbuttoned," with shirttails always tucked into trousers. Undershirts had to be white. Shoes "shall not come above the middle of the ankle." Blue jeans were forbidden, and "trousers must be worn waist-high." Mustaches and beards were taboo, along with sideburns "longer than the middle of the ear." "Hair may not be combed forward." Nor was bleach allowed, for boy or girl.[17]

In attire as in many other things, most young people in late 1964 seemed to emulate grown-up ways. (Later, it would often be the other way around.) Most middle-class American adults dressed as conservatively as they had in the 1950s. Though a few adventurous women dared to be seen in pantsuits, middle-class women rarely wore slacks in public.[18] If they could afford it, they reported every week or so to their hairdresser, who would stiff-spray and pile their locks high.[19] When traveling on planes or trains, eating out at fine restaurants, or going to the movies, American adults did not appear in sweat suits, flip-flops, baseball caps, jeans, shorts, or T-shirts, nor did they let their shirts hang out over their trousers. The same was true of dress at religious services, which some 45 percent of Americans—members of one of the Western world's most churchgoing societies—attended every week.[20]

Key manifestations of popular culture reflected these and other traditional patterns of thought and behavior as of early 1965. Developments in popular music, to be sure, hinted at dramatic changes that were to emerge later that year and to spread thereafter. Beginning with the hugely hyped arrival of the Beatles in the United States in February 1964, the "British invasion" of that year imparted a new vitality to rock music. Within a few years, as the scholar Morris Dickstein was to observe, "Rock music became the organized religion of the sixties—the nexus not only of music and language but also of dance, sex, and dope, which all came together into a single ritual of self-expression and spiritual tripping."[21]

But most popular rock music in 1964, such as that of the Beach Boys or of the Supremes (whose "Come See About Me" topped the singles charts that December), continued to be bouncy, melodic, and sweet. The Beatles, too, were unchallenging in 1964. Their "I Want to Hold Your Hand," which remained phenomenally popular throughout the year, threatened no one. What complaints it did receive were largely related to taste. One critic commented on the song by declaring, "I Want to Hold My Nose." Another dismissed it as "elevator music." As of the end of 1964, few people could have predicted that developments in rock music would help transform American popular culture.[22]

Other major forms of popular culture hardly changed at all during the early 1960s. Television, which Federal Communications Commission chair Newton Minow had described in 1961 as a "vast wasteland," continued to feature wholesome, mostly family-oriented entertainment aimed at middle-class, white viewers. Some popular programs in 1964—*The Dick Van Dyke Show*, a situation comedy, and *ABC's Wide World of Sports*—were of high quality. *The Ed Sullivan Show*, a hit in prime time since 1948, retained its extraordinary popularity. But most of the widely watched prime-time offerings—*Bonanza*, *The Beverly Hillbillies*, *Gomer Pyle, U.S.M.C.*, *Gilligan's Island*, *The Andy Griffith Show*—were risk-averse programs that many critics bemoaned. Though some shows in the late 1960s (*Julia*, with Diahann Carroll; *I Spy*, with Bill Cosby) broke ground by focusing on black people, it was not until *All in the Family* (1971) that a top prime-time program would dare to seriously challenge familiar conventions.[23]

Movies, too, aimed safely at mass audiences in 1964, reinforcing the prevailing cultural narrative of power and authority. The most popular film late in the year was *Goldfinger*, the third James Bond movie. Julie Andrews would win an Oscar for her part in *Mary Poppins*, and *My Fair Lady* would win eight, including one for Rex Harrison as best actor. Only in 1967, when *Bonnie and Clyde* and *The Graduate* appeared, did Hollywood release movies that are widely associated with the Sixties and that upended the well-established moral standards of mass entertainment.[24]

Hollywood continued to maintain the Motion Picture Association of America's prim Production Code, which had been enforced since 1934. The code was a laundry list of "thou shalt not's." No profanity, blasphemy, nudity, miscegenation, childbirth, or reference to venereal disease. Audiences should not be exposed to words such as "pansy," "virgin," or "pregnant" or to anything else that might "lower the moral standards of those who see it." Few people with cultural power in late 1964 were fully prepared to query the definition of "moral standards," much less systematically challenge those norms.

IN MATTERS SEXUAL, IT WAS INDEED HARD TO PERCEIVE SIGNIFICANT changes in America as of early 1965. To be sure, it was widely assumed at the time that young people were more sexually active than had been the case in the 1950s. The proportion of out-of-wedlock births was beginning to increase rapidly, mainly among lower-class black teenagers. Helen Gurley Brown's *Sex and the Single Girl*, a best-selling book published in 1962, encouraged young women to have sex as a way to get ahead in the world of work, offering pointers on "Squirming, Worming, Inching, and Pinching Your Way to the Top."[25] But books like this were considered scandalous, descriptive of social outliers, not as guidebooks to the behavior of young working women.

There was as yet little talk of a "sexual revolution"—a term that mainly gained popular parlance later in the 1960s. Established norms about sexual conduct, including the double standard, remained strong. States firmly enforced prohibitions on abortion and the criminalization of homosexuality.[26] Until the late 1960s, most colleges and universities maintained strict parietal rules: college women were not allowed to stay out late, and students caught having sex risked expulsion.[27]

Young single women talked frankly of petting but claimed to hold the line against "going all the way." They had ample reason to be careful, because even if 81 percent of Americans (including 78 percent of Catholics) told pollsters that they favored making birth control information widely available "to anyone who wants it," reliable contraception was not all that easy for young unmarried people to obtain.[28] In 1964, the Vatican Council asserted that the church would continue to oppose contraception.[29] Until 1965, the American Medical Association actively resisted the dissemination of "propaganda intended to promote artificial birth control."[30] Most doctors dissociated themselves from sex education. Several states forbade the use of contraceptive devices, even by married couples—a prohibition that would be the subject of a Supreme Court challenge in 1965.

The Pill had become available in 1960. But as of 1965, not very many high school girls or college-age women dared to tell their parents they were sexually active or visit the family doctor for an examination, which was required for a prescription. Because of the force of traditional attitudes such as these, and for other reasons (for one, it was not cheap), the Pill was more widely used by married women in the early 1960s than by those who were young or unmarried.[31] Only in September 1965 would an American university health officer, Dr. Roswell Johnson at Brown University, prescribe the Pill to students: two seniors who were over twenty-one, had consulted with their ministers, and intended to marry their boyfriends. Dr. Johnson emphasized that he would not prescribe for women under the age of twenty-one and added, "I want to feel I'm contributing to a solid relationship and not contributing to unmitigated promiscuity." The *New York Times* and national magazines like *Time* and *Newsweek* reported this landmark event.[32]

—

ASIDE FROM CIVIL RIGHTS ACTIVISM AND THE FREE-SPEECH EVENTS in Berkeley, politically oriented protest among young people was also relatively uncommon in late 1964. Bob Dylan might sing that the times they were a-changin', but the change young American liberals seemed to be seeking at the time was hardly subversive. Many embraced visions inspired by Kennedy's New Frontier, which called for domestic reforms but also supported America's unyielding Cold War policies against international communism. Boomers in 1964 seemed to be nearly as apolitical as teenagers had been in the 1950s.

Indeed, except for civil rights, there did not appear to be very pressing political or social causes for young activists to rally behind in 1964. Americans were reflexively anticommunist in 1964 and approved of advancing their national interests in a Cold War world, but they did not otherwise pay great attention to foreign affairs. The formation of the Palestine Liberation Organization that May received little media coverage, nor were most Americans greatly concerned when China detonated its first nuclear bomb in mid-October. With the unnerving Cuban Missile Crisis of 1962 two years in the past, Fidel Castro's island nation had become less of a concern, and fears of nuclear conflict had abated. Nations with the Bomb—the United States, the Soviet Union, France, and Great Britain—had agreed in 1963 to a treaty banning nuclear tests in outer space, under water, and in the atmosphere. A "hotline" linked the White House and the Kremlin. The world was still a very dangerous place, but few Americans in 1964 were agitating for agreements that might lessen tensions between the United States and communist nations such as the USSR or China.

The American people, moreover, had reason to feel secure. The government, spending some $50 billion a year on defense (half the federal budget), was harnessing awesome military strength—so much so that President Eisenhower had publicly warned in early 1961 of the power of a "military-industrial complex." And though the Cold War remained intense, the Soviet Union was coping with its own internal struggles, which culminated in mid-October with the sacking of Nikita Khrushchev as premier and head of the Communist Party. Leonid Brezhnev replaced him as the most powerful man in the USSR.

The simmering conflict in Vietnam did not preoccupy the American public in late 1964, in spite of the subtly escalating US presence in the country. Some 23,000 American military personnel were stationed in Vietnam at the end of 1964 (an increase of approximately 7,000 since Johnson had become president in November 1963). Some of them, unbeknownst to most Americans, were seeing combat. But like JFK, LBJ referred to them as noncombat "military advisers." For these reasons, few young Americans in late 1964 were protesting against the draft. Like their older siblings born in the pre-boomer years, they accepted military service, however reluctantly, as one of a number of obligations young men in a rules-oriented culture had to meet. They would have found it hard to believe that hundreds of thousands of American soldiers would soon fight or that more than 58,000 of them would die and more than 303,000 would be wounded as a result of serving in Southeast Asia between 1965 and 1973.[33]

Many other causes that were later to engage rights-conscious protestors in the Sixties were barely emergent in 1964. Though Rachel Carson's *Silent Spring* (1962) had alerted Americans to ecological matters, notably danger from pesticides, and advocates of conservation applauded passage of the Wilderness Act in late 1964, a broader, tough-minded environmentalism did not gather significant strength until the late 1960s or peak until the 1970s. Climate change had not become a salient issue. The first Earth Day commemoration occurred in 1970, and the Environmental Protection Agency got its start in 1972.

Other reform efforts later to become powerful were also insignificant—indeed, scarcely heard from—in 1964. Very few Americans at the time were campaigning on behalf of marginalized groups such as American Indians, people with disabilities, or lesbians and gay men. These groups, inspired by the rights-consciousness that surged through American life in the wake of the civil rights movement, began to organize effectively only later in the 1960s and received serious attention from the media considerably later than that.

American women, too, had yet to mobilize. Though Kennedy had established a President's Commission on the Status of Women, it had not attracted much notice as of late 1964. The paperback version of Betty Friedan's *The Feminine Mystique* (1963) sold 1.4 million copies in 1964, indicating that the pioneering author had surely struck a nerve. But Friedan's call was mainly for individual action, not for political mobilization of the sort that the civil rights movement had developed. Nor did she have much to say about the plight of working-class or minority women. A majority of American women, yet to coalesce into a feminist or women's rights movement, continued in 1964 to accept conventional assumptions about gender roles: men were the breadwinners, women the homemakers. Since World War II, a rapidly rising number of women had joined the work force: 26.7 million were gainfully employed by 1964, representing 36.7 percent of all women sixteen years old or more. But most of them faced widespread discrimination in hiring, promotions, and pay. Medical and law school admissions officials discriminated blatantly against women.[34] Help-wanted ads carried separate listings of jobs open to men and women (as well as to whites and blacks). Many careers were essentially closed to women.

Even in militant civil rights and leftist student groups, women were undervalued. Mary King and Casey Hayden, SNCC activists engaged in Freedom Summer in Mississippi, issued a position paper in July arguing, "the woman in SNCC is often in the same position as that token Negro hired in a corporation." But their efforts received little attention at the time. Women were one-third of the membership of the leading New Left group, Students for a Democratic Society (SDS), which prided itself on practicing "participatory democracy" in its discussions and decision making. But SDS women held only 6 percent of executive committee seats. As one male SDS leader noted later of the place of female members (usually referred to as "girls"), "women made peanut butter, waited on tables, cleaned up, got laid. That was their role." Later, when young men began resisting the military draft, one of their antiwar slogans played on this sexist view: "Girls say yes to guys who say no."[35]

President Johnson's summons to address the problems of the poor did engage the attention of some Americans in 1964, especially after Congress approved a War on Poverty. But it was unclear in late 1964 what that war, struggling to define itself, would manage to accomplish. Leaders of SDS had already been focusing that summer on mobilizing poor people in the inner cities. But like SDS itself, this effort was small, and at the end of the year, many of these campaigns were foundering. Poor people, it seemed, were very hard to organize.

On December 30, 1964, when SDS held its convention, it was hardly an effective group, let alone a mass movement. Having been formed by young people in 1960 as a less rigid alternative to the old (mostly Marxist but still anticommunist) Left, it was composed mainly—though by no means entirely—of students from prestigious private colleges or state universities. It had only 1,365 paid-up members, most of whom focused on civil rights activism, community organization, and resistance to corporate domination of foreign policy. Because members tended to be leery of carefully structured, hierarchical organization and took seriously their faith in "participatory democracy," they often labored through long and exhausting debates over priorities.

Though many SDS delegates at the December convention still hoped to concentrate on mobilizing the poor, others were becoming increasingly eager to organize against war. At the last moment, an antiwar faction won out, securing a majority in favor of staging a demonstration in Washington in April. SDS leaders hoped that at least two thousand people would take part, but although the decision was relayed in a press release to the media, it received no notice in the *New York Times*.[36]

—

WHY WAS ORGANIZED PROTEST, EXCEPT FOR THE CIVIL RIGHTS movement, so paltry in the United States in 1964? One explanation is compelling: the vibrant health of the economy. Since April 1961, uninterrupted economic growth had been extraordinarily strong, enabling Americans to enjoy unparalleled prosperity and to anticipate even more of it in the future. The Gross National Product rose from $504 billion in 1960 to $632 billion in 1964—that is, by 25 percent. The unemployment rate plummeted (from 5.7 percent in 1963 to 4.1 percent by the end of 1965). Prices were stable; inflation hovered around 1 percent per year. More than any other single development, economic growth defined what many exuberant Americans in the early 1960s considered to be the unparalleled "greatness" of the United States.[37]

Income inequality, moreover, had declined since the 1930s and was historically modest as of 1965 for a variety of reasons. Corporate salaries, while enabling a very comfortable lifestyle for those near the top, were far less remunerative than in later years. The federal government's top marginal income tax rates were still high: they had been at 90 percent until a tax cut in early 1964 dropped them to a still hefty 70 percent, or twice what they were to become at the turn of the twenty-first century. To be sure, the United States was by no means an egalitarian society: in 1964, 34.6 million people (more than 17 percent of the population) lived below the government's official poverty lines. For a family of four, this was $3,130 a year.[38] America's social safety net, having expanded only slowly since World War II, remained more porous than those in northern European nations. Labor unions, which had grown substantially since the 1930s, were starting to weaken. Still, income inequality was as low in early 1965 as it ever had been in the modern history of the country.

And life seemed likely to become more comfortable over time. As in the 1940s and 1950s, millions of Americans were continuing to buy homes, move into the suburbs, and rise into the middle classes. Americans were also spending freely on cars, televisions, and other expensive consumer goods, and their children were swelling the enrollments of colleges and universities. It appeared that upward economic mobility—the American Dream—would grow even stronger over time. No wonder people had high expectations about the future.

Thanks to these gratifying economic developments, the United States in 1964 also avoided many of the "us versus them" resentments that flourished in more class-conscious societies such as Great Britain. It was not until the 1970s that the Great Compression, as this relatively egalitarian situation was to be labeled, began to be replaced by the Great Divergence of income (and wealth) inequality that was thereafter to storm ahead and foment rising dissatisfactions in American culture.[39]

A second reason for the lack in 1964 of significant protest movements other than for civil rights had to do with American society's increasingly homogenous ethnic mix. As a result in large part of highly restrictive and racist laws promulgated in the early 1920s, immigration to America had been modest for more than forty years. Only 297,000 legal immigrants arrived in the United States in 1964. The percentage of the American population that was foreign-born—around 5 percent—had been declining for decades, and it would bottom out at an all-time modern low of 4.7 percent in 1970.[40]

Ethnic tensions had surely not disappeared; the widely heralded Melting Pot had by no means amalgamated America's large multiethnic and multiracial population.[41] Dissent, especially among black Americans, was obviously rising. But the religious intolerance that had long been a factor in American life was declining, as evidenced by the presidential election victory in 1960 of Kennedy, a Catholic. And few citizens of the United States in 1964 were demanding curbs on immigration or fretting about the then-insignificant number of people present in the country illegally. Liberal reformers hoped to abolish the discriminatory aspects of immigration law, not to cut back the number of foreigners who came to American shores.

WHEN LYNDON JOHNSON LIT THE NATIONAL CHRISTMAS TREE IN December 1964, he presided over a nation at once hopeful and complacent, largely trusting its institutions and feeling assured about its future path, even as certain deprived groups, notably black people, were complaining angrily of exploitation. Phenomenal economic growth and unprecedented prosperity, along with the absence of extreme inequality and of large-scale immigration, helped to explain why the United States seemed to be a remarkably stable and confident place to live. It was hardly surprising that a great many Americans, including millions of young people who were nearing adulthood, had developed high expectations. No people in the modern history of the world had had it so good.

2

GATHERING STORMS

Politics and Vietnam
in Late 1964

A WEEK BEFORE THE 1964 PRESIDENTIAL ELECTION, RONALD REAGAN, a well-known though fading Hollywood actor (his final film, earlier in the year, was *The Killers*), delivered a nationally televised oration on behalf of Senator Barry Goldwater of Arizona, the ultraconservative GOP nominee. Titled "A Time for Choosing," Reagan's speech was a ringing denunciation of Big Government. The "issue of this election," Reagan declared,

> is whether we believe in our capacity for self-government or whether we abandon the American Revolution and confess that a little intellectual elite in a far-distant capital can plan our lives better for us than we can plan them ourselves. . . . You and I are told increasingly that we have to choose between a left and a right. There is only an up or down: up to man's age-old dream— the ultimate in individual freedom consistent with law and order—or down to the ant-heap of totalitarianism. . . . You and I have a rendezvous with destiny. We will preserve for our children

this, the last hope of man on earth, or we will sentence them to
take the last step into a thousand years of darkness.

"The Speech," as Reagan's widely known address became called,
captivated conservatives. Columnist David Broder was moved to call it
"the most successful national debut since William Jennings Bryan
electrified the 1896 Democratic convention in the 'Cross of Gold' address." A signal of ideological conflict to come, the speech propelled
Reagan onto a political path that rejuvenated conservatism in 1965
and culminated at the end of that year in his decision to challenge Pat
Brown for the governorship of California in 1966.[1]

But during the 1964 campaign, Reagan's efforts went for naught,
in part because Goldwater was a flawed presidential candidate. Having
voted against the Civil Rights Act, he had had no chance of winning
the votes of blacks or of white supporters of the movement. And he
often shot from the hip. When he accepted the GOP nomination in
July, he alarmed moderates by exclaiming, "Extremism in the defense of liberty is no vice! . . . Moderation in the pursuit of justice is
no virtue!" Such a call to arms roused organizations like Young Americans for Freedom, a conservative group that had been founded at
the Connecticut home of commentator William Buckley in 1960, but
it frightened or appalled many others.

Goldwater also seemed to go out of his way to lose votes. In
Knoxville, at the heart of the region served by the Tennessee Valley
Authority, he announced his opposition to public power. In West Virginia, one of the nation's poorest states, he denounced the War on
Poverty. In Florida, where many retirees lived, he said that Social Security should be voluntary. A fierce anticommunist (and a major general in the US Air Force Reserve), he talked nonchalantly about
lobbing nuclear bombs into the men's room at the Kremlin and of using "low-yield atomic weapons" if necessary to protect South Vietnam
from the communist-dominated North.[2]

Though Lyndon Johnson had to manage a few troubles during
the campaign—notably during the convention fight with the Mississippi Freedom Democratic Party delegation—he knew he would win
the election. "Right here," he told an aide, "is the reason I'm going to
win this thing so big. You ask a voter who classifies himself as a liberal

what he thinks I am and he says a liberal. You ask a voter who calls himself a conservative what he thinks I am and he says I'm a conservative. . . . They all think I'm on their side."[3] Still, Johnson was always an aggressive and near-frenzied political campaigner, seizing every chance he could to identify himself with the policies of the martyred JFK and hailing the potential of programs he said would create the Great Society. Fourteen high-level task forces, he boasted, were already designing new and transformative federal social programs.[4]

LBJ and his advisers worked especially hard to demonize the opposition. Mocking Goldwater's slogan "In your heart, you know he's right!" Democrats retorted, "In your guts, you know he's nuts!" In early September, they aired a particularly controversial television ad, which appeared as a commercial break in the movie *David and Bathsheba* (starring Gregory Peck and Susan Hayward) that some fifty million people were watching on prime-time TV. It showed a little girl counting up slowly—"one . . . two . . . three . . . "—as she picks petals one at a time from a daisy. As she nears "ten," a menacing male voice, echoing as if from a loudspeaker at a nuclear missile site, begins counting down, "ten, nine, eight . . . one." At this point a nuclear explosion blackens the screen, and the image of the girl dissolves into a mushroom-shaped cloud. A voice, unmistakably Johnson's, announces, "These are the stakes—to make a world in which all of God's children can live, or to go into the dark. We must either love each other, or we must die." With the screen dark, a message appears in white: "Vote for President Johnson on November 3." The audio concludes, "The stakes are too high for you to stay at home."[5]

The "Daisy Spot," as it became known, ignited a barrage of protests from the GOP. Democrats, under fire, pulled it from the air. But partisan warfare over the ad was so hot that television stations ran it again and again as part of newscasts covering the controversy. Still, it was by no means the only Democratic ad that savaged Goldwater as a warmonger. Republicans fought back with vilification of their own, though neither so creatively nor so memorably. The election campaign of 1964, more negative than others of the post–World War II era, signaled the coming of an ideologically confrontational political world that would become a feature of the Sixties.

OVER THE NEXT FOUR YEARS LBJ WOULD PROVE HIMSELF FAR FROM the prophet of peace he claimed to be during the campaign. Like presidents Truman, Eisenhower, and Kennedy before him, he believed that the United States had an obligation to protect the independence of South Vietnam from communist aggression by the North. Three days after Kennedy's assassination, he had informed Henry Cabot Lodge, America's ambassador in Saigon, "I'm not going to lose Vietnam. I'm not going to be the president who saw Southeast Asia go the way China went." In April 1964, he told Lodge, "As far as I am concerned, you must have whatever you need to help the Vietnamese do the job, and I assure you I will act at once to eliminate obstacles or restraints wherever they may appear."[6] Publicly, LBJ also professed enormous confidence in the capacity of the United States to prevail whenever it might decide to engage its military forces. Addressing Secretary of Defense Robert McNamara and the Joint Chiefs of Staff at the Pentagon in July, he proclaimed: "We are the richest nation in the history of the world. We can afford to spend whatever is needed to keep this country safe and to keep our freedom secure. And we shall do just that."[7]

This did not mean that Johnson was eager to send combat troops to Southeast Asia. On the contrary, the political and military situation in South Vietnam, which was deteriorating week by week throughout 1964, greatly troubled him. In May, he had asked McGeorge Bundy, his national security adviser, to come up with constructive proposals to deal with the situation. "The more I stayed awake last night thinking about this thing," he told Bundy, "the more . . . it looks like to me we're gettin' into another Korea. . . . I don't think it's worth fightin' for and I don't think we can get out. And it's just the biggest damn mess. . . . I look at this sergeant of mine this morning; he's got six little ole kids and what in the hell am I ordering him out there for? What in the hell is Vietnam worth to me. . . . What is it worth to this country?"

But Johnson would not back down, especially while Goldwater was posing as an indomitable Cold Warrior. He reminded Bundy, "if you start running [from] the Communists, they may just chase you right into your own kitchen."[8] On another occasion, using a characteristically crude analogy, he observed, "if you let a bully come into your front yard one day, the next day he'll be up on your porch, and the day after that he'll rape your wife in your own bed."[9] Throughout 1964 LBJ greatly increased economic and military aid to South Vietnam.[10]

Ho Chi Minh, North Vietnam's leader, retaliated by rapidly bolstering his own armed forces. By the end of the year, Hanoi—aided by China and the Soviet Union—had sent large amounts of supplies and weaponry, as well as perhaps ten thousand army regulars, to aid the Vietcong, as the enemy in the South came to be called.[11] North Vietnam also took energetic steps to carve out reliable supply routes into the South. The result by early 1965 was a sinuous and complex network of improved jungle paths—the so-called Ho Chi Minh Trail—that wound from North Vietnam through Laos and Cambodia into South Vietnam. Overhung with a jungle canopy, many of the paths were virtually invisible from the air and for the most part safe from bombing attacks. Ho Chi Minh again and again made it clear that he would continue to back the Vietcong unless the United States agreed to remove its troops from the South and accept Vietcong participation in a neutral South Vietnamese coalition government.[12]

Rejecting such an outcome, LBJ took a major step toward American military confrontation. On August 4, 1964, he told the American public that North Vietnamese patrol boats had just attacked US destroyers in the Tonkin Gulf off the coast of North Vietnam.[13] Though the commander of one of the destroyers, reversing an earlier message in which he had reported enemy fire, relayed serious doubts that any North Vietnamese military action had occurred that night, LBJ did not wait to nail down all the facts.[14] Nor did he reveal that American naval vessels had for some time been engaged in electronic surveillance of North Vietnamese military installations in the area, that the vessels had been abetting South Vietnamese commando raids on North Vietnamese offshore islands, or that an American destroyer, USS *Maddox*, and US carrier-based jets—reacting to reports on August 2 of enemy attacks—had previously sunk a North Vietnamese patrol boat and damaged two others.

Instead, in a nationally televised speech, Johnson not only told of "a number of hostile vessels attacking two U.S. destroyers with torpedoes" but also disclosed that he had already ordered carrier-based fighter planes to retaliate against a nearby North Vietnamese oil depot and patrol-boat bases. The raids, which were fierce, damaged or destroyed twenty-five boats and wiped out an estimated 90 percent of the depot's oil supply. Two American planes were lost, and one pilot was captured, becoming America's first POW in the war. He was not released until US troops left Vietnam eight years later.

Johnson further used the alleged attacks of August 4 as a pretext to call on Congress to approve a joint resolution, which he had had aides begin preparing two months earlier. This would authorize him as commander in chief to take "all necessary measures to repel any armed attack against the United States and to prevent further aggression" in the area. Senator Ernest Gruening of Alaska, a liberal Democrat, dissented, declaring, "All Vietnam is not worth the life of a single American boy."[15] But neither the *Washington Post* nor the *New York Times* reported Gruening's speech, and two days later Congress approved the resolution, unanimously in the House and with only two dissenting votes (by Gruening and Wayne Morse, a Democrat from Oregon) in the Senate. Polls soon afterward indicated that 85 percent of Americans supported Johnson's action.[16]

In seeking the Tonkin Gulf Resolution, as it was called, LBJ did not intend to jump into a war. Indeed, he hoped that a show of American steel might cause North Vietnam to back off and therefore make American military involvement *less* likely. Still, the struggles in Vietnam continued to tear at him; he believed it would be difficult for the government of South Vietnam to prevail. He also yearned to secure passage of Great Society legislation before having to bite a Vietnam-related bullet that would foment dissent. But he maintained that the United States could and would pay for guns as well as butter. "Let no one doubt for a moment," he said after the Tonkin Gulf Resolution had passed, "that we have the resources and we have the will to follow this course as long as it may take us."[17]

Johnson, who was ever protective of his political position, also remembered vividly that in the late 1940s and early 1950s partisan Republicans and McCarthyites had charged President Truman with "losing" China to the Reds. During the election campaign of 1964 (and later) he was determined that no such accusation would stick to him. The Tonkin Gulf Resolution was in part an election-year ploy.

Still, the resolution was a turning point in the history of American involvement in the Vietnam War. The North Vietnamese government, realizing that the United States might send combat soldiers to fight in the war, rapidly expanded its People's Army of Vietnam and escalated its aid to the Vietcong, thereby further destabilizing the succession of shaky regimes that struggled to survive in Saigon.[18] The resolution, moreover, gave Johnson what he claimed was the legal authority to wage war in Vietnam. Congress never declared war, as the Constitution says it should. As LBJ later put it, the Tonkin Gulf Resolution was "like grandma's nightshirt—it covered everything."[19]

———

WELL BEFORE ELECTION DAY, POLLS PREDICTED A LANDSLIDE FOR LBJ and Humphrey, his running mate. But the president still campaigned as if he were on the verge of losing. Continuing to highlight his Great Society ambitions, he took credit for the nation's prosperity and frequently posed as a statesman who would stand firm against communism but keep out of war. In a statement that would come to haunt him, he said in late October, "We are not about to send American boys nine or ten thousand miles away from home to do what Asian boys ought to be doing for themselves."[20]

Two days before the election, Vietcong forces burst from the fields and villages surrounding an American air base at Bien Hoa, twenty miles northeast of Saigon, in a predawn raid that killed five Americans and wounded seventy-six and damaged or destroyed twenty-seven US aircraft. The daring assault signaled that no American installation in South Vietnam was safe. The Joint Chiefs of Staff, which for some time had been urging hawkish military responses, called on Johnson to retaliate with air strikes on the North. General Curtis LeMay, the air force chief, was especially insistent, having already complained that America had "been swatting flies when we should be going after the manure pile."[21] Secretary of State Dean Rusk soon informed General Maxwell Taylor, who had earlier replaced Lodge as America's ambassador in Saigon, that if the enemy continued to launch such attacks, "we [the United States] would initiate in January a program of slowly

graduated military actions against the North, in conjunction with negotiating moves." But LBJ, maintaining his pose as a calm and cau-
tious captain, chose not to rock the boat before the election.[22] The
moment passed.

The results of the election were extraordinary. As Johnson had
predicted after signing the Civil Rights Act, Goldwater proved to be
popular among Southern whites, winning a majority of their votes in
every Southern state except Texas. He took 87 percent of the white
vote in Mississippi and 70 percent of it in Alabama. But Goldwater
carried only six states—five in the Deep South and his home state of
Arizona. Johnson received 61.1 percent of the ballots—a percentage
that eclipsed FDR's record (of 60.8 percent) in 1936—and outpolled
his opponent by sixteen million votes. The new Congress would be
heavily Democratic—295 to 140 in the House (a Democratic gain of
37), and 68 to 32 in the Senate (a gain of two). These were the largest
Democratic margins since the late 1930s. LBJ, elated, emerged from
the campaign confident that Americans did not oppose his Vietnam
policies and that Congress would be eager to enact his Great Society
measures.

Many political commentators were so awed by these results that
they wondered if conservatism—or even the two-party system—would
survive. Political columnist James Reston of the *New York Times* wrote,
"The election has finished the Goldwater school of political reaction."
Ignoring the adulation that Reagan had received, *Time* added, "The
conservative cause whose championship Goldwater assumed suffered
a crippling setback. . . . The humiliation of their defeat was so complete that they will not have another shot at party domination for
some time to come."[23]

It later became evident that pundits heralding the end of the
conservative moment exaggerated the staying power of the liberal
surge. As events in 1965 were to demonstrate, moderate as well as
conservative Republicans soon began to rise from the ashes. Drawing
on historically powerful popular distrust of Washington and the
specter of Big Government, they would regroup to become a political
force by the end of that year.

The Democratic political coalition, moreover, was as unwieldy as it
was large. Faced with a right-wing foe like Goldwater, it held together

to carry the election. But it contained "haves" as well as "have-nots," urban liberal professionals, blue-collar unionists, and a great many eager interest groups. Many of these lobbies spoke the contagious but often self-serving language of "rights," thereby nourishing a clamorous claimant culture. It remained to be seen whether the Johnson administration could satisfy the high expectations of the ever-growing numbers of Americans who were accelerating the Rights Revolution of the Sixties.

—

WITH THE ELECTION OVER, THE MEDIA PAID INCREASINGLY CLOSE attention to worrisome events in Southeast Asia, where Buddhists, students, and others were mounting tumultuous demonstrations against the corrupt and unpopular leaders of South Vietnam. The South Vietnamese army seemed reluctant to fight. *Time*, which pursued a strongly anticommunist editorial policy, ran a cover story in its December 4 issue that focused on these events, writing ominously, "The latest U.S.-backed government [in Saigon] is struggling to cope with student riots," and adding, "Communist guerrillas roam freely over more than half of the country." Wishfully, it concluded, "most military men believe that extension [of the war] offers the only possible solution." LBJ, however, still held back. Though he could be willful and impulsive, he did not stumble impetuously into what later critics would call the "quagmire" that ultimately trapped the United States in Vietnam. On the contrary, he knew he had to move deliberately before making what he understood would be a historic decision that could divide the American people and threaten his domestic program. To prepare for such a decision, he held frequent conferences in November and December with his civilian and military advisers.[24]

A few of these officials, notably Undersecretary of State George Ball, an experienced diplomat who believed that Europe, not Asia, was the major arena for the United States to be concerned with, spoke out against American military engagement.[25] Tolerated by LBJ, he acted as a devil's advocate in many such meetings throughout 1965. Ball, backed by a few lesser advisers, also dismissed what was known as the "domino theory," the notion that if South Vietnam fell to communism, other nations in Southeast Asia—Laos, Cambodia, the Philippines, Indonesia, Thailand—would topple, too. They reminded Johnson that the French, hoping to protect their colonial interests, had sent a quarter of a million troops to Indochina, only to suffer defeat. North Vietnam, they argued, could and would match whatever additional troop commitments America might make.

These advisers, including some in the CIA, further maintained that bombing North Vietnam would not deter Ho Chi Minh, an iron-willed revolutionary.[26] Nor would it succeed in preventing men and supplies from reaching the South via the Ho Chi Minh trail. North Vietnam, Johnson was cautioned, was fighting what was a civil war, and it was prepared to suffer huge losses of resources and manpower until it achieved its ultimate goal—uniting the two Vietnams under its control. Others to whom LBJ talked during this critical time also counseled restraint. European allies, including President Charles de Gaulle of France, reminded him that past American statements of support for South Vietnam—notably by Eisenhower and Kennedy—did not require the United States to engage its bombers or combat troops. The United States, they stressed, would not lose "credibility" in the world—a major concern of the president—if it declined to escalate its involvement.

Some political leaders, including Mike Mansfield of Montana, a former professor of Asian history who was the well-regarded majority leader in the Senate, were equally cool to the notion of outright military intervention. Arguing that Vietnam was not a place of strategic importance to American interests, they urged LBJ to agree to negotiations with Hanoi—in the hope that the North Vietnamese might settle for having its southern allies represented in a coalition government in South Vietnam. Ambassador Maxwell Taylor, a general renowned for his exploits in World War II, recommended retaliatory bombing of North Vietnamese installations, but in messages from Saigon he regularly cautioned Johnson that American soldiers were poorly trained to fight a jungle war against determined guerrillas on their home ground.[27]

Yet another advocate of restraint was Richard Russell, a Georgia Democrat who for many years had headed the Senate's important Armed Services Committee. Russell, a bachelor, had been LBJ's mentor and closest friend on Capitol Hill in the 1950s, and well before 1964 he had become virtually a member of the Johnson family circle. Although he was a staunch Cold Warrior who consistently supported the military, the thought of sending American combat soldiers to Vietnam unnerved him. In November, he repeated warnings he had first given Johnson in May, when he told him that Vietnam was "just one of those places where you can't win." If the United States became seriously involved there, it would be "a Korea on a much larger scale . . . the most expensive venture this country ever went into." One way for America to withdraw from such a troubled country, Russell concluded, was to have "a man running the government over there that told us to get out."[28]

These and other warnings confirmed Johnson's sense that South Vietnam, even with vast increases of American economic and military aid, could not expect to win the war. But he nonetheless resisted the conclusions of those who urged accommodation with the enemy. Instead, he listened to his closest advisers—McNamara, Rusk, and Bundy. All were Kennedy appointees, men whom the writer David Halberstam would describe in 1972, not without irony, as "the best and the brightest" foreign policy and defense specialists the nation possessed. Men who prided themselves on their energy, expertise, and style, they did not always serve Johnson well. By late 1964, they had given up hope that negotiations with North Vietnam might end in a deal protecting the independence of South Vietnam. Instead, they were coming to the conclusion that if the situation in the South further deteriorated, America must send in combat troops and bomb North Vietnam.

If Johnson had focused on foreign affairs rather than domestic policy during his extensive congressional career, which had begun in 1937, and as vice president under JFK, he might not have heeded the advice of these Kennedy men. But, unsure of himself, he relied heavily on this inner circle of defense and foreign policy advisers.

And why not? McNamara, who exuded certainty and authority, excelled at using pointers, flip charts, and graphs to demonstrate his grasp of technology and of a range of complicated military issues. Having run the Ford Motor Company before becoming JFK's secretary of defense, he was called by Halberstam the "can-do man in the can-do society in the can-do era." Johnson, in awe of McNamara's talent, relied heavily on him in 1964 and 1965. Rusk, a former Rhodes scholar and president of the Rockefeller Foundation, had considerable experience in the world of diplomacy, especially regarding Asia. He was an ardent Cold Warrior who believed in the existence of an international communist conspiracy, led by China and the USSR, that was enabling North Vietnam to overrun the South. Should that succeed, he warned, the United States would suffer a terrible Cold War defeat. Bundy, described by a critic as a man who could "chill a polar bear with his codfish-cold scorn," had become Harvard's dean of faculty at the age of thirty-four, remaining in that high-level post for eight commanding years before becoming Kennedy's national security advisor. Continuing at that post under LBJ, he was orderly, articulate, and brimming with self-confidence.[29] Though Johnson made a point of listening to doubters such as George Ball in meetings, it was clear to his inner circle by late 1964 that such gatherings had become set pieces: he had all but made up his mind to intervene militarily in the war.

His conviction still did not impel him to act immediately. Having long since ordered the Pentagon to select North Vietnamese bombing targets, he was well prepared to set the air force loose. But he was aware that results of strategic bombing in World War II had often been overrated, and he was skeptical of large claims for aerial bombardment. "I have never felt the war will be won from the air," he cabled Ambassador Taylor in January. "What is needed is more effective strength on the ground."[30] He complained that the Joint Chiefs kept coming to see him in the early morning in order to chant, "Bomb, Bomb, Bomb." And that they would return in the afternoon and go after him again, "Bomb, Bomb, Bomb."[31]

As Johnson had earlier revealed in his comments to Lodge, however, he was afraid of appearing to be weak in the face of hostile powers and of being the president who would "lose" Vietnam. Those who urged him to give in, he sneered, suffered from "Nobel Prize fever."[32] Like many Americans of his generation, he also believed in what was often called the "Munich analogy"—that appeasement of Hitler at a Munich conference in 1938 had backfired, leading the Nazis to undertake aggressive military moves. Any such appeasement of North Vietnam, he believed, would encourage communist aggression not only in Southeast Asia but also throughout the world. If he were to back away from what he believed were long-standing American commitments to preserve the freedom and independence of South Vietnam, he would badly damage the all-important credibility of the United States, leader of the Free World. (History offers many such questionable lessons.)

Having settled on such a course, Johnson made a decision in early December. When and if the political and military situation in Vietnam seemed to call for it, he would rely on the Tonkin Gulf Resolution and escalate America's military presence in Vietnam.

He did not, however, share this decision with the American people—or with the media. Neither then, when it might have mattered, nor later was there anything approaching an open or high-level public debate in the United States over Vietnam policy. Unaware of Johnson's intentions, *Time*, for instance, concluded in its December 4 story that American escalation was improbable. It quoted the president as saying that any ideas about widening the war were "premature." LBJ, it added, had observed, "When you crawl out on a limb, you always have to find another one to crawl back on." *Time* concluded, "The likelihood is that the President has no intention now of extending the Vietnamese war in any meaningful way."[33]

———

THOUGH THE MEDIA RAN DISCOURAGING NEWS ACCOUNTS ABOUT Vietnam later in December, these did not seem to upset many Americans. Even word of a Christmas Eve bloodbath that killed two Americans and injured fifty-eight in Saigon itself—Vietcong forces had planted a bomb in a hotel housing American officers—did not arouse great popular alarm. After all, the United States did not have combat troops in Vietnam, only military "advisers." And the president, who had said he would keep the nation out of war, tried to downplay the seriousness of the attack and refrained from retaliating during the Christmas season.[34]

Instead of worrying about Vietnam, most Americans continued to concern themselves in December with their jobs and other matters closer to home. Christmas shoppers flocked to the stores. Millions watched the animated TV movie *Rudolph the Red-Nosed Reindeer.* Throughout December and into 1965, television featured specials on the inspirational deeds of heroes from JFK's *Profiles in Courage.* The hero in mid-December was Sam Houston, the soldier-statesman from the Republic of Texas who had led its struggles against Mexico in the 1830s and 1840s. If LBJ, whose brother was named Sam Houston Johnson, had watched it, he would surely have been delighted.

—

IT WAS AT THIS LARGELY CONFIDENT TIME THAT PRESIDENT JOHNSON, lighting the National Christmas Tree, made his memorable observation, "These are the most hopeful times in all the years since Christ was born in Bethlehem." Given the good news that had graced the year, and the widespread though misplaced sense that Johnson would manage to keep the nation out of war, it is unsurprising that this statement, ludicrous though it would have seemed if uttered during the contentious atmosphere that had blanketed the nation by December 1965, did not seem extreme.

3

LBJ

Big Man in a Big Hurry

As THE CRYSTAL BALL DROPPED SLOWLY DOWN THE FLAGPOLE ATOP One Times Square, heralding the arrival of 1965, crowds of people were on hand to rejoice. Merrymakers then dispersed, some for revels that would ring in the New Year. Similarly joyful gatherings elsewhere in the United States highlighted the upbeat tenor of American life at the close of 1964.

Had the celebrants paused to ponder the controversies simmering abroad and elsewhere in America, they might well have been sobered. One of the most troubling of these controversies concerned race. On January 2, Martin Luther King announced in Selma, Alabama, that black civil rights advocates were determined to demonstrate for their right to vote. "We must be willing," he told seven hundred cheering supporters, "to go to jail by the thousands. We are not asking, we are demanding the ballot."[1] Within the next few weeks, King and other protestors were beaten and jailed. White-incited racial violence seemed likely to explode.[2]

Troubles overseas also disturbed the peace. Some of these, remote in place and interest for Americans, elicited little concern: chronic civil war in the Congo, fighting in Nigeria between Islamists and their foes, rebels battling against Portuguese rule in Mozambique, Greeks struggling against Turks over Cyprus, tensions between India and Pakistan (which were to erupt into warfare later in the year), and artillery duels between Syria and Israel. Unrest was rising in the Dominican Republic. President Sukarno of Indonesia pulled his country out of the United Nations after it awarded a temporary seat on the Security Council to Malaysia, with which Indonesia was then at war.[3]

Harder for Americans to ignore in January 1965 were the latest salvos in the Cold War. On New Year's Day, the Soviet Union announced, "Let this be a year of further strengthening of the fraternal friendship of the countries of Socialism, a year of strengthening of the unity of the international communist movement"—a declaration that portended intensified Soviet support of "national liberation" struggles throughout the world.[4] Reports in the press of military developments in "Red China"—it was said to have amassed an army of 2.3 million men—were also unsettling, leading *Life* in early January to warn of dangers from "Chinese imperialism."[5]

And then there was Vietnam. As 1965 dawned, fierce fighting that had raged since December 28 intensified in the village of Binh Gia, which was only forty-five miles southeast of Saigon. Featuring armored vehicles and sophisticated weaponry, it was the first large-scale battle between South Vietnamese regular forces and the Vietcong. When it ended, the Vietcong were victorious, tightening a noose around Saigon. Some two hundred South Vietnamese soldiers (and five American military advisers) had been killed.[6]

The political situation in Saigon was also continuing to deteriorate. Despite American economic aid and military presence, a newly installed regime in the capital was already in danger of collapse. Reports of fresh combat and of government instability led to heightened alarm. The *New York Times* editorialized, "the dilemma [for the United States] is that no one has an alternate course to suggest that does not involve the enormous risks of an expanded war or the abandonment of all our commitments to the area."[7] A few days after Binh Gia, a lead editorial, "To L.B.J.: What *Is* Our Aim in Vietnam?" appeared in *Life*, which (like *Time*, its sister magazine under publisher Henry Luce) was staunchly anticommunist. Complaining of LBJ's secretiveness, the editorial told the president that he owed the American people "a fuller statement of our aims in Vietnam." It also demanded to know why 136 American military "advisers"—men who were not supposed to be fighting there—had been "killed in action" in 1964.[8]

———

AMERICANS, HOWEVER, HAD MANY WAYS OF TUNING OUT UNPLEASANT overseas developments such as these. On New Year's Eve, millions watched Johnny Carson's *Late Show,* whose guests included Jayne Mansfield, the voluptuous blonde movie star who epitomized the still prevalent 1950s ideal of female pulchritude. If they stayed up until midnight, they likely turned to CBS, which still featured—as it had since 1956—Guy Lombardo's orchestra playing "Auld Lang Syne." On January 1, they could tune into the Orange Bowl, which for the first time in history was played at night. It featured Alabama, the national championship team, against Texas. Reflecting the growing importance of television revenue to high-level intercollegiate sports, Paul "Bear" Bryant, the legendary 'Bama coach, declared, "I'll play at midnight if that's what TV wants."[9]

Most reassuring of all, the economy seemed headed for unimaginable successes. On New Year's Day, the *New York Times* headlined, "Banner Year on Big Board Saw Records Toppled Like Tenpins," reporting that the Dow Industrial Index had jumped 144 points in 1964 (and by 44 percent over the previous two years) to close the year at 874.13. The paper's prediction of further gains was prescient—the Dow topped 900 for the first time in its history on January 29 and continued to rise during the next few months.

On Inauguration Day, January 20, James Reston of the *New York Times* further hailed the state of the economy, writing that Johnson would be entering his four-year term "riding on the greatest economic boom in peacetime history." *Time* ran an essay, "Boom Without Bust?" in which it rhapsodized, "Economic policy has begun to liberate itself from the preoccupations of an earlier day and from the bitterness of class or partisan division that becloud rational discussion and hamper national action."[10] No single event better revealed the fact that money was awash in the culture than the signing of Joe Namath, Alabama's star quarterback, to a professional football contract with the American Football

League's New York Jets. The signing ceremony, featured on newspapers' front pages, took place on January 2, the day after Namath had played in the Orange Bowl. He received a three-year deal, including a bonus and various perks, which totaled $427,000. This was by far the biggest contract in the history of the sport. The Jets also threw in a Jet-green Lincoln convertible. "With that kind of salary," Bob Hope cracked, "Joe Namath will be playing quarterback in a business suit."[11]

MANY OF THE BIGGEST STORIES OF EARLY 1965 FOCUSED ON THE doings of President Johnson. Indeed, coverage of *Time*'s fifty-six-year-old 1964 Man of the Year—especially of his efforts to enact Great Society programs—blanketed the nation throughout the early months of 1965.

Johnson, who only a few days after Kennedy's assassination had called for a civil rights act to honor his memory, persisted thereafter in linking his goals with those of his martyred predecessor. Given the sense of loss that many people still felt following JFK's assassination, this was important in enabling Americans to feel a sense of continuity amid tragedy. It was also shrewd and effective politics. Moreover, LBJ knew that Americans in early 1965 were confident about the capacity of the federal government. Polls indicated that more than 75 percent of people believed they "could trust government to do the right thing most of the time."[12] Seizing the moment in January, LBJ wasted no time in driving for his Great Society programs. On January 4, the day after the start of the congressional session, he used his State of the Union address—delivered in the evening for the first time in American history so it could be seen on prime-time television—to outline his list of goals. It was estimated that thirty-one million people tuned in.

What they heard, delivered in LBJ's characteristically measured fashion, echoed the optimism he had offered while lighting the National Christmas Tree in December. Touching briefly on foreign affairs, he proudly declared he would stand firm against communist aggression in South Vietnam—a pledge, he reiterated, made by his three predecessors as president. He also hoped for better relations with Latin American nations and with the Soviet Union.

But Johnson cared most deeply about domestic policy. Having digested the task force reports he had commissioned in mid-1964, he called for passage of a huge bundle of programs he would urge on Congress in the coming months: an education bill that that would aid disadvantaged public school students; a government effort (labeled Medicare) that would provide health care for the elderly via Social Security; laws to advance clean air, clean water, and the landscaping of highways; increased funding for the War on Poverty; repeal of a controversial clause, Section 14(b), of the Taft-Hartley Act—a goal of union leaders—and creation of a National Foundation on the Arts.[13]

LBJ also asked for a "substantial" cut in excise taxes; extension of federal minimum wage coverage to millions of unprotected workers; "unified long-range policies for metropolitan areas," to be managed by a proposed Department of Housing and Urban Development; "new efforts to control and prevent crime and delinquency"; regional development programs to aid distressed areas; and (with the Selma protests in mind) elimination of "every remaining obstacle to the right and opportunity to vote." LBJ even called for funding in support of "test projects" for high-speed rail service that would move people from Boston to Washington in less than four hours.

Liberals, having been stymied by conservatives in Congress for nearly thirty years, ever since the later days of FDR's New Deal, were understandably delighted. Like Johnson, they were all but hypnotized by the strength of the economy. The nation, they believed, could easily afford to establish the ambitious programs LBJ had in mind. In this sense, the liberal surge accompanying the quest for a Great Society (like Kennedy's quest for a New Frontier, only much stronger) was different from the bread-and-butter liberalism FDR had fashioned as emergency measures intended to lift the nation out of the depths of the Depression.

The quest for a Great Society was in truth an unusual reform movement in American history. Though it drew on a popular sense that large problems needed to be addressed, notably those concerning race and poverty, it also benefited from popular pride and satisfaction in the nation's accomplishments, rather than from a widespread sense that the nation's economic and social contract with its citizens was broken and needed to be fixed. Johnson and his ambitious fellow liberals exuded confidence—even hubris—about the capacity of the nation to prosper and of the government to accomplish wonderful things.

This Great Society venture would not mean an undertaking of politically perilous ventures to redistribute income or assail vested interests—LBJ, a pragmatist seeking consensus, was hardly a radical. Nor, Johnson insisted, would Great Society programs lead to vastly increased government debt. In a budget message he gave three weeks after his State of the Union address, the president estimated that with the enactment of his proposed legislation, the government's adminis- trative budget would be $99.7 billion, only a little more than the $97.9 billion he had requested a year earlier.[14] In his search for consensus, Johnson focused not on guaranteeing expensive entitlements—or in pioneering for a Rights Revolution—but on the goal of widening the *opportunity* of people who had been denied access to the American Dream. The government, relying on rising revenue streams from prosperous taxpayers, would enact long overdue reforms and pioneer new ones to move toward equality of opportunity and enhance the quality of life for all.

The remarkable self-assurance of liberals in 1965 also stemmed from what some contemporaries referred to as a "knowledge revolu- tion," which among other things would not only promote a successful "war" against poverty but also succeed over time in placing a man on the moon. As LBJ once put the matter, "any problem could be solved." Humphrey, his ebullient vice president, agreed, explaining, "Only if we wait passively for the future to come will we be its victims rather than its masters. . . . For no matter how complex the world might be, it is still *our* world, and its complexity is in great part *our* creation."[15]

Daniel Patrick Moynihan, a bright young Kennedy appointee and intellectual gadfly who was serving as LBJ's assistant secretary of labor in 1965, emphatically agreed with such visions. He wrote proudly of the "professionalization of the middle classes," "the exponential growth of knowledge," and the "econometric revolution" that had led to all manner of possibilities for the application of governmental plan- ning. The economic policies of the Kennedy administration, he went on to say, represented "perhaps the most impressive demonstration of the capacity of organized intelligence to forecast and direct events that has yet occurred in American government of the present era."[16]

Many editorialists, caught up in these grand expectations about the ability of government to solve problems, gave near-rhapsodic support to Johnson's goals. *Life* wrote, "What Johnson is telling us is the simple truth: that the American people have more and better options than any society ever had." Although *Newsweek* worried that "South Vietnam remains the great canker—chronic, nagging, and susceptible to no quick or easy solutions," it quickly moved on, gushing that the Great Society "is an attempt to put a label on the kind of sustained national effort that hopefully could lead to a new Antonine Age—that golden time in the history of Rome which, in Gibbon's phrase, was 'possibly the only period in history in which the happiness of a great people was the sole object of government.'"[17]

Johnson, always aware of the need for quick and decisive action, prided himself on sending Congress six special messages for domestic reforms by January 17. No other president had ever exhibited such a degree of executive activism. He also busied himself planning the most magnificent inauguration ceremonies in American history. Costing an estimated $1.5 million, the extravaganza featured a host of pre-inaugural receptions and banquets, as well as gala nights of ballet, orchestral music, and singing before large audiences. Some 1.2 million spectators showed up to watch the inaugural parade. Until 2009, when bigger throngs turned out for Barack Obama, it remained by far the largest Inauguration Day crowd in American history.[18]

—

WHILE THE MEDIA UNDERSTANDABLY PAID CLOSE ATTENTION TO such public events, they were also cognizant of Johnson's skill as a behind-the-scenes persuader and manipulator. Indeed, old Washington hands knew him well, for he had been something of a fixture on Capitol Hill ever since late 1931, when as a tall, thin Texan of twenty-three he had started serving as secretary to a Democratic congressman from his home state. An ardent admirer of Franklin D. Roosevelt, Johnson was selected by FDR in 1935 to head the National Youth Administration in Texas. The NYA job, which Johnson performed with headline-capturing energy, strongly influenced his approach to politics and policies. Seeking to aid deprived young people, he developed an abiding faith in the duty of the federal government to provide opportunity for Americans who were in need and willing to work hard to get ahead. This faith, not in governmental handouts or long-term welfare support but in government as a provider of education, job training, and economic opportunity to people who deserved a leg up, remained the bedrock of his liberal political philosophy.

Though the NYA directorship was for a while a fulfilling job, Johnson was eager to return to Washington, and when the chance to compete for an open Texas seat in the US House of Representatives arose in 1937, he seized it. Running as a New Dealer, he won the race in April and returned to the Hill. There, save for wartime service in the navy, he remained until 1948. At that time, he won a hotly contested Democratic primary that helped him gain a seat in the US Senate.

LBJ was only forty years old when he was sworn in as a senator in January 1949. He moved speedily ahead, becoming Senate minority leader in 1953. When the Democrats regained control of the Senate in January 1955, LBJ was chosen as majority leader. At forty-six, he was the youngest man in American history to hold this important post. For the next six years, he worked closely with his friend and fellow Texan Sam Rayburn, Speaker of the House, in an effort to hold fractious Democrats together while Dwight Eisenhower remained in the White House.

Johnson was a stiff and ineffective speaker; soaring, JFK-style rhetoric was not his forte. Nor did he ever receive—either as a Senate leader or as president—the popular adulation that Kennedy inspired. But he was a consummate insider and wheeler-dealer as Senate leader. Indeed, then as in his White House years, politics was his religion. He read no books, had no hobbies, and could barely sit through a new movie. Boundlessly energetic, he made it his business to learn everything he could about the habits and private lives of his colleagues—and to use his know-how effectively when he needed a crucial vote.[19]

By the late 1950s, reporters and others were taking special note of what they called the "Johnson Treatment": a manner of persuading and manipulating people that remained central to his style of leadership as president. As described by the journalists Rowland Evans and Robert Novak, it relied in part on threats and accusations but also on wheedling, flattery, or even tears. The Treatment, which was relentless and often intimidating, featured physical domination. Johnson was six feet four inches tall, with long and drooping ears, a creased face, big jowls, a very large head, and a broad chest. His eyes, dark and piercing, bore in on people and added to his thoroughly commanding presence. When he applied the Treatment, he towered over people: "he moved in close, his face a scant millimeter from his target, his eyes widening and narrowing, his eyebrows rising and falling. From his pockets poured clippings, memos, statistics. Mimicry, humor, and the genius of analogy made the Treatment an almost hypnotic experience and rendered the target stunned and helpless."[20]

One recipient of the Treatment explained why he changed his mind to agree with Johnson on a matter of policy: "Lyndon got me by the lapels and put his face on top of mine and he talked and talked and talked. I figured it was either getting drowned or joining." Ben Bradlee, executive editor of the *Washington Post*, likened LBJ to a St. Bernard who "licked your face for an hour [and] pawed you all over." Hubert Humphrey, LBJ's Senate colleague, said of one experience (in an obvious exaggeration), "I came out of that session covered in blood, sweat, tears, spit, and sperm."[21]

Well before 1965, Washington insiders also came to recognize that LBJ was liberal on many matters of domestic policy. Breaking with his Southern colleagues in 1957, he was a key figure in enabling passage of that year's Civil Rights Act. Because of opposition from Southern legislators, this was necessarily a modest measure that aimed—with little success—to secure better voting rights for blacks, but it was nonetheless the first civil rights bill that had gotten through Congress since Reconstruction some ninety years earlier.

Johnson, a restlessly ambitious man, craved power—not for its own sake but to use it to implement his aspirations for domestic reforms. Having virtually conquered the Senate by the late 1950s, he yearned to become president. Though he was defeated in his quest for the Democratic presidential nomination in 1960, John F. Kennedy, hoping that placing Johnson on the ticket would help him win votes in the South, asked him to be his running mate. This was a shock to JFK's closest advisers, notably his campaign manager, Robert Kennedy, who made no secret of his loathing for the large and imperious Texan who had challenged his older brother for the nomination.

The antipathy was mutual: Johnson often privately described Kennedy's younger brother as "that little runt." While stunned by the offer, Johnson nonetheless accepted it, even though he had an essentially low opinion of JFK. Behind his back, LBJ often called him "sonny boy" and a "lightweight." And he wondered why Kennedy was so popular. "It was the goddamnedest thing," he mused later. "Here was a whippersnapper. . . . He never said a word of importance in the Senate and he never did a thing. . . . His growing hold on the American people was simply a mystery to me."[22]

Johnson was frustrated and often miserable as vice president. Though Kennedy treated him courteously, LBJ knew he was excluded from the president's inner circle and therefore isolated from any significant role in policymaking. Many of JFK's top aides, regarding him as an uncouth Southerner (a "Rufus Cornpone"), barely hid their contempt for him.[23] Some were maneuvering in 1963 to ditch him as the vice-presidential nominee in 1964. Johnson, a proud man, found belittlement of this sort deeply humiliating. But when JFK was assassinated in November 1963, LBJ quickly and ably took decisive command and associated himself with JFK's domestic and foreign policies. He also kept on some of the top Kennedy appointees, including McNamara, Rusk, and Bundy. Then and throughout 1964 and 1965, Johnson repeatedly reminded the American people that he was carrying out the New Frontier agenda of his predecessor.

—

Pressing for Great Society programs in early 1965, Johnson yearned to be loved and honored by all—and especially to outperform his idol, FDR. He would prove himself in quantitative terms by getting more and bigger domestic programs through Congress than Roosevelt had and by signing laws quickly, as FDR had done in the fabled Hundred Days of 1933. Not for nothing was Johnson often portrayed as a larger-than-life, can-do Texan.

To succeed in this quest, Johnson possessed advantages that few American presidents have enjoyed, notably the mandate that voters had given him in 1964 and the huge Democratic majorities he would command on the Hill. Having served in Congress for many years, he was well informed about key issues, and he was on good terms with most of its leaders. Among the new senators were liberals who became well known in the future—Birch Bayh of Indiana and Walter Mondale of Minnesota among them. Mike Mansfield of Montana, the majority leader, was a well-regarded figure. Though he questioned LBJ's Vietnam policies, he was a staunch liberal on domestic matters and a loyal leader who did not go public with his reservations about Vietnam. Moreover, there were sixty-five freshmen Democrats in the House, fifty-six of whom were from outside the South. One of these was Patsy Mink of Hawaii, the first woman of Asian background to be elected to the House. Another, Lee Hamilton of Indiana, explained, "The President's election and immense popularity helped me get elected. In a sense, we're all tied to him."[24] On important roll call votes throughout the session, Democratic freshmen almost unanimously followed the president's directions.

House Republicans, a small and demoralized minority, replaced their leader, Charles Halleck of Indiana, with a younger man, Gerald Ford of Michigan. (Rep. Donald Rumsfeld of Illinois, a Republican young Turk at the time, was a key Ford backer.) Ford was only a little less conservative than Halleck, but he knew he could not stop the Democratic majority, and he was not disposed to be mindlessly obstructive. Indeed, Ford and the Senate Republican leader, the colorful Everett Dirksen of Illinois, were sometimes moderate in their opposition. The congressional politics of 1965, while heated at times, included a number of aisle-crossing deal makers and was less partisan than in later years. In some areas of domestic policy—civil rights, for instance—Republicans (with tiny Southern representation) were key supporters of the administration.

Taking no chances, Johnson went out of his way to establish amicable relationships with legislators of both parties. "I am not for denouncing Congress all the time," he explained to a historian in late 1965. "I am not like . . . writers who think of congressmen as archaic buffoons with tobacco drool running down their shirts. . . . I got up at seven this morning to have breakfast with them. I don't have contempt for them."[25] In fact, LBJ spent hours on the phone with congressmen and senators, held frequent one-on-one meetings with leaders, and hosted regular Tuesday morning breakfast gatherings in the White

House, where his guests encountered an imposing chart indicating the current status of administration legislation. He also saw to it that the chairs of key congressional committees were loyalists. Wilbur Mills of Arkansas, who headed House Ways and Means, was to become especially valuable in the quest for Medicare early in the session. At the start of the session, LBJ loyalists in the House also managed to weaken the Rules Committee, which in the past had frequently blocked liberal legislation from reaching the floor. To circumvent the ultraconservative chair of the committee, Howard Smith of Virginia, the House agreed to allow the Speaker (John McCormack of Massachusetts) to force a floor vote to consider a bill twenty-one days after it reached the Rules Committee and to send bills that the House had approved to Senate-House conference committees without the approval of Rules. Johnson, delighted with the "Twenty-One-Day Rule," rejoiced, "The situation in Congress could be better, but not this side of heaven."[26]

In planning his legislative efforts, Johnson displayed a characteristically obsessive quest for political information. He installed three television sets in the Oval Office—one for each major network—that were often turned on while he worked. He also placed three TVs in his bedroom, as well as at his ranch (the LBJ Ranch) in Texas. He labored long hours, sometimes going without dinner or grabbing a bite late in the evening. When he climbed into bed, he often watched television while studying official documents or leafing through newspapers—he read several papers every day—scattered about him on the bedcovers. He conducted an immense amount of business over the telephone, secretly taping hundreds of hours of conversations.[27]

Johnson relied further on a corps of loyal and overworked aides. In 1965, these included Larry O'Brien, a Kennedy holdover who was expert as a liaison with Congress; Richard Goodwin, his chief speechwriter; Bill Moyers, a press secretary and later in 1965 his top aide; and Joseph Califano, a young man who became a key assistant in the middle of that year. With their help, LBJ, an incredibly forceful and energetic man, succeeded in 1965 in becoming the most effective congressional manager in modern American history.

It was amazing, however, that many of these aides remained loyal to their boss, because as Washington insiders knew, LBJ had epic weaknesses that coexisted with his many-splendored talents. He was a domineering, deceitful, and needy man—what his biographer Robert Dallek was to call a "flawed giant."[28] Extraordinarily difficult to work for, he was given to bellowing rages, self-pitying rants, explosions of vulgar language, and lengthy, boastful monologues. Ingratiating himself with people who could help him, he was frequently tyrannical in his treatment of others, including his long-suffering aides.

Johnson not only insisted on sycophantic service but also required that his assistants be reachable at all times. Shortly after Califano joined the White House staff, LBJ telephoned him, only to be told by Califano's secretary that he was in the bathroom. "Isn't there a phone in there?" Johnson demanded. Told no, he ordered her to have one installed right away. It was. LBJ even instructed his aides on how to wear their hair and how to dress. One time at the LBJ Ranch, he began staring at Califano's necktie. "Take the tie off," he demanded. "That four-in-hand knot looks like a limp prick. Let me show you how to tie a knot." Johnson then proceeded to place the tie around Califano's neck and secure it with a Windsor knot. When Lady Bird, his wife, walked in, he said, "Look at Joe's tie. He's got a man's knot now, not a limp one."[29]

LBJ was especially sensitive about his educational background. Though he had earned a BS degree in 1930, it was from a little-known institution, Southwest Texas State Teachers College in San Marcos, Texas. Many political leaders, he knew, regarded him as unlettered, unsophisticated, crude, and rude.[30] Understandably, he resented such attitudes, and he was often uncomfortable in the presence of intellectuals, academics, and well-educated people from the cosmopolitan Northeast. He told Eric Goldman, a Princeton professor who served for a short time in the Johnson White House, "I don't think I'll ever get credit for anything I do in foreign policy, because I didn't go to Harvard."[31]

As if to compensate for such insecurity, LBJ came across as a vain and highly egotistical man. As vice president, he had photo albums featuring his accomplishments passed out as presents to visiting dignitaries. He named his ranch after himself. A joke circulated well before he became president: "There was concern about God's mental health. He thinks he is Lyndon Johnson." Other stories about Johnson, most of them unkind, went the rounds. One had him driving his Lincoln

Continental convertible at maniacal speeds around his ranch—which he loved to do, frightening distinguished visitors half to death. He then stopped to relieve himself. A Secret Service man standing next to him felt warm liquid on his leg, looked down, and said, "Mr. President, you are urinating on me." LBJ replied, "I know I am . . . it's my prerogative."[32] Another story had Chancellor Ludwig Erhard of West Germany asking LBJ if it were true he had been born in a log cabin. "No, Mr. Chancellor," Johnson was supposed to have replied, "you have me confused with Abraham Lincoln. I was born in a manger."[33]

He could also be a bully. When he went to the White House swimming pool, he swam naked. On occasion, he demanded that (male) aides accompany him and that they, too, take off all their clothes. Sometimes, he pointed to what he called "Jumbo," his penis, and ridiculed the equipment of his aides.[34] The most disgusting stories involve his bathroom behavior. Sitting on a White House toilet, he would leave the bathroom door open and summon an aide to talk with him.

This was the boorish Johnson. But he could also be charming, compassionate, sentimental, and openhearted, often making grand gestures and offering gifts or lavish compliments to friends and assistants. John Connally, a one-time aide and a Texas governor who knew him well, observed that LBJ was "cruel and kind, generous and greedy, sensitive and insensitive, crafty and naïve, ruthless and thoughtful, simple in many ways yet extremely complex, caring and totally not caring. . . . He knew how to use people in politics in the way nobody else could that I know of."[35]

But many stories of his crudeness and bullying are true. Once he described his ideal aide as "someone who will kiss my ass in Macy's window and stand up and say, 'Boy, wasn't that sweet?'"[36] He told an assistant, "Just you remember this: There's only two kinds at the White House. There's elephants and there's piss ants. And I'm the only elephant." George Reedy, a presidential press secretary who grew disenchanted with LBJ, later observed that Johnson "as a human being was a miserable person—a bully, sadist, lout, and egoist. . . . His lapses from civilized conduct were deliberate and usually intended to subordinate someone else to do his will. He did disgusting things because he realized that other people had to pretend that they did not mind. It was his method of bending them to his desires."[37]

MANY OF JOHNSON'S UNATTRACTIVE PERSONAL CHARACTERISTICS were to receive considerable attention in the media. Highly sensitive to criticism, he later complained to a friend, "I feel like a hound bitch in heat in the country. If you run, they chase your tail off. If you stand still, they slip it to you."[38] Ultimately worn out, he decided in early 1968 not to run again for the White House. When he left office, he was a beaten and unpopular president.

In early 1965, however, the media were singing his praises, and polls showed that 65 to 70 percent of Americans approved of how he did his job. He gained extra confidence and power from knowing his legislative efforts would not have to face trouble from the Supreme Court the way Roosevelt's had. On the contrary, the Court, headed by Chief Justice Earl Warren, was the most liberal in American history. After it had struck down state-mandated school segregation in *Brown v. Board of Education* in 1954, it had issued a series of decisions—concerning the separation of church and state, the apportionment of state legislatures and the House of Representatives, freedom of the press, criminal justice, and civil rights. These had not only delighted liberals; they also paved the way for the extraordinary rise of popular rights-consciousness in the Sixties.

Still, Johnson was under no illusions about the power of the presidency. Although he had won a smashing victory in 1964 and had a mandate for change, he knew he had to move quickly. "Landslide Lyndon," he often told his friends, would all too soon become "Lame Duck Lyndon"—a president without political power. "You've got to give it all you can that first year," he explained to his aides. "Doesn't matter what kind of majority you come in with. You've got just one year when they [he meant Congress] treat you right, and before they start worrying about themselves." On another occasion he said, "Every day while I'm in office, I'm going to lose votes. . . . We've got to get this legislation fast. You've got to get it during the honeymoon."[39]

From his long experience on the Hill, Johnson also understood that legislators were fickle. They might break their word or slither out of an understanding. A president had to keep the pressure on at all times. This meant, as he well knew, that he would endlessly have to deploy his well-honed talents at persuasion—wheedling, flattering, bargaining, threatening—to secure his goals. "There is but one way for a President to deal with the Congress, and that is continuously, incessantly, and without interruption," he explained later. "If it's really going to work, the relationship between the President and the Congress has got to be almost incestuous. He's got to know them even better than they know themselves." Again and again he told his aides to find out everything they could about individual congressmen. As he put it later to Califano, "You've got to learn to mount the Congress like you mount a woman."[40]

Johnson's description of congressional relations, while crude, was deeply felt, as Califano came to understand. He wrote, "The first time I told the President I thought I had a congressman's vote on a bill, he snapped, 'Don't ever *think* about those things. Know, Know, KNOW! You've got to *know* you've got him, and there's only one way you know.' He raised his right hand and closed his fingers in the form of a fist. He looked at his right hand and said, 'And that's when you've got his pecker right here.' Johnson then pulled out his desk drawer, opened his fist as though he were dropping something, slammed the door closed and smiled."[41]

If a congressman or senator proved reluctant to go along with a piece of legislation, Johnson might invite him to the White House for a drink or two—he did this often with Senator Minority Leader Dirksen, an old friend from across the aisle—and find out what the man wanted in return for his vote. With Dirksen, a crafty trader, the price might be an appointment for a friend. LBJ would flatter and cajole and horse-trade until a deal could be struck: the friend would get the job, and the president get support for a vote. But if a senator or congressman remained recalcitrant, Johnson pulled no punches. Democratic Senator Frank Church of Idaho, opposing him on Vietnam issues, once defended himself to the president by observing that the columnist Walter Lippmann shared his views. Johnson replied, "I'll tell you what, Frank, the next time you want a dam in Idaho, you call Walter Lippmann and let him put it through for you."[42]

No American president, before or since, was more adept at amassing—and using—power than LBJ. What he managed to accomplish during the forthcoming congressional session was astonishing.

4

OUT-ROOSEVELTING ROOSEVELT

Johnson and the Great Society

DURING A PHONE CALL TO SENATOR JOHN McCLELLAN OF Arkansas on March 23, 1965, LBJ declared, "In the year 2000, we're going to have 80 percent of our people, over 300 million, living in the cities of the country. This damn world is shifting and changing so fast." He added,

> I got 38 percent of these young Nigro boys out on the streets. They've got no school to go to and no job. And by God, I'm *just scared to death* what's going to happen. . . . You take an old hard-peckered boy that sits around and got no *school* and got no *job* and got no *work* and got no *discipline*. His daddy's probably on relief, and his mama's probably taking mor-*phine.* Why, he ain't got nothing hurt if he gets shot. I mean he's better off dead than he is where he is.[1]

LBJ's characteristically colloquial observation, given to an old friend from the South, painted an unflattering picture of black family life—one held in the minds of many white Americans at the time. But his lament also revealed the depth of his concern over the miserable situation facing young black men in the United States. It was also in keeping with his broader belief that America simply had to do better— much better—in its efforts to improve the education and health of disadvantaged people, old as well as young, white as well as black.

During the first Hundred Days of the 1965 congressional session, Johnson's determination to effect transformative change led him to focus obsessively on trying to outdo (out-Roosevelt) Franklin D. Roosevelt, his idol, as America's greatest president in the realm of domestic policy. His strenuous efforts on behalf of a range of domestic causes, especially for health and education reforms, provide a textbook example of how a determined, skillful, and politically powerful chief executive, at the peak of his game as a congressional manager, can prevail.

LBJ'S PERSONAL EXPERIENCES HELPED ACCOUNT FOR HIS SERIOUS interest in health care issues, which had led him to advocate in 1964 for greater federal aid to medical research and hospitals. His father had died at age sixty-three from coronary disease, his mother had succumbed to cancer, and his grandmother had been immobilized by a stroke. In 1955 LBJ himself had suffered a major heart attack; he had fully recovered but was left haunted by how little time he might have left. "I don't like to sleep alone ever since my heart attack," he said to an aide. "If Lady Bird was away," the aide explained, "the President would often call friends . . . and ask them to stay at the White House in the room next to his. . . . 'The only deal is,' LBJ would say, 'you've got to leave your door open a crack so that if I holler someone will hear me.'"[2]

Johnson's support of governmental health programs stemmed also from deeper roots. Long before 1965, he and other American liberals had worried greatly about the situation facing the elderly. Millions of older Americans who needed medical care were at the mercy of the jobs they were retiring from or entirely dependent on their savings or their grown children. As LBJ often stated, some four-fifths of Americans age sixty-five or older (nineteen million people, nearly 10 percent of the population at the time) suffered from disability or chronic disease, nearly a third were in poverty, and almost half lacked health insurance. To deal with this situation, he pressed in 1965 for passage of what had come to be commonly called Medicare, which would provide medical care for those sixty-five or older via major amendments to the Social Security Act of 1935.[3]

The quest for some such law was hardly new. Liberals in the past had made a number of efforts, some of them hard-fought, to establish governmental health care. Truman had proposed a comprehensive national health insurance program, and Kennedy had sought a Medicare law to cover the elderly. But conservatives, led by the well-financed American Medical Association, had denounced these initiatives as "socialized medicine." Many physicians feared that any such government plan would disrupt the nationally predominant fee-for-service system of medical care, which featured doctors attending to patients and getting reimbursed out of patients' pockets and/or through private health insurance.

In 1964, with LBJ urging action, both the Senate and the House had enacted bills to broaden Social Security. The Senate bill included Medicare, but the House bill did not. Wilbur Mills of Arkansas, the powerful head of the House Ways and Means Committee, was a determined fiscal conservative, and he had remained uncommitted to the plan. A conference committee ultimately adjourned in September without resolving the differences between the bills. The president, irritated by Mills, at one point described him as a "prissy, prim and proper man" who "worried more about saving his face than . . . saving his country. He was afraid to put his reputation behind a risky bill." LBJ added, "When you run around saving your face all day, you end up losing your ass at night."[4]

The resounding triumph of Johnson and liberal Democrats in November greatly improved chances for passage of Medicare legislation, which LBJ made sure was introduced in both houses in January 1965 as bill number 1. Also promising for legislative success was the ever more impressive growth of the economy, which encouraged proponents of Medicare to insist that the government could afford it. Mills, a political realist, recognized that virtually all freshmen Democratic representatives favored such a law and that his committee would no longer have a dependable conservative majority. He then cooperated with Johnson and his aides—notably Health, Education, and Welfare assistant secretary Wilbur Cohen—to combine aspects of the bills that had passed in 1964 with other proposals, some of them designed by liberal Republicans. Johnson, though deeply involved in every stage of the drafting process, shrewdly acknowledged Mills's key role by often referring to the end product as the "Mills bill."

Completed by the Ways and Means Committee in late March, the complicated measure featured three main health care proposals. Part A of Medicare, to be supported by increased Social Security payroll taxes (on employers as well as employees), would set up a separate trust fund within the Social Security system to provide the elderly and people with disabilities with insurance for hospital care and skilled nursing-home care. Part B of Medicare, to be financed in part by deductions from Social Security checks and in part by general government revenue, would cover the services of doctors and nurses as well as diagnostic tests and other costs. Part B was voluntary but generous: when the program went into operation, the vast majority of the elderly signed up for it.

A companion program included in the bill, called Medicaid, considerably expanded existing legislation aimed at serving low-income people. To be administered by the states, it was a means-tested program that would rely on state and federal appropriations to provide care for the "medically needy." These would be people with low incomes who were already eligible for welfare: the disabled, the elderly, and families with dependent children.

The bill also included significant changes to the Social Security program. It raised the earnings base on which Social Security taxes were paid, increased benefits by 7 percent, liberalized the definition of disability, added to rehabilitation service programs for people on disability insurance, and lowered the age at which widows might receive benefits. It also increased federal payments for maternal and child health and children's services. All these provisions added considerably to the political attractiveness of the bill.[5]

Throughout the laborious process of legislative drafting, AMA conservatives continued to resist LBJ's efforts. They were not alone. Ronald Reagan, who spoke out against many Great Society efforts in

1965, complained that Medicare was the advance wave of socialism, which would "invade every area of freedom in this country" and predicted that it would force people to spend their "sunset years telling our children and our children's children what it was like in America when men were free."[6] The measure that LBJ and Mills had crafted, however, was far from socialistic. Unlike Truman's proposal, which had called for national health insurance, Medicare was a considerably less sweeping program that focused on the elderly. It was not a reform of existing medical practices but an extension of the delivery of medical care to people who were sixty-five and older. LBJ's proposals did not require patients to look for new physicians or upset the traditional fee-for-service basis of America's predominantly private medical care system.

Part B, which concerned doctors' services, was also careful not to antagonize health care providers. It specified that physicians would be paid their "reasonable and customary" fees at the prevailing rates in their areas and allowed doctors to work through Blue Shield and other carriers for the collection of payments. Thanks to reassurances such as these, the bill's advocates anticipated (correctly, as it turned out) that most physicians would ultimately cooperate with the new system.[7]

LBJ did all he could to downplay concerns about costs of Medicare and Medicaid to the government, which were anybody's guess at the time. (Medicaid alone, some believed, might cost the federal government and the states $3 billion or more per year.[8]) When Cohen warned him that Part B of Medicare concerning doctors' services might cost $500 million in its first year, LBJ replied, "Five hundred million. Is that all?" Waving his hand, he added, "Do it. Move that damn bill out now, before we lose it."[9] When Mills expressed fears about the cost, LBJ told him not to worry. "I'll take care of [the money]," he said. "I'll do that. . . . We had an old judge in Texas one time . . . and he said, when they talked to him one time that he might've abused the Constitution and he said, 'What's the Constitution between friends?' And I say . . . that $400 million's not going to separate us friends when it's for health."[10]

As LBJ had urged, Mills and his committee did move the bill: the House received it in late March and approved it on April 8, the ninety-sixth day of the congressional session, by the overwhelming margin of

313–115. Seventy of the 140 House Republicans joined a large majority of Democrats to pass the bill. It still had to wend its way through the Senate, but its chances looked very good; the House had always been the chief obstacle to passage. The House's action exhilarated LBJ and other liberal Democrats. A long-sought measure that would strengthen America's somewhat flimsy social service net now looked likely to become law.[11]

THOUGH SECURING PASSAGE OF MEDICARE IN THE HOUSE WAS A presidential priority in these early months of the congressional session, LBJ hardly ignored other domestic concerns. Between late January and early March, he bombarded Congress with special messages. Large-scale education reform was a particular goal—along with Medicare, it was LBJ's major domestic policy issue of the first Hundred Days of the Congress. As Humphrey put the matter, LBJ "was a nut on education. He felt that education was the greatest thing he could give to the people; he just believed in it, just like some people believe in miracle cures."[12] He was relentless in his quest for a new and ambitious plan, which he saw as a cornerstone of the wider War on Poverty launched by the creation of the Office of Economic Opportunity in 1964. "Education," he proclaimed, is "the only valid passport from poverty."

Having taught impoverished Mexican Americans in Texas as a young man in 1927–1928, LBJ had seen firsthand the linkage among poverty, education, and economic opportunity. As he showed in his phone call to Senator McClellan, he knew that blacks in particular suffered from limited educational prospects. But in his quest for political consensus, he described the issue as one that went beyond race, insisting that the nation as a whole would greatly benefit from better schools. As he put the matter, "If every person born could acquire all the education that their intelligence quotient would permit them to take, God only knows what our gross national product would be—and the strength we would add to our nation, militarily, diplomatically, economically, is too large even to imagine."[13] Johnson, in short, was passionately committed to the idea that reform of education was the key to moving young people out of poverty, and he believed that the federal government had to spend generously to make it possible. He also understood that passion was not enough: ever since the Truman years, many aid-to-education bills had gone to the Hill, only to fail. These failures, like those of health insurance bills in the past, revealed with special clarity the power of interest groups in American politics.

Racial considerations had killed some previous measures. Liberals, believing in the blessings of federal aid, generally favored federal government support of the schools. But some liberals, led by Congressman Adam Clayton Powell Jr., a Harlem-based African American who headed the House Education and Labor Committee, had in the late 1950s supported an amendment (the Powell Amendment) that barred federal financial assistance to segregated schools. Although many Southern congressmen and senators favored federal aid in principle—the South, a relatively poor region, suffered from badly financed public schools—they refused to support legislation with any such stipulation. Powell supporters and Southerners would combine to doom the bills.

Religious considerations had defeated an effort by President Kennedy. Seeking to counter the accusation that as a Catholic he supported aid to parochial schools, he had pressed for a bill that would direct federal funds only to public schools. In an exhausting fight in 1962, the National Education Association, which spoke for public school teachers, combined with the National Council of Churches to oppose federal aid to parochial schools, thereby tangling angrily with the National Catholic Welfare Conference. (Anti-Catholic rumors circulated that the Statue of Liberty was about to be renamed Our Lady of the Harbor.) Two Catholic congressmen—one of them was Thomas P. "Tip" O'Neill of Massachusetts, who represented the district that Kennedy had previously served—ultimately provided votes that helped beat Kennedy's initiative in the Rules Committee.[14]

Federal aid-to-education bills also faced opposition from those congressmen and senators, most of them conservatives, who believed that support of public schools was not a federal but a local responsibility. This had indeed been the case throughout American history: except for special situations, local tax dollars, not federal revenue, had sustained the nation's public education system. In

1962, the National School Boards Association, a lobbying group, had fought against general federal aid for public schools; the key to improving the schools did not lie in federal money, its president said, but in "re-awakening our local communities to the importance of the principle of self-autonomy."[15]

Johnson, navigating around interest groups and ideologies, had political assets that Kennedy had not enjoyed. First (as in the case of Medicare), the wonderfully buoyant state of the economy made it easier for him to press for costly public programs—greater revenue raised from income taxes would support them. Second, liberals were stronger than ever in the Congress of 1965. Third, thanks to Title VI of the Civil Rights Act of 1964, which authorized the federal government to withhold aid from segregated institutions, racial concerns that had motivated Powell and others had ceased to be relevant. Congress no longer needed to consider a Powell Amendment.

Religious concerns had also become more manageable by 1965. The National Education Association (NEA), having learned that persisting in its stand would kill federal efforts to support public schools, dropped its opposition to aid to parochial schools in 1963. Moreover, because LBJ was not a Catholic, he did not have to worry that he would be perceived as religiously motivated if he backed a bill that aided parochial as well as public schools. When he established a task force on the subject in 1964, he had also been careful to work closely with the National Catholic Welfare Conference (NCWC).

Early in 1965, he and his aides (notably Education Commissioner Francis Keppel and Health, Education, and Welfare Assistant Secretary Cohen), having enlisted the backing of the NEA and the NCWC, had also devised a clever formula for distributing federal aid. Highlighted as an essential arm of the War on Poverty, this provided a way to circumvent opposition to support for parochial schools. The formula targeted federal aid not at individual schools but at disadvantaged students—a "child benefit" approach that would provide "compensatory education" for the poor. Amounts to be allocated to school districts would depend on the number of students from low-income families—whether in public or parochial schools—that qualified under the formula.[16]

Johnson also secured language in the bill to reassure conservatives worried about intrusive federal oversight of local schools. "Nothing contained in this act," the language read,

> shall be construed to authorize any department, agency, officer, or employee of the United States to exercise any direction, super-vision, or control over the curriculum, program of instruction, administration, or personnel of any educational institution or school system, or over the selection of library resources, text-books, or other printed or published instructional materials by any educational institution or school system.[17]

Having helped to mollify the contending interest groups, John-son drove hard for his measure, which he introduced to Congress on January 12. It called for spending $1.2 billion of federal money on elementary and secondary schools, roughly $1 billion of which would support Title I of the act, the child benefit plan. Confronting Keppel, he explained—as he often did to aides—that new presidents lose popular support at a rate of about a million voters a month. He demanded to know when congressional subcommittee hearings on the bill would start, telling Keppel, "I want to see this coonskin on the wall."[18]

Adam Clayton Powell, who had backed Johnson's presidential run in 1960, seemed ready by early February to push the measure through his Education and Labor Committee. But Powell, a loose cannon, was also insisting that the House increase its financial support of the committee's operating expenses, and he retreated from Washington in early February for a sojourn in Bimini and Puerto Rico. Alarmed and irritated, Speaker of the House John McCormack and Larry O'Brien, LBJ's liaison with Congress, tried to track him down. Powell would not answer the phone. It was not until the end of the month that he returned to Washington, at which point he let it be known that he expected the House to authorize an additional $400,000 to cover the committee's expenses. Powell also alleged that a clause in the administration's $1.1 billion Appalachian aid bill, then near pas-sage, was "anti-Negro."

When Johnson learned of Powell's return, he was deeply engaged in implementing Operation Rolling Thunder, a massive bombing effort about to start in Vietnam. But in a classic demonstration of his forceful congressional leadership, he was quick to go after Powell. With Lady Bird sitting nearby, he telephoned him at 9:32 PM on March 1 and let him have it. The conversation was taped:

> LBJ: Adam, what the hell has been happening to your committee? I thought you told me two months ago that you were going to pass a bill for me.
> POWELL: . . . All hell has broken loose.
> LBJ: What the hell are you blackmailing me on a—
> POWELL: Let me—
> LBJ: The hell you didn't! You wanted a $400,000 appropriation for you. . . . You damn near defeated the best education bill I've got! I hope you're going to be proud of it!

When Powell interjected to argue his case about the Appalachia bill and his office needs, LBJ again cut him off, reminding the chair of his promise to get the education bill quickly to the floor.

> POWELL: By March first, I told you.
> LBJ: Oh, *hell no!* You didn't say March first. You told me you were going to *do* it. Then you ran off for three weeks and they couldn't even locate you. . . . This [the education bill] is the thing we ran on all over the country. Your people [blacks] are being damn well taken care of in it.

After Powell wheedled some more, LBJ berated him because committee opponents of the education bill had riddled it with amendments while he had been away.

> LBJ: . . . They *used* you for three weeks and murdered me! They got *thirty-two* amendments written while you were gone. They got the *hell* raised in the Senate. . . . You got every fascist organization in the country working while *you* are trying to get $400,000. . . . I want that bill reported out

tomorrow morning . . . and what you want me to do, I'll try
to do.

This was Johnson at his most commanding—direct, coarse, and
insistent. No conversation better illustrated his capacity to read the
riot act to congressmen who crossed him. Lady Bird loved it. "It was
really a virtuoso performance," she wrote in her diary. "He gave [Pow-
ell] all the reasons why he ought to get that bill out of his committee
in words that were dazzling, homey, and unanswerable. If I had been
on the other end of the line, I would have ended by saying yes without
waiting to quite decide why."[19]

With Powell back on track, the bill moved quickly to the Rules Committee and then to the floor of the House.[20] As anticipated, conservative Republicans attacked it. One of them, Clarence Brown of Ohio,
blasted the bill as "one of the most dangerous measures that has come
before us in my time." Even Charles Goodell, a liberal Republican from
New York, asserted that the measure would "radically change our historic structure of education by a dramatic shift of power to the Federal
level."[21] More than three-quarters of House Republicans ultimately
voted against the final bill. But LBJ's powerful majority overrode all
opposition, and the bill, unfriendly amendments shorn, passed by a
vote of 263 to 153 on March 26. It authorized an expenditure of $1.3
billion, $1.03 billion of which was to be used for Title I's support of
compensatory education.

The bill then went to the Senate, where, as in the House, angry
conservatives spoke against it, none of them more forceful (or more
prophetic) than Senator John Williams, a veteran Republican from
Delaware. "Make no mistake about it," he warned, "this bill . . . is
merely the beginning. It contains within it the seeds of the first federal education system, which will be nurtured by its supporters in the
years to come long after the current excuse of aiding the poverty-
stricken is forgotten. . . . The flood of federal control is ready to sweep
the land."[22]

But the Senate rejected all amendments. On April 9, the ninety-
seventh day of the congressional session, the bill passed, 73–18. The
majority included 18 of the chamber's 30 Republicans. That it sailed
through both houses so easily—and that the Senate did not change a

word of the House bill—meant that a Senate-House conference committee would not have to convene. The concurrence of both houses, highly unusual for such an important measure, reflected the power of the liberal Democrats on the Hill and the iron discipline that LBJ was able to exert in the early months of the 1965 congressional session.

Johnson was immensely proud of the Elementary and Secondary Education Act (ESEA), as it was called. Eager to sign it with a flourish before the hundredth day of the session, he flew to Stonewall, Texas, where he had attended a one-room elementary school. There, at a dilapidated little building a mile and half from his ranch, he signed the bill into law. In attendance were his first teacher, a former classmate, and some of the Mexican Americans he had taught in 1927 and 1928. (Lady Bird wrote in her diary that it was a "corny, warm setting."[23]) "No law I have ever signed," LBJ proclaimed, "or will ever sign means more to the future of America."

Several months later, he was still euphoric about what he called "my" act. Franklin Roosevelt, he told an aide, "did get things done. There was regulation of business, but that was unimportant. Social Security and the Wagner Act were all that really amounted to much. And none of it compared to my education act."[24]

IN ONE SIGNIFICANT RESPECT, LBJ'S HYPERBOLE HAD MERIT: enactment of the Elementary and Secondary Education Act was a major turning point—the first large-scale venture of the federal government into the financing of general education in America's public schools. It was also the first major law of a congressional session whose legislative activism made 1965 a banner year in the history of American liberalism.

The law, moreover, left a permanent imprint on American educational policy. As Williams predicted, Congress in later years enacted additional education programs, notably Special Education and English as a Second Language, which considerably expanded the federal role in education. As early as 1980, the Department of Education (created in 1979) was operating some five hundred different educational programs.[25] In 2001, the No Child Left Behind Act, passed with bipartisan support, was an amendment to ESEA; it represented a degree of federal involvement in school practices that would have been unimaginable in 1965.

The compensatory education feature of ESEA also proved in future years to be politically popular with Congress. That is not because it worked educational wonders for low-income children—it did not—but because the complicated aid formula, agreed on after considerable horse-trading in the House, was crafted so as to direct federal money into practically every congressional district, thereby lessening the financial burden borne by state and local authorities. As early as 1967–1968, when annual funding for Title I had risen to $2 billion, compensatory education money amounted to 8.8 percent of all government spending—federal, state, and local—for America's public schools. It had been 4.4 percent in 1963–1964.[26]

Has Title I money fulfilled Johnson's goals? Most people over the years have agreed with LBJ's premise that millions of children in low-income areas—disproportionate numbers of them in black ghettos—need much better schooling. Some experts also believe that the involvement of the federal government has spurred state and local officials to direct greater attention to educational questions.[27] But critics of Title I compensatory education have scored valid points. Some note simply that federal funding for such a purpose, though politically welcome at the local level, has always been far too small to cope with the very large and complex problems it aims to remedy. Considering the number of school children in poor families in 1965 (estimated at ten million or more), $1 billion in compensatory education money could not and did not go very far.

Other critics emphasize that a considerable amount of Title I funding has historically failed to reach schools with large percentages of low-income students. This was because the formula ultimately adopted by Congress stipulated that funding amounts be calculated by multiplying the number of qualifying students by 50 percent of a state's per capita spending on education. This benefited children in wealthier states—mostly in the North—that were already offering more support, per capita, for their schools. Later studies estimated that 81 percent of poor children eligible for Title I aid were concentrated in only 32 percent of America's school districts, but that 95 percent of the districts received money.[28]

The ESEA also did not specify clear guidelines on how the money should be used. The Office of Education, which was charged with disbursing the funds, was at that time a small bureaucracy within the Department of Health, Education, and Welfare. Weak and disinclined to assert itself, the office could not and did not insist that the money go primarily to the poor. Some school administrators tried to direct funds to disadvantaged students; others—then and in later years—have also used it for various forms of budget relief. Critics (especially conservative ones) have called the ESEA an educational pork barrel.

This is another way of saying that the ESEA, like most Great Society laws, was not a radical act. Because the measure included no mechanism for terminating aid that was misdirected, the Office of Education could not ride herd on local education officials. Nor was the office authorized to shake up existing curricula or address deep-seated social and economic problems afflicting the neighborhoods where low-income children lived. Instead, by supplementing school resources, ESEA aimed at widening the opportunity—always LBJ's key goal—afforded to such children.

Moreover, though Johnson relied on his education task force, he and his supporters, anxious to act while their political mandate lasted, had been in a big hurry. They did not know very much about what should or should not be taught to masses of underprivileged students or understand how their cognitive or social skills might be significantly improved. In general, they seriously underestimated the depth and complexity of educational issues facing disadvantaged children, thereby opening themselves up to subsequent critiques from conservatives and others who complained that they were jumping too quickly into reform campaigns. Those who touted the "knowledge revolution," it was later clear, oversold the ability of the federal government to solve social problems.

For all these reasons, the ESEA, oversold, was to fall well short of the expectations that LBJ's characteristically expansive rhetoric aroused; the billions of dollars that Congress has appropriated for compensatory education since 1965 (including more than $14 billion by 2010) have done little to narrow the gaps that existed—and persist—between the measurable educational achievement of poor and not-so-poor students. These cognitive gaps, which originate in deep-seated socioeconomic problems—poverty, racism, chaotic neighborhoods—are formidable before children enter school, and they have proved to be extraordinarily difficult for even the best teachers and schools to shrink.

In time, when the limitations of ESEA began to become clear, a degree of popular disillusion with LBJ—and with the expansive promises of Big Government—set in. In early 1965, however, liberals understandably hailed Johnson and his advisers for securing passage of the law. LBJ had plunged into the notoriously treacherous realm of educational politics with the well-intentioned conviction that poor children needed better education and that federal money would help to provide it. Sensing that his popular mandate might not last long, he decided to move quickly. He navigated skillfully to satisfy interest groups, bulldozed his bill through Congress, and signed it within ninety-nine days of the start of the congressional session. It was no wonder that he was immensely proud of his accomplishment and that his liberal followers in the early months of 1965 had high hopes for the political success of other administration proposals.

It was indeed a gratifying start to his quest for a Great Society, which now seemed all but certain to have clear sailing in Congress. Lady Bird, writing in her diary after passage of the education law, remarked that her husband had just observed, "Never has there been such a Hundred Days." She added, "And what a week this has been! Thursday, the House passed Medicare . . . and then the success of the education bill. This was a week to put a golden circle around."[29]

5

BLOODY SUNDAY

Struggles for Justice in Selma

TWO MONTHS INTO NATIONALLY TELEVISED VOTING RIGHTS demonstrations that Martin Luther King had been leading since January in Selma, Alabama, white deputies and state troopers tore into some six hundred nonviolent civil rights marchers crossing a bridge on their way to demonstrate at the state capital of Montgomery. Wielding clubs, nightsticks, and electric cattle prods, they battered the marchers and chased them back into the city. Many demonstrators, badly beaten, had to be hospitalized.

This was March 7, "Bloody Sunday," one of the most memorable days in the history of the civil rights movement. Along with other acts of violence by Selma-area law enforcement officials, the day's brutality enraged civil rights activists, many of whom would grow more militant in the months to come. Bloody Sunday also led to a resounding political triumph that had been politically elusive up until then: passage that summer of an effective Voting Rights Act.

The next day, March 8, a second event took place that would define the year: thirty-five hundred marines, the first American combat troops to land in Asia since the Korean War, splashed ashore at Danang, on the South Vietnamese coast, 375 miles north of Saigon.

Smiling Vietnamese girls greeted the soldiers with garlands and displayed a poster proclaiming, "Welcome to the Gallant Marines."[1]

But the landing represented a fateful escalation in the hostilities that had been mounting since February 7, when 300 Vietcong raiders armed with AK-47 rifles had staged a mortar attack on an American helicopter base near the village of Pleiku, 240 miles north of Saigon in the central highlands of South Vietnam.[2] The predawn raid, launched while many of the men were sleeping, killed 8 Americans and wounded 126, and destroyed ten aircraft and damaged fifteen. US casualties were the largest of any encounter up to that time in Vietnam. Almost all the attackers escaped.

Responding quickly, LBJ ordered sustained air raids on North Vietnamese installations, in the first American strikes since the Gulf of Tonkin incident of August 1964. But when the bombing failed to deter the Vietcong, General William Westmoreland, America's chisel-jawed, supremely self-confident commanding general in Vietnam, pressed for the dispatch of the combat troops to Danang, the site of an American airfield from which many bombing runs had been launched after Pleiku.

These military decisions, countered by unyielding enemy opposition, led to a seemingly inexorable escalation of American military involvement in the war. By 1969, when the US ground combat effort peaked, more than 550,000 American troops were stationed in Vietnam. Before the United States finally extricated itself from the conflict in 1973, the fighting had devastated much of South Vietnam. More than a million North Vietnamese troops, 250,000 South Vietnamese troops, and 800,000 Vietnamese civilians had been killed. Some 58,000 Americans lost their lives; more than 300,000 were wounded.[3]

That these two events—Bloody Sunday and the landing of American combat troops in Vietnam—took place at nearly the same time was coincidental. Each received worldwide attention, and each would prove among the most pivotal events of the decade. More than any other happenings, they pulled the United States into the contentious era that Americans now think of as the Sixties.

—

KING'S DECISION TO LEAD DEMONSTRATIONS IN SELMA WAS ONE OF many signs of the intensifying militancy of American civil rights advocates in early 1965. As a survey by the pollster Louis Harris indicated at the time, blacks were "caught up in an exhilarating sense of progress." But progress, as is often the case in history, whetted still higher expectations. *Newsweek*, reporting the poll's findings, explained that "Negroes have not backed down from their basic demands for an end to discrimination in all its forms—or from the majority view that the pace of progress is still too slow. They regard the trophies of two revolutionary summers, including the civil rights act, as promissory notes still to be paid in full. . . . They won't stop making demands."[4]

Such restlessness was hardly surprising. Notwithstanding the passage of the 1964 Civil Rights Act, Southern schools still remained segregated. Anger among blacks in the North, where de facto segregation and discrimination were unchanged, was mounting. Unemployment remained more than twice as high among blacks as among whites, and poverty roughly three times as high. Most blacks, the Harris poll concluded, believed that white racism had declined. But while a majority of whites opposed Southern-style segregation, they were not so liberal when it came to supporting programs to advance social and economic equality. A Gallup Poll taken in early 1965 reported that 48 percent of white Americans (42 percent in the North, 72 percent in the South) favored the state-level miscegenation laws. Only 46 percent of white Americans opposed them.[5]

Increasingly impatient with the slow pace of change, many black leaders were setting forth wide-ranging demands in early 1965. Bayard Rustin, perhaps the most brilliant civil rights strategist, emphasized in February that the activism of black protestors had expanded to become a broad social movement involving labor leaders and other militants.[6] Malcolm X, having broken with the Nation of Islam in 1964, was invited to Mississippi by members of the integrationist Mississippi Freedom Democratic Party (MFDP) to address its conference in February.[7] Malcolm, who seemed to be edging toward support of interracial civil rights activities, initially accepted but nonetheless continued to speak angrily about the racism of "white devils," reject nonviolence, and stress the virtues of black self-determination and self-defense.[8]

Legal developments stemming from the shocking gangland-style executions by Ku Klux Klansmen of three young civil rights workers in Philadelphia, Mississippi, in June 1964 further inflamed black Americans in early 1965.[9] In mid-January, a federal grand jury indicted seventeen white people, including a sheriff and a deputy, charging them with having conspired to deprive the victims of their constitutional rights to life and liberty without due process of law. A felony indictment, it raised the spirits of civil rights activists. On February 24, however, federal district judge William Harold Cox, a segregationist who had been appointed by Kennedy, dismissed the indictments. He held instead that the defendants should be tried on a lesser charge (a misdemeanor) of violating the victims' civil rights. The maximum penalty for people found guilty on such a count would be one year in jail and a fine of $1,000.[10]

From the start of the year, however, it was the bitter racial strife in Selma that most aroused attention around the country. As black protests mounted, white authorities increasingly resorted to violence, which was to receive graphic attention on network television.

King and his allies had a powerful case: the systematic deprivation by whites of black voting rights that persisted in early 1965 had a long and dismal history. In 1870, the Fifteenth Amendment to the Constitution had stated, "The right of citizens of the United States to vote shall not be denied or abridged by the United States or by any State on account of race, color, or previous condition of servitude." But Southern whites quickly evaded the Amendment, perfecting ruses, including poll taxes and literacy tests, to block blacks (and many poor whites as well) from voting. The US Supreme Court, reflecting the racist temper of the times, declared these ploys to be constitutional. By 1900, politics in many parts of the South was for whites only.

Civil rights acts in 1957 and 1960 had made an effort to rectify this situation, but though the legislation established the federal Civil Rights Commission, Southern congressional opposition had so weakened the laws that they had little impact. The Civil Rights Act of 1964, while a powerful force against segregation, had touched only briefly on voting issues. During the 1964 elections, as before, blacks in the Deep South faced unyielding resistance when they tried to register or vote.

Voter registration statistics clearly revealed the region's methodical and pervasive discrimination. As protestors were demonstrating in Selma, less than one-third of blacks of voting age in five Deep South states were eligible to vote.[11] In some of these states, the numbers were staggeringly low: less than one-quarter of African Americans of voting age were registered to vote in Alabama, and only 6.7 percent were registered in Mississippi. It was figures such as these that had outraged civil rights workers during 1964's Freedom Summer in Mississippi and that had led to the creation of the MFDP.

Selma, a city of nearly thirty thousand people, was the seat of Dallas County, situated in the heart of the Black Belt of central Alabama. Lying fifty-four miles to the east was the state capital of Montgomery, where George Wallace, a fervent segregationist, was governor and commander of state troopers. Selma was also the headquarters of the state's White Citizens' Council, a staunchly segregationist organization. Meanwhile, many black people in the county and in surrounding rural areas were desperately poor and isolated: King recalled meeting some black people in the region who had never seen paper currency or a water faucet.[12]

The Student Nonviolent Coordinating Committee (SNCC) had been staging a voting rights drive in Selma since 1963, but to no avail. In 1964, approximately fifteen thousand blacks of voting age lived in Selma and surrounding Dallas County. They constituted 57 percent of the population of voting age in the county, but only 2.2 percent of them had been allowed to register. Registered whites were 99 percent of the people on the voting rolls.[13]

The largest obstacles facing aspiring black voters in Selma, as in many parts of the South, were so-called literacy tests given at voter-registration offices.[14] In Dallas County, this office was open only two days a month. Black people who were determined enough to line up at the office might have to cool their heels for a good part of the day. If they finally reached the head of the line, they were likely to be disqualified if they failed to cross a *t* while filling out forms. Registrars asked extraordinarily difficult questions, some dealing with obscure and irrelevant matters, others about complicated matters of government. Many people were asked to recite the exact language of lengthy parts of the Constitution. Each month, only sixty people, almost all of them white, were registered to vote in Selma.[15]

Though statistics such as these made Dallas County an obvious site for a voting rights campaign, King, who was an able strategist, chose it for another reason: the nature of the white authorities who would have to cope with such a drive. Some of these authorities, King judged, were relatively moderate, including the mayor of Selma and the city's director of public safety. The sheriff of Dallas County, however, was Jim Clark, widely known as a hot-tempered white racist. As if chosen by Central Casting for the role, he was a jowly, corpulent figure who wore a tight-fitting uniform and a helmet with a Confederate flag on it. Advertising his hatred of desegregation, he once called black people the "lowest form of humanity." He proudly stuck on his lapel the label "NEVER" to tell blacks that nothing would ever change.[16]

King knew his man. He anticipated that Clark, who had earlier used electric cattle prods and tear gas against peaceful blacks who were testing enforcement of the Civil Rights Act of 1964, would take full advantage of his authority as county sheriff to shape events at the county courthouse in Selma, where the registrar's office was located. He would lose his temper at civil rights protestors, throw them in jail, and abuse them. Physical attacks by white authorities, King understood, would heighten the zeal of his followers, who as nonviolent protestors were trained not to fight back. Clark's violent reaction, displayed on national television, would dramatize the differences between Christlike civil rights supporters and brutal white deputies and troopers.

King's strategy was a calculating if not devious form of nonviolent protest. In developing it, he knew that at least some of his nonviolent followers would not be fully aware of the dangers ahead. Some were likely to get hurt. But he had come to believe that white violence—as had flared at Birmingham in 1963—was necessary for his cause to succeed. Millions of Americans, disgusted by scenes of brutality on television, would exert political pressure on elected officials to act. Johnson and Congress, King believed, would then have to back a strong federal voting rights bill.

King was also a pragmatic and effective political manager. Though he was known above all for his brilliance as an orator, he was expert at resolving the seemingly endless factional disputes within the civil rights movement. As his organization, the Southern Christian Leadership Conference (SCLC), geared up for a campaign in Selma, he sought the support of other civil rights advocates. But intramovement tensions between the SCLC, which was headed by King and other ministers, and younger militants in organizations such as CORE and SNCC had long threatened the unity of the civil rights cause, and fractures such as these reappeared in Selma. Some militants, notably SNCC activists, resented King's interference with their efforts and refused to cooperate. But King did win over John Lewis, a founder and chair of SNCC. Lewis, the son of an Alabama sharecropper, was a pacifist. Only twenty-five, steadfast and heroic in his activism, he had already been beaten and jailed in other campaigns. When he agreed to join the protests at Selma on his own, he became a valiant ally in the struggles that ensued.

———

BECAUSE KING'S GOAL WAS TO SECURE A STRONG VOTING RIGHTS act, he was especially intent on winning President Johnson's support. Given LBJ's backing for civil rights, this might not have seemed like a difficult task. As a Southerner of liberal instincts, Johnson was eager to free his section of the country from its racist reputation and thereby to advance its social and economic development. He was well aware that the Civil Rights Act of 1964 did not protect black voters in the South and that civil rights leaders would press hard for a law that ensured the suffrage of black citizens. Such a law also promised to help Johnson politically. In 1964, his support of the Civil Rights Act had hurt him in the Deep South states, which Barry Goldwater, his Republican opponent, captured. Elsewhere in the South, however, racist practices were less widespread, and as King reminded him, black people who had been allowed to vote in Arkansas, Tennessee, Florida, Virginia, and North Carolina had helped the president carry those states. If the Democratic Party hoped to maintain a decent foothold in the South, it had to ensure that blacks would be allowed to register and vote.

LBJ had yet another reason to seek a strong voting rights law. Keenly aware of political trends, he recognized that black civil rights leaders were not only becoming increasingly militant but also yearning to take full charge of the movement themselves. After all, it was *their* cause. Yet Johnson was leery of allowing civil rights organizations, a contentious array of groups with a variety of strategies, to eclipse the centralized authority and disciplined direction of the federal government. To back a voting rights law, in Johnson's mind, was one way to stay in control of the movement.

With these concerns in mind, Johnson in mid-November 1964 had directed Nicholas Katzenbach, acting attorney general, to begin drafting voting rights legislation.[17] Katzenbach and his staff set about putting a bill together, although he believed it might be necessary to craft a constitutional amendment prohibiting states from interfering with voting rights. Johnson, too, wondered if such an amendment would be needed. But both men knew that the process of amending the Constitution would be laborious and time-consuming. Over the course of the next few weeks, they considered their options.

During this period, LBJ also held back from pressing voting rights on Congress as a major goal for 1965. His reasoning rested in large part on his consideration of political realities. Thanks to obstructive tactics by Southern opponents in the Senate, it had taken months to pass the Civil Rights Act of 1964. Trying to enact yet another civil rights bill would infuriate Southern senators, who would again resort to filibustering. Amid the rancor that would poison the air, LBJ's cherished Great Society goals—his education bill, government health care for the elderly, and a host of other measures— might fail to pass.

Johnson temporized through December and early January. Shortly after he started Katzenbach on the drafting process, he told King that he could not promise to prioritize the issue—which led King to reply that civil rights advocates, eager for reform, would open demonstrations in Selma. Though the president appealed in his State of the Union message on January 4 for the "elimination of every remaining obstacle to the right and opportunity to vote," he did not highlight the cause. King, a persistent lobbyist, soon telephoned him. When Johnson called back on January 15, King's thirty-sixth birthday, King pressed him to name a Negro to the cabinet. Such an appointment would have been a first in American history. Again, Johnson was evasive. There were several excellent prospects for such a post, he said—notably

Robert Weaver, whom he was considering as the head of a department that would be concerned with cities and housing.[18] (Approved later in 1965, this became the Department of Housing and Urban Development, and Weaver was named to head it in early 1966.)

Characteristically loquacious, LBJ tried to dominate the twenty-four-minute conversation with King, among other things urging him to offer public support for Great Society measures. As if he were a political science professor, he also explained how the voting rights issue could be dramatized and win popular support. What King should do, the president said, would be to publicize specific examples of questions that racist registrars were posing to prospective black registrants. "Find the most ridiculous illustration you can on voting," LBJ advised, "and point it up and repeat it and get everybody else to do it."

In the course of the telephone conversation, it was obvious that Johnson was closely following the protests in Selma, which had already become tense. At last, he made it clear to King that he hoped to secure a voting rights law in 1965. He told King, "The greatest achievement of my administration was the passage of the 1964 Civil Rights Act, but I think this [a voting rights act] will be bigger because it will do things that even that 1964 act didn't do."[19]

—

THREE DAYS LATER, WHEN KING TRAVELED TO SELMA, THE STRUGGLE turned ugly. He arrived at a hotel in the city and by his very presence integrated it. As he did, a white man, a member of the National States Rights Party, punched him in the head, knocked him down, and kicked him in the groin before others intervened and the man was arrested. The next day, Sheriff Clark, wielding a club, grabbed Amelia Boynton, a black community leader who was helping local people to register at the county courthouse in Selma, held her by her coat collar, and shoved her along the street to a police car. Television covered the manhandling of Boynton, as did newspapers. Photos of the incident ran in the *New York Times* and the *Washington Post.* King, interviewed on TV, pronounced her arrest to be "one of the most brutal and unlawful acts I have seen an officer commit."[20]

Many such arrests and acts of white violence marred Selma during the next two weeks. On January 22, Clark and his men used nightsticks and electric cattle prods to beat back 110 schoolteachers—virtually the entire membership of the Selma Negro Teachers Association—who had marched to the courthouse to register to vote and demonstrate against the arrest of Boynton. Their march was a pivotal moment in the struggle—perhaps the first time in the civil rights movement as a whole that middle-class black teachers had participated publicly, and as a group, in protest. Bruised but unbowed, the teachers returned to the Brown Chapel in Selma, a headquarters of the movement. Some 300 of their students cheered them on. On January 25, King led 250 followers to the courthouse steps. When Clark approached a fifty-three-year-old woman and twisted her arm, she responded by knocking him down. Clark beat her with his nightstick, while three of his deputies pinned her to the ground. These scenes, too, appeared on national TV.

Though Clark had vastly overreacted, his actions to that point had not yet backfired. King and his allies, counting on newspaper and television reporters to cover their activities, decided to dramatize their cause by getting arrested. On February 1, a drizzly day, he led hundreds of protestors from the chapel toward the courthouse. Local police arrested and jailed most of them, including King and his top aide in the SCLC, the Reverend Ralph Abernathy. As planned, scores of people, many of them children and high school students, marched to the county courthouse, where Clark and his men, chasing some of the protestors in police cars and pickup trucks, arrested and jailed them, too. In the next few days, white authorities incarcerated many more, filling every cell in the area with prisoners. Estimates of the total number imprisoned in and around Selma during the five weeks of demonstrations to that time ran as high as three thousand.[21] King, refusing bail for four days and nights, remained in jail until February 5. Right after King's release, Johnson made it known that he would ask Congress for a voting rights bill.

Four days later, King journeyed to Washington, where he found Johnson absorbed in responding to the February 7 Vietcong attack near Pleiku. With American bombers blasting North Vietnamese installations, it was an extraordinarily tense and hectic time for King to be lobbying the preoccupied president on behalf of civil rights. King's trip was nevertheless satisfying; the direct action demonstrations of civil rights activists—and the bravery and sacrifices of nonviolent local people—were proving in Selma to be a widely reported protest strategy, even if it had not yet succeeded in registering black voters or changing the proscriptions against opening the voting franchise. Media coverage of the roughing up and jailing of peaceful citizens was rallying many Americans to the cause.

Johnson, even as he recognized that nasty struggles lay ahead, affirmed to King his commitment to a strong voting rights bill. At the same time he made it publicly clear that he would use Title VI of the 1964 Civil Rights Act, which authorized him to cut off federal aid to institutions, such as hospitals, universities, and schools, that continued to segregate.[22]

The voting rights bill, which Katzenbach and his staff had been working hard to craft, was indeed shaping up to be a far-reaching measure. It covered voting rights in state as well as federal elections. Rather than relying (like earlier voting rights bills) on enforcement through the courts, the bill, seeking to crush the arbitrary activities of local voting registrars, prohibited literacy tests and provided for enforcement of the measure by federal registrars on the scene. Justice Department officials needed only to fine-tune the bill so that it would be likely to satisfy congressional leaders and the courts. The measure was certain to outrage Southerners and provoke angry fights on the Hill.[23]

Selma continued to be a battleground. Widely publicized demonstrations, many of them organized by a top King associate, the Reverend James Bevel, persisted. On February 10, the day after King went to Washington, Sheriff Clark lost his temper again when 160 youthful blacks attempted to register to vote. Each time they were rejected, they returned to the back of the line to try again. Enraged, Clark and his deputies used clubs and electric cattle prods to drive the young people on a three-mile-long forced march and run into the countryside. Many protestors—exhausted, singed, beaten, and vomiting—collapsed by the wayside.[24] On February 16, Clark ordered the Reverend C. T. Vivian, an SCLC leader, to move off the courthouse steps. Vivian, proclaiming his right to be there, refused to budge. He also compared Clark to Hitler. Clark punched him in the face, sending him reeling down the steps, and arrested him. Television coverage of this dramatic one-on-one confrontation further shocked viewers throughout the country.

No incident up to that time was more infuriating to civil rights advocates than what happened two evenings later in Marion, a small town near Selma, in Perry County, where no black people were registered to vote. Some five hundred civil rights protestors staged a nighttime march from a church to the jail, where a civil rights worker was being held. Marion was not within the domain of Sheriff Clark, but local police and state troopers emulated him, running amok in an ambush of the protestors and clubbing them with nightsticks. Jimmie Lee Jackson, a twenty-six-year-old Baptist deacon, intervened to protect his mother from the assaults. One of the troopers, firing at close range, shot him twice in the abdomen. Mortally wounded, Jackson was taken along with other injured demonstrators to the hospital in Selma. He died eight days later.

On the morning of March 3, some two thousand mourners filed by Jackson's casket in Selma, and most of them journeyed thirty miles for a funeral service in Marion. There King declared, "Jimmie Lee Jackson is speaking to us from the casket, and he is saying to us that we must substitute courage for caution. . . . We must not be bitter, and we must not harbor ideas of retaliation with violence. We must not lose faith in our white brothers." More than one thousand people walked three miles in the rain to bury the young man on a pine hill.[25]

———

ON FEBRUARY 21, AS JACKSON WAS FIGHTING FOR HIS LIFE IN Selma, another shooting made headline news: an assassination in New York City. Malcolm X was gunned to death in full view of some four hundred African Americans as he began a speech that afternoon at the crowded Audubon Ballroom in Washington Heights. His pregnant wife, Betty Shabazz, and their four children were seated near the front of the stage. In the pandemonium that followed, three men loyal to the Nation of Islam, which was widely believed to have been behind recent plots to assassinate him, were charged with and ultimately convicted of the killing.[26]

Few white Americans at that time mourned Malcolm X's death. On the contrary, most white people who knew of his activities thought of him not as a man who might be open to working with interracial civil rights groups but as a fierce and uncompromising black nationalist. Many imagined that his refusal to be bound by nonviolence would spur a black insurrection. Law enforcement officials regarded him as a radical and a criminal who posed a danger to society. The *New York Times* described him as "an extraordinary and twisted man." *Time* branded him as a "disaster to the civil rights movement." *Newsweek* called him a "spiritual desperado . . . a demagogue who titillated slum Negroes and frightened whites."

Though few black people at the time endorsed Malcolm's nationalistic cause, many were deeply saddened by his killing. This was especially the case with Northern blacks—most of them in the cities—who admired his hard-hitting and uncompromising denunciations of white America. Indeed, in death he was to become a near iconic symbol of black resistance and an inspirational champion of black liberation.[27] It was estimated that between fourteen thousand and thirty thousand people paid their respects to him during a four-day public viewing of his body. Some one thousand people crammed a Harlem church for his funeral on February 27. Many others listened outside via loudspeakers. The outpouring of grief and respect attested to the following that Malcolm X, a protean figure, was attracting by the time of his death.[28]

Because Malcolm X had often ridiculed civil rights advocates, King included, as integrationist Uncle Toms and as "professional beggars" who depended on white people, they might not have been expected to grieve deeply over his death. Some activists, however, showed their respect for his work. King (who had met him only once) telegrammed his widow to express his sorrow. He wrote, "While we did not always see eye-to-eye on methods to solve the race problem, I always had a deep affection for Malcolm. . . . He was an eloquent spokesman for his point of view." Some movement activists also recognized that as of late 1964 Malcolm X was seeming to indicate a willingness to work with civil rights leaders and that he had earlier agreed to speak to the

MFDP. They also remembered that he had visited Selma three weeks earlier, only to fail in his effort to talk with King, who was then in jail. John Lewis and Bayard Rustin were among the many integrationist civil rights leaders who attended the funeral.

———

THE ASSASSINATION OF MALCOLM X DID NOT DIRECTLY AFFECT THE movement for justice in Selma. What mattered most to civil rights activists there was the murder of Jimmie Lee Jackson. His killing led Bevel, King, and others to adopt a fateful strategy: protestors would march to Montgomery, where they would petition Governor Wallace for protection of black citizens who wished to register. King had hoped to schedule the march for March 9, by which time he expected a federal judge, Frank Johnson, would have voided an order by Wallace to ban it. A march to Montgomery, therefore, would be court-approved.

Younger activists, however, demanded the group move earlier, on Sunday, March 7. Many members of SNCC, still at odds with SCLC, did not join the march. But some, including Lewis, did. He acted as co-leader with SCLC's Hosea Williams. (King, who faced death threats in Alabama, and Abernathy were preaching in Atlanta that day.) Early in the afternoon, six hundred civil rights protestors left their headquarters and headed for the Edmund Pettus Bridge, which would take them over the Alabama River and put them on the road to Montgomery.

The demonstrators knew they faced danger. Wallace, having vowed to ban the march, had warned the day before, "I'm not going to have a bunch of niggers walking along a highway as long as I'm governor." Selma's police anticipated violence. But the mayor said that Wallace had promised there would be peace, and many of the marchers, expecting a walk of several days, carried sleeping bags. As they came to the crest of the bridge, however, they espied a formidable array of opponents waiting for them. Shoulder-to-shoulder at the end of the bridge were Wallace's forces: a hundred helmeted state troopers, who wore masks to protect themselves from tear gas. Lining the sides of the bridge were a hundred of Clark's men on horseback, armed with clubs, bullwhips, and lengths of rubber tubing wrapped in barbed wire.

When the marchers reached the troopers, Major John Cloud, their commander, blocked the way. He gave them two minutes to turn around and return to Selma. But as Lewis, Williams, and others began to confer about what to do next, the troopers suddenly formed a flying wedge and charged. Clark's men, screaming rebel yells, joined them. Swinging nightsticks, cattle prods, and barbed-wired rubber tubing, the troopers and deputies tore indiscriminately into the un-armed and nonviolent men and women who had dared to march.[29]

Some of the protestors, including Lewis, tried to stand their ground. Cracked on the head, he suffered a fractured skull. Other marchers, beaten, bleeding, or suffering from the effects of tear gas, were forced back, many of them chased by Clark and his deputies all the way to the chapel from which they had started. Five women were clubbed so severely that they lost consciousness and collapsed on the bridge. A total of seventy-eight protestors had to be taken to the hospital. Lewis, who knew that LBJ was authorizing the dispatch of combat marines to Vietnam, cried out, "I don't see how President Johnson can send troops to Vietnam . . . and can't send troops to Selma, Alabama." He added, "Next time we march, we may have to keep going until we get to Montgomery. We may have to go to Washington."[30]

Bloody Sunday represented an even more barbaric form of violence than King and his aides might have expected when they selected Selma as the site for their protest. But it vindicated the wisdom of his belief that white-inflicted brutality would backfire and aid the civil rights cause. That evening, some forty-eight million Americans were watching the television premiere of *Judgment at Nuremberg*, a film starring Spencer Tracy, Burt Lancaster, and Richard Widmark about the post–World War II trials of Axis war criminals. ABC broke into the movie, captivating viewers with fifteen minutes of footage from Selma. Many other Americans read about or saw photographs and televised shots of the mayhem of March 7 over the course of the next several days.

Millions of Americans from outside the South were outraged. Editorialists and political leaders denounced Clark, Wallace, and the troopers, and demanded federal intervention. As urged by King and others, supporters of civil rights, including many hundreds of white ministers and students, began descending on Selma to show their support of the movement. SNCC, too, rejoined the struggle. Bloody Sunday, a pivotal date in the history of the civil rights movement, made the passage of a strong voting rights bill much more likely.

Matters on the ground in Selma, however, remained tense and complicated. King, having opposed the March 7 march, faced a rebellion from SNCC militants. Led by James Forman, who took over while Lewis was in the hospital, the more radical group was determined to march toward Montgomery on March 9, even without protection by federal troops. Thousands of local people, along with Northerners who were still descending on the city, were eager to join them. King, seeking to retain his standing as a leader, declared that he would lead the trek. On March 8, however, Judge Johnson, fearing the march would be met with violence, issued a temporary restraining order that enjoined the protestors from marching, pending a hearing on Wallace's request for a ban. King, having never defied a federal court order, was now in a bind.

President Johnson, who had been anxiously keeping track of the marine landings in Vietnam—and the escalation of bombing in North Vietnam—was also reluctant to become publicly involved. Though appalled by Bloody Sunday, he, too, opposed the defiance of a court order. Instead, he urged King to await the judge's final decision. He also resisted demands that he send federal troops to protect the marchers. Furious white people throughout the South, he knew, would denounce such an act as the beginning of a second Reconstruction—a repeat of the Northern military presence that had antagonized the white South following the Civil War. Governor Wallace would be hailed as a hero by his followers when he decried federal intervention. Johnson insisted shrewdly that it was the governor's responsibility to guarantee the right of peaceful protestors to march in safety on the roads of Alabama.[31]

Following meetings and telephone conversations that lasted half the night of March 8–9, King and a mediator representing Johnson crafted an awkward compromise. After receiving a promise that Alabama police would not harm the protestors, King quietly decided to lead the march on March 9. His presence would emphasize the seriousness of the cause. But, he determined, it would be a token demonstration. At the other end of the Pettus Bridge, to avoid the risk of violence and in deference to the federal court order, he would turn around and go back.

On March 9, some two thousand marchers, including a number of white people, followed King to the bridge. Many were laughing and singing "Ain't Gonna Let Nobody Turn Me 'Round." Others sang "We Shall Overcome." Only a few—confidants of King—knew that he planned to return to Selma. Confronting the protestors at the bridge was a force of law enforcement officers that was a good deal larger than the one that had attacked on Bloody Sunday. Some five hundred state troopers led by Major Cloud were armed and ready for action. They, too, were aware of King's compromise, and when he came to within fifty feet of them, Cloud blocked his way and ordered, "This march will not continue." King asked to pray—a request that Cloud granted. But Cloud then moved his men to the sides of the road. The road to Montgomery was open!

It was a moment of major decision for King. With the way clear, the goal of the marchers—to walk to Montgomery—seemed within reach. But King had agreed to the plan to turn around, and he did not keep walking. Instead, he shouted, "We will go back to the church now!" He then headed back toward Selma. Perplexed by what had happened, some of the marchers grumbled. But they, too, retraced their steps. The march was over.[32]

Many of the demonstrators were furious with King: their leader, they thought, had backed away from the enemy. In cities throughout the North—Cleveland, Chicago, New York, Detroit, Oakland—black activists staged protest marches of their own. Many branded the aborted march as "Turnabout Tuesday." Others demanded that Congress act quickly to pass a voting rights act. Relations between SCLC and SNCC, crumbling further, could not be repaired, opening the door wider to the demands of more militant voices within the ever more divided movement.

Yet another act of violence soon angered civil rights advocates. That evening, white hoodlums in Selma accosted three white Unitarian-Universalist ministers who had come to the city to support the cause. One of them, the Reverend James Reeb, was clubbed on the head. He died on the evening of March 11.[33] Though the death of Jackson, a black man, had outraged advocates for civil rights, the killing of Reeb infuriated a great many people—white as well as black—throughout the United States. His murder galvanized the national struggle for a voting rights measure as much as anything to that time had managed to do.

Long after Bloody Sunday and the events of March 9, critics took King to task for his decision to turn back. In fact, King had acted prudently. Distrusting assurances from Wallace, he had maneuvered so as to avert a bloodbath on March 9. He had also avoided disobeying a federal court order. Johnson, too, had been wise in not sending federal troops or ignoring the courts—acts that would also have enraged Southern whites.

———

LBJ's FIRST MOVE THEREAFTER WAS TO ACCEPT WALLACE'S REQUEST for a meeting, which took place at the White House on March 13. Wallace, a feisty foe, began by complaining that "outside agitators" were inciting trouble in his state. But Johnson, having carefully orchestrated the encounter and intending to knock Wallace off balance, had seen to it that the governor, a short man, would be seated in a low, squishy sofa where he had to lean back and look up, while LBJ, sitting very close by, loomed above him in a rocking chair.

The president then proceeded to harangue his antagonist for more than two hours, switching back and forth from expletive-laden insults to appeals to Wallace's better nature. When Wallace said he could not persuade local officials to register black voters, LBJ snapped, "Don't shit me about your persuasive powers, George. I saw you [on television] attacking me. And you know what? You were so damn persuasive that I had to turn off the set before you had me changing my mind." Later he asked Wallace not to think of 1968 (when the governor was expected to run for president) but of 1988. "You and me," Johnson said, "we'll be dead and gone then. George . . . do you want a Great . . . Big . . . Marble monument that reads, 'George Wallace—He Built'? . . . Or do you want a little piece of scrawny pine board lying across that harsh, caliche soil, that reads, 'George Wallace—He Hated'?"

Having cowed Wallace, LBJ led him to the Rose Garden, where reporters were waiting. He told the press that the governor had agreed that blacks should be registered and marchers protected. He added that he would send a voting rights bill to Congress right away. Wallace did not challenge the president. He told reporters as he was leaving, "Hell, if I'd stayed in there much longer, he'd have had me coming out for civil rights."[34]

LBJ's next move, two days later, was to address Congress on Monday night, March 15. It was the first time in nineteen years that a president had made such a special congressional appearance at night. Television networks aired the address for all of America to watch.[35] Well prepared, LBJ moved his listeners, drawing forty bursts of applause and two standing ovations in a slowly delivered oration that took forty-five minutes to complete. He placed the events at Selma in a broad historical and moral framework:

> I speak tonight for the dignity of man and the destiny of democracy. . . . At times history and fate meet at a single time in a single place to shape a turning point in man's unending search for freedom. . . . So it was a century ago at Appomattox. So it was last week in Selma, Alabama. . . . What happened in Selma is part of a far larger movement which reaches into every section and state of America. It is the effort of American Negroes to secure for themselves the full blessings of American life. Their cause must be our cause too. Because it is not just Negroes, but really it is *all* of us who must overcome the crippling legacy of bigotry and injustice.

At this point Johnson paused. Raising his arms, he repeated key words from the Baptist hymn that had become a major marching song of the movement: "And . . . we . . . *shall* . . . overcome!"[36] Swept up in the emotion of that moment, virtually everyone in the House chamber and in the gallery rose to give him a standing ovation. Chief Justice Earl Warren, also on his feet, was smiling and applauding. Martin Luther King watched the speech on television. When LBJ spoke, "We . . . shall . . . overcome," tears ran down King's cheek.

TWO DAYS LATER, MARCH 17, CONGRESS SET TO WORK ON A VOTING rights bill, focusing at first on banning poll taxes in state elections. Though Southerners were certain to oppose the measure (Senator Richard Russell, breaking with his old friend, told a colleague that LBJ was a "turncoat"), the events at Selma had given it an enormous push forward. Polls taken between March 18 and 25 indicated that 76 percent of Americans, including 49 percent of Southerners, favored passage of a bill.[37] And on March 17, Judge Johnson issued his decision: the march to Montgomery could take place. The judge also enjoined Alabama and state officials from interfering with the marchers and ordered them to protect them. The event was scheduled for March 21, two weeks after Bloody Sunday.

Wallace, however, remained recalcitrant. Hearing of Judge Johnson's decision, he called him a "low-down, carpetbaggin', scalawagin', race-mixin' liar."[38] He then reneged on the assurances he had given to the president on March 13. Alabama, he now maintained, could not financially afford to protect the marchers. His stance outraged LBJ. Talking the next night with Buford Ellington, a former governor of Tennessee who was acting as his liaison with Wallace, he exclaimed, "You're dealing with a very treacherous guy. You must not even come in quoting him anymore. Because he's a no good son of a *bitch*! . . . He is absolutely treacherous." LBJ closed the conversation saying, "I'm going to issue a statement here that kind of burns his tail."[39]

Johnson's most important move was to ensure that the march would take place—and safely. He federalized eighteen hundred members of the Alabama National Guard and reinforced them with federal marshals and units from the US Army. On March 21, some thirty-two hundred jubilant people stepped off on a cool and sunny day for the fifty-four-mile trek through the exposed and potentially dangerous territory of Lowndes County. King, his wife, Coretta, and Lewis, released from the hospital, led the throng.

Sullen white onlookers held up placards, "Bye, Bye, Blackbird," "Nigger Lover," and "Martin Luther Coon." Children chanted "white nigger" and "nigger lover" at white participants. But reporters and guardsmen virtually surrounded the marchers, most of whom, often singing, paid little heed to the heckling. King did not march the whole way, but thousands of others—local people and supporters both white and black—swelled the procession as it moved ahead. Celebrities also arrived, Harry Belafonte and Leonard Bernstein among them. When the marchers, singing "We Shall Overcome" (or, triumphantly, "We *Have* Overcome Today"), reached the outskirts of Montgomery four days later, it was estimated that their numbers had increased to at least twenty-five thousand.

That evening at a conference center on the outskirts of the city, the marchers, in a celebratory mood, enjoyed the singing of Belafonte, Sammy Davis Jr., Nina Simone, Odetta, and Tony Bennett. Dick Gregory and Nipsey Russell provided stand-up comedy. Mike Nichols and Elaine May also entertained.

The next day, March 25, King and a host of civil rights activists led the marchers through the streets of Montgomery to a square in front of the state capitol (where the Confederate flag flew over the dome). Many religious and labor leaders joined them. All three TV networks covered the event. With twenty-five thousand or more still in attendance, the assemblage was the largest in the history of civil rights demonstrations in the South.

There, the people sang,

> Keep your eyes on the prize, hold on, hold on
> I've never been to heaven, but I think I'm right
> You won't find George Wallace anywhere in sight.
> Oh, keep your eyes on the prize, hold on, hold on.

By then it was mid-afternoon. King, moving to the steps of the capitol, closed the festivities with an uplifting oration, some of which was punctuated by thunderous rounds of applause and by responses from the crowd ("Yes, sir!" "Speak!"). Praising the bravery of supporters—including those who had participated in the Montgomery bus boycott of 1955–1956—King also lauded LBJ's role in the struggle. He emphasized that the civil rights movement was interracial and thanked white Americans "who cherish their democratic traditions over the ugly customs and privileges of generations and come forth boldly to join hands with us."

King ended on another positive note, predicting that racial justice would not take too much time to achieve: "I come to say to you this afternoon, however difficult the moment, however frustrating the hour, it will not be long. Because truth crushed to earth will rise again." Again he asked, "How long?" and replied, "Not long, because no lie can live forever." And a third time he asked "How long?" He replied, "Not long, because you still reap what you sow." He closed with words from the "Battle Hymn of the Republic": "Mine eyes have seen the glory of the coming of the Lord. / He is trampling out the vintage where the grapes of *wrath* are stored. / He has loosed the fateful lightning of his *terrible* swift sword. / His truth is marching on."

Speaking rapidly, King moved through another stanza of the hymn. Then he slowed a bit, only to hurl himself into a spoken chorus:

> He has sounded forth the trumpet that shall never call retreat
> He is sifting out the hearts of men before his judgment seat
> Oh, be swift my soul to answer him, be jubilant my feet
> Our God is marching on
> Glory! Hallelujah!
> Glory! Hallelujah!
> Glory! Hallelujah!
> His truth is marching on![40]

WHILE PROPONENTS OF RACIAL JUSTICE CELEBRATED NOT ONLY IN the United States but also in many cities around the world, a deadly coda marred the otherwise triumphant occasion. That evening, four members of the Ku Klux Klan followed Viola Liuzzo, a thirty-nine-year-old white Detroit housewife and mother of five who, as one of the many out-of-state volunteers, had been shuttling marchers between Selma and Montgomery in her car. As she drove that night from Selma toward Montgomery on a deserted stretch of highway in Lowndes County, the Klansmen's car drew even with her. Rifle bullets smashed through her car window and hit her in the head. She died instantly.[41]

Because one of the Klansmen was an undercover FBI agent (who said later he had fired in the air), the killers were quickly identified and arrested. FBI director J. Edgar Hoover (without disclosing that an undercover agent had been in the Klansmen's car) announced he had broken the case. LBJ, who had been talking urgently on the phone with Hoover and Attorney General Katzenbach into the early morning following the shooting, took time out the next day from last-minute oversight of passage of Medicare in the House to appear with Hoover at the White House. There he called for a national campaign against "the terrorists of the Ku Klux Klan" and lauded Hoover for his success. The *New York Times* saluted Hoover the next day by referring to him as "an authentic American folk hero . . . the incorruptible idol of generations of American youngsters and the symbol of the 'honest cop' to millions of their elders."[42]

Given Hoover's abysmal record concerning civil rights (he had earlier referred to King as "the most notorious liar in the country" and as a "'tomcat' with obsessive degenerate sexual urges"), the *Times*'s comment was uninformed, to say the least. More important, however, the arrest of the Klansmen hardly mollified Americans who were enraged by the killing of Liuzzo. Her murder was one more reminder of the hate-filled white violence that had shaken Selma and poisoned American race relations since the start of the year.[43]

King and his fellow civil rights leaders, moreover, had not yet reached their goal: the eradication of discrimination against black voters in the South. When a small group of black Alabamans tried to deliver the marchers' petition to Wallace (who had watched the ceremonies through his office blinds), they were turned away at the capitol door. While it was clear that a voting rights bill would be passed—hearings were already underway in the House and Senate—it was also likely that the process of hammering out a final version would take a considerable amount of time. Meanwhile, racist white authorities, Sheriff Clark included, still dominated the local scene. Over the next few months, most would-be black registrants continued to be rejected.

In the early spring of 1965 the future of the civil rights movement was also unclear. Disputes over strategies at Selma had widened the already substantial divisions between the SCLC and SNCC. Moreover, SNCC was itself divided. Some of its members, like Lewis, continued to pursue nonviolent and interracial strategies, mainly in the South. Others were beginning to emphasize that blacks must take the lead in the freedom struggle and embrace a broader range of egalitarian goals. As an incisive commentary was later to put the matter,

> The year 1965 may be known as the time when the civil rights movement discovered, in the sense of becoming explicitly aware, that abolishing legal racism would not produce legal equality. [Black people had come to realize that] *de facto* segregation and subtle racism were tied to our most fundamental socioeconomic institutions. . . . After they had integrated the lunch counter they didn't like the menu.[44]

The controversies in Selma, finally, focused on Southern injustices. When Congress succeeded in passing a strong voting rights act, one of the most flagrant aspects of racism in the South would become history. This would be a great accomplishment—one that the struggles in Selma had helped mightily to achieve and that could scarcely have been imagined in early 1964. But what of the North, where de facto segregation and discrimination persisted? Would civil rights leaders—or federal officials—be able to satisfy the yearnings and demands rising in the poverty-stricken inner cities of the nation?

For all these reasons, it was hard to predict in the early spring of 1965 how civil rights activists would proceed and whether LBJ, who dearly hoped to lead them, would be able to control the situation. If he could not, race relations in the United States, which had improved enormously since the 1950s, might well worsen again, thereby fomenting interracial tensions that might tear LBJ's liberal coalition apart and usher in even more implacable racial confrontations in the United States.

6

FORK IN THE ROAD

Escalation in Vietnam

THE STRUGGLES IN SELMA ULTIMATELY HAD A POSITIVE OUTCOME: voting rights legislation. The second development of early 1965 that would greatly change America, however, had no benign results: America's military escalation in Vietnam. More than any other event of the year, it spurred the polarization that characterized the Sixties in the United States.

—

THOUGH THE FEBRUARY 7 PREDAWN ATTACK NEAR PLEIKU SURPRISED American soldiers, LBJ and his top advisers were well aware that some such provocation might occur. The political and military position of the unstable South Vietnamese government had deteriorated considerably in January. Buddhist protests and fasts had been mounting. A number of monks, as well as a seventeen-year-old girl, had burned themselves to death—acts that were widely reported in the press and on TV, making the troubles in Vietnam vivid to millions of Americans. Some five thousand Vietnamese students had sacked the US Information Service library in Hue.

On January 27, as yet another reorganization was destabilizing the South Vietnamese government in Saigon, Secretary of Defense Robert McNamara and National Security Advisor McGeorge Bundy sent LBJ their most urgent memo yet.[1] The United States, they wrote, had reached a "fork in the road." Emphasizing that "our current policy can lead only to disastrous defeat," they called on Johnson to authorize the bombing of North Vietnam. Meanwhile, former vice president Richard Nixon, a major force in the Republican Party and a potential presidential candidate in 1968, gave a widely reported speech in which he declared, "We are losing the war in Vietnam." American security, he said, required that "we end the war by winning it." He, too, advocated bombing the North.[2]

In response to the "fork in the road" memo, Johnson sent Bundy to Vietnam to assess the situation. It was his first visit there. At the same time, pressure for America to escalate was mounting from influential media. On February 5, *Life* featured a story, based on a "secret report," bewailing the plight of South Vietnam. Vietcong forces in the South numbered around a hundred thousand, of whom thirty-five thousand were "hard-core combat troops who are fanatically loyal Communists." The article conceded that Saigon's army had four times as many soldiers but stressed that a ten-to-one edge was necessary to prevail in a guerrilla war.

The story in *Life*—like other publications headed by the fervently anticommunist Henry Luce—was militant. (*Time*'s editors, also echoing Luce's views, regularly rewrote dispatches from their own correspondents in Vietnam, thereby excising accurate descriptions of the incompetence of Saigon's military and political leaders. The magazine also referred to antiwar protestors as "Vietniks."[3]) Yet the anticommunist stance of Luce publications was hardly unique at the time: until then, major newspapers, including the *New York Times*, and the national TV networks (NBC, ABC, and CBS) had tended to be gentle in their coverage of the administration's foreign policies.[4]

Most prominent politicians, sharing this anticommunist Cold War mentality, were unwilling to say that the president should abandon his support of South Vietnamese independence. Many, including GOP leaders like Everett Dirksen in the Senate and Gerald Ford in the

House and influential Democrats like House Speaker John McCormack and Senate Armed Services Committee chair John Stennis of Mississippi, were hawks who offered vigorous support for LBJ's moves.

To be sure, some prominent figures were skeptical about escalating the war. In the Senate they included not only Majority Leader Mike Mansfield but also Democratic liberals like George McGovern of South Dakota, Frank Church of Idaho, Al Gore Sr. of Tennessee, and—as during the Bay of Tonkin crisis—Ernest Gruening of Alaska and Wayne Morse of Oregon. J. William Fulbright, chair of the Senate Foreign Relations Committee, had grown cool to administration policy, causing LBJ to complain privately, "Fulbright is a cry baby—and I can't continue to kiss him every morning before breakfast."[5] Republican senators George Aiken of Vermont and John Sherman Cooper of Kentucky also took a dim view of escalation.[6] Aside from Gruening and Morse, however, legislators dubious about the war generally refrained from strong public attacks on the administration's policies in early 1965. Nor did they dare to oppose funding of military efforts. Most congressional foes of American military involvement hoped instead that the administration would root out corruption and incompetence in the South and embark on negotiations with the North that might end the war.

In this increasingly tense atmosphere, Johnson's room to maneuver was restricted. Unlike Kennedy, who in late 1963 might (or might not) have been seriously thinking about withdrawing some or all American military "advisers," LBJ had the misfortune to be president when the political and military situation in South Vietnam had grown far more unnerving. The demands on the president to act decisively—either to accept the likely collapse of South Vietnam or to back up American commitments militarily—had become much more urgent than in late 1963.

After his use of force at the Gulf of Tonkin, Johnson had declined to undertake military action. As he did in early 1965, he had recognized that Saigon had little if any chance of actually winning the war. And he had hoped that the fall of South Vietnam might not necessarily cause the communization of other nations in Southeast Asia. He often called Vietnam (which had only eighteen million people) a "damn little piss-ant country."

In early 1965, LBJ also resisted the temptation to launch all-out war against communism in Southeast Asia. Anxious to keep China and the Soviet Union out of the fighting, he had no intention of provoking them by bombing Hanoi or by dispatching American troops to invade North Vietnam. Johnson and his aides remembered vividly the disastrous consequences that had ensued when the United States decided during the Korean War to chase enemy soldiers northward toward the Chinese border: that effort brought China into the war and led to two more years of bloodshed. LBJ also determined that if America entered the conflict in Vietnam, it should not attack Cambodia or Laos, even though these nations had been serving as sanctuaries for the enemy.

Finally, Johnson had held back before Pleiku for a reason that remained close to his heart: his sense that American military escalation would divide the nation, weaken his political coalition, and damage chances for passage of his ambitious Great Society agenda. He expressed this feeling with memorable force years later in a conversation with the historian Doris Kearns:

> I knew from the start that I was bound to be crucified either way I moved. If I left the woman I really loved—the Great Society—in order to get involved with that bitch of a war on the other side of the world, then I would lose everything at home. All my programs. All my hopes to feed the hungry and shelter the homeless. All my desires to provide education and medical care to the browns and the blacks and the lame and the poor. But if I . . . let the Communists take over South Vietnam, then I would be seen as a coward and my nation would be seen as an appeaser and we would both find it impossible to accomplish anything for anybody anywhere on the entire globe. Oh, I could see it coming all right. . . . Once the war began, then all those conservatives in Congress would use it as a weapon against the Great Society. . . . Oh, I could see it coming. And I didn't like the smell of it.[7]

Still, having prepared for military escalation in 1964, Johnson had come to believe by February 1965 that getting more deeply entangled in "that bitch of a war" was all but inevitable. With South Vietnam in terrible straits—corruption was rampant, desertions from its army were increasing—he recognized that unless the political and military situation could be turned around, the North would overrun the South.

Johnson also remained fearful of being called an appeaser and suffering the political fate that had befallen Truman when China went communist in 1949. He continued to worry that politicos on the right—Goldwater, Reagan, Dirksen, and others—would savage him if he did not stand up to communism. So he remained steadfast in support of the commitment he believed his predecessors in the White House had made: to preserve the independence of a noncommunist South Vietnam. As he did throughout his long and agonizing involvement in Southeast Asia, he emphasized the necessity of maintaining the international credibility of the United States. The Free World, its leader declared, must not back away from its promises.

—

FOR ALL THESE REASONS, JOHNSON'S DECISION TO ESCALATE IN February 1965 was predictable. To brush off the bloodshed at Pleiku as if it were unfortunate but tolerable had become a highly unattractive option. In hindsight, given the horrors that followed American military engagement in the war, it is evident he should have resisted the incremental but ultimately vast American escalation that followed the attack near Pleiku.

It is arguable that he would not have suffered politically had he refrained from escalating. As earlier, none of America's major allies was anxious to see the United States tied up in a war in Southeast Asia. Mansfield and a number of others in Congress had made it clear that they opposed a strong military response. So did Vice President Humphrey, who after Pleiku sent LBJ a memo detailing the political and military risks of further escalation. And while public opinion polls were generally to indicate that majorities of the American people backed Johnson's military moves in 1965, this support was neither deep nor well informed in February.[8]

It is also unlikely that hawks, even if they were to ally with conservatives in struggles over domestic policies, would have succeeded in blocking Great Society programs as retaliation against a dovish Johnson policy approach to Vietnam. LBJ's skills as a congressional manager, together with the ardent support for domestic reforms he enjoyed from substantial liberal majorities on Hill, would likely have combined to see the Great Society through. Though increasing numbers of congressional liberals and moderates were later to turn against Johnson's management of the war, most continued to be loyal backers of his domestic ideals throughout 1965.

Such speculations remain among the many "might have beens" of history. The fact is that Johnson was determined—as he had been since becoming president in November 1963—to sustain America's commitment to South Vietnam. He would *not* be the president who would appease aggressors or "lose" Vietnam to the communists. Bundy, still in Saigon, hurried with Ambassador Taylor and General Westmoreland to Pleiku, where he was horrified by the bloodshed and relayed his feelings of outrage to the White House. Furious, Johnson decided that America must fight back.

Quickly calling a meeting of the National Security Council (with Mansfield and McCormack also present), LBJ exploded, "We have kept our guns over the mantel and our shells in the cupboard for a long time now. And what was the result? They are killing our men while they sleep in the night. I can't ask our American soldiers out there to continue to fight with one hand tied behind their backs."[9] After a brief discussion, he authorized immediate bombing of North Vietnamese installations. Within twelve hours, some 150 planes set off on bombing missions. Though Mansfield and Humphrey disagreed with this decision, all of LBJ's major advisers—McNamara, Secretary of State Rusk, Bundy, Undersecretary of State Ball, Taylor, Westmoreland, and General Earle Wheeler, chair of the Joint Chiefs of Staff—supported it. Bundy, aware that the war would be fierce and sustained, cautioned LBJ to alert the American people that "the struggle in Vietnam will be long" and that "there is no shortcut to success." Humphrey, too, recommended that he make the situation clear to the nation. But Johnson, not yet certain how long he would maintain the bombing, was reluctant to detail his policies before the people. He also feared that an open and high-level debate over the war might undermine his efforts for the Great Society. He rejected Bundy's advice.[10]

Indeed, he never accepted it. Then as later, Johnson was secretive about his decisions and about the course of the war. But it was impossible to conceal everything that the United States was doing. Well-informed members of the news media, resenting his attitude, were quick to complain. James Reston of the *New York Times* wrote in mid-February, "The time has come to call a spade a bloody shovel. This country is in an undeclared and unexplained war in Vietnam. Our masters have a lot of long and fancy names for it, like escalation and retaliation, but it is a war just the same."[11]

When Johnson had unleashed American air power at the Gulf of Tonkin in August 1964, he had called it off quickly. Indeed, he continued to doubt that bombing would save the day for South Vietnam. As the Joint Chiefs themselves conceded, North Vietnam possessed little in the way of an industrial infrastructure, and most of the fighting was taking place in rural areas of the South. Nonetheless, this time he sustained the bombing. The next day, February 8, American and South Vietnamese planes attacked again. The enemy, unfazed, blew up a hotel housing American enlisted men at Qui Nhon, seventy-five miles east of Pleiku and on the coast of South Vietnam. The raid killed twenty-three American soldiers and wounded twenty-two. The United States retaliated on February 11 in the biggest air response yet, with hundreds of planes blasting enemy supply and staging bases just north of the seventeenth parallel, the partition line dividing the North from the South.

If Johnson, who prided himself on his ability to bring fence-sitting legislators to his way of thinking, allowed himself to hope after Pleiku that incremental increases in bombing might some day achieve similar success with the North Vietnamese—that is, get them to compromise at a bargaining table—he was doomed to disappointment. The North Vietnamese were fighting a revolution, and they were not to be shaken from their course. Johnson, trapped, quietly decided on February 13 to launch daily and gradually more powerful air strikes against North Vietnamese targets.

These massive attacks, officially labeled Operation Rolling Thunder, started in earnest on March 2. During the course of the bombing, which increased over the next eight years, three times the tonnage of explosives fell on North Vietnam as had been unleashed over Europe during World War II. The effort was to engross the president, who later held regular Tuesday lunches to designate targets. Johnson often stayed up far into the night—or arose in the early hours after midnight—to check on results of the raids. "They can't even bomb an outhouse without my approval," he said.[12]

Because Johnson remained nervous about making moves that would bring Chinese or Soviet troops into Vietnam, he did not order strikes close to Hanoi or Haiphong, the North's major port. But Operation Rolling Thunder was nonetheless costly to the United States: some five hundred American aircraft were lost in 1965 and 1966.[13] The bombing was also savage. Though the attacks were supposed to hit carefully identified targets, they were far from precise, often blasting villages and towns and unleashing floods of desperate refugees. American bombing during the war killed an estimated hundred thousand civilians.[14]

Johnson also authorized the dropping of incendiary bombs, including napalm, a gasoline-based defoliant and antipersonnel weapon. Victims of napalm, some of them caught up in firestorms, often died from severe burns. Toxic herbicides and defoliants such as Agent Orange, sprayed by helicopters and low-flying aircraft to eradicate enemy cover and food crops, killed or maimed civilians and resulted in birth defects. Agent Orange ultimately destroyed five million acres of land in Vietnam. A motto of bombing crews satirized the slogan of Smokey the Bear: "Only You Can Prevent Forests."

Shortly after the enemy assault near Pleiku, polls indicated that 70 to 80 percent of Americans agreed with Johnson's response.[15] So did a number of political figures. Senator Gale McGee, a Democratic senator from Wyoming, declared, "This is no time for another Munich. If Red China is prepared to expand its sphere of influence and territory in Southeast Asia, we might as well find out now before it is too late."[16] Dirksen and others emphatically and publicly agreed. Views such as these were hardly surprising—Americans generally back their commanders in chief in the immediate aftermath of bold and daring decisions—and public opposition to escalation of the war in early February remained scattered and small.

By late February, however, polls and editorial opinions suggested that hawkish Americans might be cooling off. Many people, more anguished than angry, appeared to believe that negotiating would be a good idea.[17] Congressional skeptics, notably major figures like Fulbright and Mansfield, continued to express their doubts to Johnson. Walter Lippmann, America's most influential political columnist, was an especially sharp critic of the new war. In his regular *Newsweek* column on February 15, he emphasized that the United States, the strongest power in the world, "need have no fear to negotiate."[18]

Other prominent intellectuals, notably Reinhold Niebuhr, George Kennan, and Hans Morgenthau, also spoke out against escalation. For the most part, seasoned observers such as these did not argue—as many younger antiwar critics on the Left were later to do—that the United States was fundamentally an imperialist country or that the insatiable appetites of American capitalism generated warlike public policies.[19] Rather, their "realist" position, like Lippmann's, held that going to war to protect South Vietnam from communism was a costly overcommitment and not in the national interest of the United States. In short, America should seek a negotiated settlement of the conflict.

Martin Luther King seconded this view, saying at a convocation at Howard University on March 2 that while he sympathized with Johnson's "serious problem" concerning Vietnam, he saw no solution in violence. Because American military engagement in the conflict was "accomplishing nothing," he argued that the United States should negotiate with Hanoi.[20] It was King's first public comment on the war, which he was to oppose with increasing forcefulness until his death in 1968. A number of liberal Democratic senators agreed. "It is not appeasement," McGovern declared, "to recognize that the problem of Southeast Asia does not lend itself to a military solution." Church argued, "If the people themselves [of South Vietnam] will not support the government, we cannot save it. . . . The question is really not whether we should negotiate, but when."[21]

Still, LBJ's decision did not provoke immediate large-scale protests. Early coverage in Luce publications continued to back the president. On February 19, *Life* devoted six pages of photos to the attack at Pleiku, one of which depicted a wounded GI.[22] On the same day, *Time* featured on its cover a drawing of General Westmoreland, a handsome soldier's soldier who had been first captain of cadets at West Point and had fought during World War II in North Africa,

Sicily, and Normandy, and later in the Korean War.[23] One of *Time*'s photos depicted blood-splattered soldiers' bunks at Pleiku. Another showed flag-draped coffins aboard a homebound US plane, under which a caption stated, "No mere misunderstanding, the aims are simple and long-range."

Time also cited McNamara, who declared that because there were Americans at two hundred installations in Vietnam, the United States would need fifty military police battalions and two hundred thousand troops to guard these bases adequately. McNamara added, "We may be certain that we would have to face this problem all over again in another place, or permit the Communists to have all of Southeast Asia by default." The article concluded, "There are obviously dangers in the new U.S. firmness. But the perils of pulling back, or showing a lack of resolution are greater, the chief one being that Red China's expansionist government would see U.S. weakness as an invitation to crawl over Southeast Asia."[24]

THE WAR, HOWEVER, WENT BADLY FOR THE SOUTH VIETNAMESE. The North reacted sharply to the bombing and further increased its aid to the Vietcong in the South. Even as Operation Rolling Thunder got under way on March 2, desertions from the South Vietnamese army were continuing to rise. (Disgusted, *Newsweek* wrote that the deserters were like the children's book character Ferdinand the Bull—"they like to smell the flowers and do not like to fight.")[25] As it became clear to Westmoreland that American air bases needed better security, he agitated for more help. On February 22, he urged Johnson to send him two marine battalions—thirty-five hundred men—to protect America's air base at Danang.

The request was hardly a surprise to LBJ, who had expected the war to be costly. Ambassador Taylor, fearful that America would get sucked into a ground-based jungle war like the one that had ended in defeat for France, expressed "grave reservations." But LBJ's top advisers in Washington again backed the general's call. Johnson quietly granted Westmoreland's request, though making it appear in official statements that the landing, which would take place on March 8, was a short-term expedient.

But the dispatch of combat troops to Vietnam was in fact a very large step—greater than the bombing decision of February 7. For the first time since the Korean War, American combat troops would be exposed to fighting on the Asian mainland. If the marines encountered enemy forces, as was certain to happen, some would be killed. Their superiors would demand reinforcements. Johnson would then face an excruciating decision: whether to risk still wider war with the enemy.

As the marines were preparing to land, he called Senator Richard Russell. "Dick," he complained on March 6, "a man can fight if he can see daylight down the road somewhere. But there ain't no daylight in Vietnam. There's not a bit." Russell concurred: "There's no end to the road. There's just nothing." Johnson agreed: "The more bombs you drop," he said, "the more nations you scare, the more people you get mad."[26] Russell sympathized, saying, "It's just awful. . . . It's the biggest—it's the worst mess I ever saw in my life. You couldn't have inherited a worse mess." To which LBJ replied, "Well, if they'd say I *inherited*, I'll be lucky. But they'll say I *created* it!"

Lady Bird recorded in her diary how LBJ felt that night. The next day (which was Bloody Sunday in Selma) she wrote, "In talking about the Vietnam situation, Lyndon summed it up quite simply—'I can't get out, and I can't finish it with what I have. And I don't know what the hell to do.'"[27]

Some of the marines, far more innocent, appeared to think they would win in a walk. After all, they were met by smiling Vietnamese girls presenting them with garlands of flowers. One of those who landed that day, Philip Caputo, later wrote a widely praised book, *A Rumor of War*, in which he recalled the orders of his skipper before they landed at Danang. "I don't want anyone going in there thinking he's going to be John Wayne," he said. "We're to provide security and that's all. We're not going to fight, but to free the ARVNs [the Army of the Republic of Viet Nam] to fight. It's their war."

After the marines had landed without resistance, Caputo, who was twenty-three years old at the time, was bored and uncomfortable. The conditions, he wrote, were miserable—dusty, hot, and humid.

Ever-present bugs were eating him alive. But, he wrote in a section titled "Splendid Little War," he was certain that he and his comrades in arms, if attacked, would triumph: "We had acquired the conviction that we could win the brushfire war, and win it quickly, if we were only turned loose to fight. By 'we,' I do not mean the United States, but our brigade alone, and by 'quickly,' I mean very quickly." This, Caputo added, was because they were American marines.

> We believed all the myths created by that most articulate and elegant mythmaker, John Kennedy. If he was the King of Camelot, then we were his knights and Vietnam our crusade. There was nothing we could not do because we were Americans, and for the same reason, whatever we did was right.[28]

Within a short time the marines encountered Vietcong forces and had to fight. The enemy, moreover, was pummeling the ARVN in many areas of South Vietnam. Westmoreland, believing that there was "no solution . . . other than to put our own finger in the dike," quickly requested reinforcements. Emphasizing that "a good offense is the best defense," he also sought authorization for offensive missions to punish the enemy.[29] A marine leader, concurring, said that offensives would enable his men "to start killing the VC instead of sitting on their ditty box."[30] As Johnson pondered these appeals, he recognized that a decision to further escalate the ground war was fraught with peril.

—

WHILE JOHNSON WAS CONSIDERING WESTMORELAND'S REQUESTS, he was also trying to cope with events following Bloody Sunday at Selma and press his Great Society legislation through Congress. As he well knew, chances of success in these efforts depended in part on his ability to persuade the American people of his skill in managing the situation in Vietnam.

It turned out that he did not need to persuade Congress very much at that time. Once "American boys" were engaged in combat, it was politically perilous for elected officials to oppose the appropriations he sought or to severely criticize the war. No one exhibited this response more strongly than Russell, who had never considered Vietnam to be of strategic importance to the United States. "We are there now," he said after the troops were under fire. If we "scuttle and run, it would shake the confidence of the free world in any commitment we might make."[31]

Russell and his colleagues on the Hill made certain that requests for military funding received quick approval. At the opening of the session, LBJ had estimated that spending related to Vietnam in the coming fiscal year might total $1.5 billion, but it was already obvious that far more money would be needed, not only to support the escalating ground combat effort but also to create the enormous infrastructure necessary to protect the Danang air base and other sprawling US installations. Ongoing construction of these in early 1965 indicated to reporters in Vietnam that the American engagement would be both large-scale and long-range. In early May, bowing to administration requests, the House would vote by a margin of 408 to 7 and the Senate 88 to 3 in support of a supplemental $700 million appropriation for the fighting in Vietnam. It was just one of many special appropriations that Congress approved in subsequent years.

SOME AMERICANS BECAME INCREASINGLY OUTSPOKEN AS THE fighting intensified. After US combat troops arrived in Vietnam, student opposition to the war began to mount. On March 24, the first "teach-in," organized by antiwar faculty members, took place at the University of Michigan at Ann Arbor. The event's name was inspired by the highly newsworthy sit-ins that civil rights advocates had been staging since 1960. To the consternation of many prowar Americans, more than three thousand students and two hundred faculty members packed lecture halls and classrooms in the early evening (after the end of regular classes) to attend antiwar lectures, watch films, listen to music, and engage in debates and discussions. Despite bomb scares and heckling from about eighty prowar attendees (whose signs read, "Better Red Than Dead" and "Drop the Bomb"), the teach-in was judged a huge success. Some six hundred students were still discussing the war at eight the next morning. During the next two months, the teach-in movement spread to many more campuses.

Opposition to the war also began slowly to mobilize the student-dominated New Left. Leaders of SDS, having decided at its December convention to focus on antiwar activity, spoke out with special fervor after the start of combat operations in March. Some who began to join SDS at the time—or who attended their meetings—worried especially about the recent increase in draft calls of young men into the military.[32] A few protestors were starting to look like "radicals"—that is, the men wore long hair and beards, the women long hair and no lipstick. SDS leaders began to hope that their long-planned antiwar rally in Washington, scheduled for April 17, would attract widespread participation.[33]

—

IN FACT, OVERT ANTIWAR ACTIVITY BETWEEN EARLY FEBRUARY AND early April remained scattered. The number of combat troops in Vietnam was small, and Johnson was not telling the American people very much. Many headlines, especially after Bloody Sunday on March 7, continued to focus on the dramatic and unsettling confrontations in Selma.

Moreover, then as later that year, most Americans, enjoying unparalleled prosperity, attended primarily to matters near to home, paying little regard to events in faraway Southeast Asia. Consumer spending, stronger than ever, continued to spark glowing predictions of future economic growth. Following reports that the TV networks would turn heavily to color programming in the fall, Americans flocked to purchase color sets.[34]

Rather than dwell on news reports of Operation Rolling Thunder, Americans could turn on their TVs to watch the Division I NCAA men's basketball tournament, which lasted from March 8 to March 20.[35] In early April, 42,652 people turned out to see the Philadelphia Phillies beat the Houston Astros, 2–0, in the first regular season major league baseball game to be played at the indoor Astrodome.

During the time between Pleiku and early April, Americans also continued to enjoy a wide variety of diverting entertainments. A new movie, *How to Murder Your Wife* (featuring Jack Lemmon as a carefree bachelor who gets waylaid into matrimony), attracted large audiences. Maria Callas returned to the Metropolitan Opera after a seven-year absence and dazzled her audience in Puccini's *Tosca*; she received sixteen curtain calls. Feel-good songs—the Beatles' "Eight Days a Week," the Righteous Brothers' "You've Lost That Lovin' Feelin'," and the Supremes' "Stop! In the Name of Love"—topped the charts. Like most pop tunes, these dealt with love and personal feelings, not with matters of national or international concern. (The Beatles, who didn't think much of their own song, never performed it live.)

Even Bob Dylan, who released his fifth album (*Bringing It All Back Home*) on March 22, distanced himself from protest themes that had long been beloved by folk-music fans. Instead, many of his lyrics were personal and abstract. Supported for the first time by an electrically amplified rock 'n' roll band on some of his songs, he alienated a portion of his admirers, who expected him, like other folk musicians, to sing with acoustic guitar and no backup. Still, the album—which included acoustic versions of "Mr. Tambourine Man" and "It's Alright, Ma (I'm Only Bleeding)"—was his first to make *Billboard*'s top ten, peaking at number 6. Its lead song, "Subterranean Homesick Blues," did reasonably well on the singles charts.[36]

On March 2, the day Rolling Thunder started in earnest, a new film, *The Sound of Music*, opened in theaters across the country. Based on a Rodgers and Hammerstein musical that had opened on Broadway in 1959, it romanticized the real-life travails of the von Trapp family, who at the end of the movie scale the Alps to Switzerland (a choir sings "Climb Ev'ry Mountain") to escape from Nazi-controlled Austria. The movie did not impress reviewers. *Newsweek* praised the singing of Julie Andrews, who starred as the von Trapp governess, but complained of the "fatuousness" of the plot and commented, "Its rickety bones show through everywhere." In *McCall's*, the critic Pauline Kael ridiculed the film as a "sugar-coated lie people seem to want to eat." (For her temerity, she was fired.) Christopher Plummer, who played Baron von Trapp, was alleged to have said on the set that the production should have been titled *The Sound of Mucus*.[37]

But Americans flocked to the film, which packed theaters throughout 1965. Ultimately grossing more than $158 million in the United

States and Canada, an all-time high, it won five Oscars.[38] The fact that such an old-fashioned, sentimental movie could entice millions of people when the conflict in Vietnam was rapidly escalating has prompted the suggestion that viewers, worried about the war, found the film to be a means of escape. A better explanation, however, is that people who watched *The Sound of Music* (or who loved the Beatles or the Supremes) simply liked feel-good amusements. *Time*, for instance, wrote that *The Sound of Music* was "tuneful, cheerful, and colorful," that it "celebrates courage," and that it was "wholesome family entertainment."[39]

In any event, no survey of American popular opinion between February and early April revealed the existence of significant popular opposition to the war. Gallup polls, for instance, while subject to varying interpretations, tend to confirm the conclusion that most people at the time were not greatly exercised about developments in Vietnam. One found that 41 percent of respondents between March 11 and March 16 (immediately after the marines' landing at Danang) favored greater efforts on behalf of negotiation, and that 42 percent favored the dispatch of more troops. Polls between April 2 and April 7, however, indicated that 55 percent of people thought the United States was handling affairs in Vietnam "as well as could be expected," compared to 26 percent who thought the administration was managing the situation "badly."[40] Some two-thirds of Americans at the time continued to have a good opinion of President Johnson's decisions as president.

Newsweek published a special feature, "Campus 1965," on March 22, reporting on scattered student protests, many of which involved issues of employee, faculty, or student rights, including relaxation of parietal rules. Describing college students as more liberal concerning racial matters than their parents' generation, the magazine noted that some of the campus demonstrations raised racial issues, including protests against university investments in South Africa and against racial discrimination by fraternities and sororities.

But *Newsweek* mentioned only one recent campus demonstration against the war: a 200-student march at Harvard. It added that the membership of SDS, the most significant organization on the Left, had grown a little since late 1964 but still numbered only 2,000. By comparison, it continued, the Young Democrats claimed 450,000 members, the Young Republicans 135,000, and the Young Americans for Freedom, the leading conservative group on the campuses, 15,000 or more. (Total college and university enrollment in the United States was 5.2 million at the time.) Conveying the impression that the campuses were calm, *Newsweek* generalized, "Indications are that American youth is asking for a truce in the endless war between generations." It quoted the editor of the University of Michigan's student paper: "Students just don't want to take part in outside activities, they worry too much about getting into law or medical school."[41]

Newsweek's dismissal of antiwar sentiment among college students was hardly unique at the time. Many mainstream media accounts, including those appearing in magazines and newspapers that had hailed the courage of civil rights protestors at Selma, rallied behind LBJ's war policies and deprecated, marginalized, and trivialized antiwar young people. Students participating in teach-ins or raising questions about the war were "just kids." Some press and TV accounts were soon to become harsher, perceiving protestors not only as too young to be well informed but also as radical, unpatriotic, deviant, and menacing dangers to society.[42]

In any event, Johnson did not let stirrings of antiwar activism worry him. He concentrated instead on managing the war effort. On March 30, Vietcong operatives set off a bomb outside the CIA station in Saigon, killing at least twenty people in the street and a CIA secretary, blinding two CIA officers, and injuring sixty more. This bold action showed that virtually no American preserve in Vietnam was safe.[43] The next day, April 1, LBJ backed Westmoreland's request for help by authorizing the sending of another thirty-five hundred combat marines to Vietnam, along with twenty thousand additional logistical personnel. He also secretly granted his general's request to allow American combat soldiers to mount offensive moves against Vietcong forces that were raiding American bases.[44] Escalation, having begun with bombing in February and increased with the dispatch of troops in early March, was gaining momentum.

Nevertheless, the president hoped to dampen antiwar opposition and was eager to appear a flexible and reasonable leader. With such concerns in mind, he invited Walter Lippmann, still one of his most consistent critics, to the White House to tell him about a conciliatory speech, "Peace Without Conquest," he was scheduled to give the next day at Johns Hopkins University. But when Lippmann proved unsympathetic, Johnson shot back, "I'm not just going to pull up my pants and run out on Vietnam. Don't you know the church is on fire over there? . . . You say to negotiate, but there's nobody over there to negotiate with. So the only thing there is to do is to hang on. And that's what I am going to do."[45]

Though LBJ the next day proclaimed "we will not withdraw" from Vietnam, Johnson did try to sound generous and reasonable. If North Vietnam agreed to guarantee South Vietnamese independence, he said, it could expect to receive some of $1 billion in funding that he would seek for a "greatly expanded cooperative effort for development" throughout Southeast Asia. This would feature a complex of dams, power plants, and agricultural facilities in the Mekong Delta region. Such an effort, he proclaimed, would "dwarf even our own TVA."[46] Johnson also maintained that he was willing to conduct "unconditional discussions" with Hanoi.

The *New York Times*, pleased, wrote that the president's speech was one "in which the country can take pride." Though Lippmann continued to criticize the president, both Mansfield and Fulbright also praised LBJ's willingness to begin discussions.[47] Perhaps, they allowed themselves to hope, the United States and North Vietnam would sit down and talk.

But Fulbright nevertheless continued to snipe at LBJ's policies, thereby annoying him. "This damn fool Fulbright fights me on everything," he complained to former president Truman on the phone.[48] And Johnson did not reduce the military pressure: even as he spoke, massive bombing raids were continuing to target enemy installations, and troop reinforcements, as approved earlier, were arriving in Vietnam. He also knew that Hanoi would refuse to negotiate. Though he told Bill Moyers, an aide, "Old Ho can't turn me down," he also remarked to his staff, "If I were Ho Chi Minh, I would never negotiate." He was right about that. Hanoi immediately restated its basic and consistent position: America must pull its military personnel out of South Vietnam, end its hostile actions (such as bombing), agree to the formation of a coalition government in Saigon that would be "in accordance with the program of the National Liberation Front" (the political arm of the Vietcong), and accept a peaceful reunification of Vietnam without foreign interference.

By this time, Johnson had also managed to alienate influential people in the press. As early as March 3, *Time*, though continuing to support his policies, let him know how angry it had become with the president it had chosen as its Man of the Year for 1964. It objected first to Johnson's practice of calling sudden and unscheduled press conferences and of being "evasive" when asked questions. *Time* went on to complain that in private he referred to inquiring journalists as "crybabies" and "bellyachers" and that ("furious at leaks") he ordered his aides not to talk to reporters. Joseph Alsop, an outspoken hawk, wrote in his syndicated column of the "almost hysterical secretiveness which the Johnson administration has been carrying to extremes quite unimagined by anyone in any previous American government."[49]

Alsop's word "secretiveness" best described the way that Johnson and his top aides were continuing to behave with regard to Vietnam in the weeks after the marines had landed in early March. Though many Americans were aware of the major events—Pleiku, the bombing, the arrival of the marines—few people as yet had a clear idea of the escalating nastiness of the fighting taking place on the ground. And Johnson, fearful that open debate might polarize the nation, still did not explain how much the war would cost, and he made no effort to call up the reserves—an act that would have revealed how serious the situation was and that would have yanked a great many men out of their jobs and away from home. Outside of a slow increase in draft calls, he asked no sacrifices of civilians. Taxes would not be raised.

In the weeks and months ahead, the administration continued to do its best to conceal the broadening scope of the fighting. But even in April, doubters were becoming highly suspicious, believing that Johnson was not telling them anything like the whole truth. And the die having been cast, there was no returning to the more confident world of late 1964. The Sixties, launched above all by American escalation of the Vietnam War, had arrived to stay.

7

"MAXIMUM FEASIBLE PARTICIPATION"

Complications on the Domestic Front

PERHAPS NO MAGAZINE PIECE TRIED HARDER TO CAPTURE AN upbeat mood during the spring of 1965 than a May cover story in *Time*. Titled "Rock 'n' Roll: The Sound of the Sixties," it featured photos of super-energetic people—middle-aged as well as young—moving to the "Jerk," the "Monkey," and other dances in the loud and crowded clubs of New York City. Musicians jumped around the stage, playing their electric guitars behind their backs. "The big beat," *Time* marveled, "is everywhere. It resounds over TV and radio, in saloons and soda shops, fraternity houses and dance halls. It has become, in fact, the international anthem of a new and restless generation, the pulse beat for new modes of dress, dance, art, and morality."[1]

In the course of its story, *Time* understandably failed to mention that Vladimir Horowitz, the world-famous pianist, had emerged from a twelve-year retirement in early May to give a concert at Carnegie Hall. Or to report that Barbra Streisand, who made her TV debut, *My Name Is Barbra*, in late April, brought out a hit album with that name in May. (It later won an Emmy award.) Instead, the magazine highlighted the music of Herman's Hermits, a popular quintet of clean-cut British singers whose catchy song "Mrs. Brown, You've Got a Lovely Daughter" had recently topped the singles charts. Most of the other pop performers *Time* praised were also well known: the Rolling Stones, the Beach Boys, the Supremes, and, of course, the Beatles. The Fab Four's latest hit, "Ticket to Ride," was even then rising to the number 1 spot on the singles charts, and their second movie, *Help!*, was being readied for release.

It was also at that time that Sidney Lumet's controversial movie *The Pawnbroker* opened in American movie theaters. Unlike *Time*'s effusion, it was far from upbeat. Starring Rod Steiger as a cynical and embittered survivor of a Nazi concentration camp, the darkly serious film was a pioneering movie, dealing with the Holocaust from the point of view of a survivor. Steiger's character, running a pawnshop in Manhattan, had seen his two children die and his wife raped by Nazi officers.

The movie also sparked debate because it was the first American film to show (briefly) a woman's bare breasts. In so doing, *The Pawnbroker* marked the beginning of the end to Hollywood's restrictive Production Code and the arrival—as of 1967–1968—of more sexually explicit movies associated with the Sixties. The film was otherwise in no way titillating, nor was it a big draw at the ticket office. *The Sound of Music* and still-popular films from 1964—*Zorba the Greek*, *Goldfinger*, and *Mary Poppins*—indicated that the movie theater would largely continue to be a realm of reassurance. Not everything changed in 1965.

Major sporting events also continued to offer heroics and heroes to the American public. Early in April, Jack Nicklaus, only twenty-five, won his second Masters Golf Tournament, overwhelming Arnold Palmer and Gary Player, his closest competitors, by a record margin of nine strokes.[2] Several weeks later in Lewiston, Maine, a younger but far more colorful athlete, twenty-three-year-old Muhammad Ali, delivered a first-round "phantom punch" to knock out Sonny Liston and retain his heavyweight boxing championship. Disbelieving spectators, believing that Liston had taken a dive, shouted, "Fake! Fake! Fake!" and "Fix! Fix!" The *New York Times* (which like most other papers referred to the champ not as Muhammad Ali but by his birth name of Cassius Clay) reported that Liston, the "shuffling, sullen-faced former champion . . . collapsed slowly, like a falling building. . . . Clay danced around him, waving at him, taunting him."[3]

Ali was not yet the iconic figure he was to become. His identity as a figure of social and political consequence developed mainly after 1967, when he refused to be inducted into the army and was stripped of his title. Thereafter he was hailed around the world, especially by blacks, as a man of conviction who would stand up against authority. "I ain't got no quarrel with them Viet Cong," he said in 1966. "No Viet Cong ever called me nigger." But like Malcolm, Ali, having joined the Nation of Islam in 1963, had already emerged in 1965 as a proud and assertive black man. Guarded by Black Muslims after dropping Liston, he leaned against the ropes and told derisive fans to "shaddup." His victory, he said, was a triumph of the "righteous life."

Technological triumphs also continued to excite Americans in the spring of 1965. Many of these were associated with the space program. In late March, *Ranger 9* landed on the lunar surface, sending back photos. Two days later, Gus Grissom and John Young became the first two-man team of American astronauts to orbit the earth. In April, Communications Satellite Corporation (COMSAT) made headlines by launching an eighty-five-pound satellite, *Early Bird*, twenty-three thousand miles into space. When the system became operational in June, *Early Bird* enabled the first direct and nearly instantaneous telephone messages and TV broadcasts between Europe and the United States.[4]

Computers, which were essential to the space program, evoked anticipation and hope about their futuristic applications. In April, *Time* ran a cover story, "The Computer in Society," which announced the arrival of the "Cybernated Generation."[5] More than twenty American companies, it reported, were engaged in the computer business, which in 1964 had employed 650,000 people and reaped some $5 billion in sales. IBM, which dominated the trade, had by then installed some thirteen thousand computers in the United States and three thousand in Europe. The computer companies were not marketing personal computers, which were years away. But Digital Equipment Corp was even then advertising the first successful "mini-computer," the PDP-8. It was still large—the size of a refrigerator—and it cost $18,000, but as a second-generation model it was considerably smaller than the enormous mainframes that had earlier dominated the business.

As contemporary accounts were quick to point out, these computers had many and varied uses, not only for the space program but also for the military (among other things monitoring underground nuclear explosions). NASA and the Pentagon were among the first of many government departments and agencies, such as the post office and the IRS, that accelerated the growth of the computer industry in America. But corporations were investing in them, too. Computers were helping to route long-distance telephone calls, manufacture cars, navigate ships and planes, prepare weather forecasts, aid in traffic control, manage inventories, and send out monthly bills and bank statements. The New York Stock Exchange was relying on a "talking computer" to provide instant stock quotations over a special telephone. The New York Central Railroad scored a first among the world's railroads by installing computer-fed TV devices that would disseminate instant information concerning the location of any of 125,000 freight cars on Central's ten thousand miles of track.[6]

Claims for the wonderful potential of computers were credible, in part, because by May 1965 the American economy was booming as never before. The Dow Industrial Index reached an all-time high in mid-May of 939.62. General Motors ran up the biggest profits in the history of American business—$636 million for the quarter. Ford and Chrysler also reported unprecedented first-quarter profits. AT&T, the second largest American company behind GM, announced a profit for the quarter of $424 million. Delighted, the *New York Times* wrote that the "record expansion" of the American auto industry (not yet seriously challenged by "tinny Japanese cars") was the key to the health of the economy as a whole.[7]

A month later, the *New York Times* ran two articles on the same day highlighting important improvements in the overall well-being of the American people. The first reported that Connecticut had enacted a bill requiring fluoridation of water supplies in all communities in the state with populations of twenty thousand or more. This was not a revolutionary move: some forty-eight million Americans in 2,792 communities were already drinking fluoridated water. But fluoridation, which many conservatives had denounced as an unwarranted and dangerous intervention by Big Government—or as a communist-inspired plot—remained controversial in parts of the United States in the mid-1960s.

(In Stanley Kubrick's satiric film *Dr. Strangelove*, which premiered in late 1964, the paranoid character Jack D. Ripper insists that communists were backing fluoridation in order to "sap and impurify" the "precious bodily fluids" of Americans.) Connecticut's law delighted fluoridation advocates, who praised it as enabling an important attack on tooth decay, which had long been a major public health problem.[8]

The second *Times* article—considerably broader in its implications—indicated how extraordinarily healthy the American people were becoming as a result of better nutrition and easier living during the post–World War II years. It drew on a national survey that showed American young men to be the tallest and heaviest in the world. Men between the ages of eighteen and twenty-four averaged 5 feet 9 inches in height, 2.1 inches higher than the height of their parents thirty years earlier, marking "the greatest short-term increase for a population of people ever measured."[9]

———

IN SPITE OF THE DEEPENING TROUBLES IN VIETNAM, JOHNSON, too, had reasons for satisfaction. Congressional support of his domestic policies continued to please him. On April 9, he told Larry O'Brien, "Roosevelt's got eleven [bills through]. . . . They were not major bills at all. But you'll have one major one really with education. Now, Appalachia's a supermajor one, and then the others are about like Roosevelt. But on the 12th, you'll have the best Hundred Days. Better than he did!"[10]

Needless to say, LBJ's successes irked conservatives, who complained that he was ramming great lumps of legislation down their throats. Now and again, moreover, one could hear complaints from the left. William Shannon, Washington correspondent for *Commonweal*, wrote in early April that LBJ was the "master of the America-is-a-great-wonderful-barbecue school of politics." Shannon added, "His programs are designed to evade rather than confront the hard issues. He believes in consensus, not conflict. The barbecue school of politics is not based on any belief in redistributing wealth or disturbing anyone's existing privileges; rather, it presupposes that there is enough meat, and gravy, too, for everyone at the tables."[11] As historians were later to conclude, there was truth in this analysis: with notable exceptions, such as voting rights legislation, LBJ sought to avoid protracted fights with powerful opponents or interest groups. He continued to be a liberal who believed that the federal government should advance equal opportunity; he was not a radical or social democrat who sought to tame Big Business, fight against income inequality, ensure equal economic outcomes for people, or guarantee a host of special rights and entitlements.

Still, Johnson continued to deploy all his well-honed weapons in support of his ambitions. Ever more fearful that the war in Vietnam might ultimately weaken his mandate, he drove Congress hard so that it would enact his legislative measures before escalation seriously endangered his political standing. In early April and May, congressional forces led by Senator Edmund Muskie of Maine initiated hearings on clean air legislation. At the same time, LBJ urged the extension of the federal minimum wage to millions of additional American workers. He announced that the War on Poverty would sponsor an eight-week Project Head Start summer program for some half million preschool children. Late in May, he sent Congress yet another special message: he proposed a law that would advance the beautification of America's highways, many of which featured roadsides lined with billboards and cluttered with automobile graveyards.

But not all of LBJ's already established Great Society programs were running smoothly in the spring of 1965. One effort, the War on Poverty, was already encountering criticisms. Like those that were to beset the ESEA and other highly ambitious efforts of his administration, they revealed how difficult it could be for governmental initiatives to remedy large and complicated social problems in the United States. Some critics began to wonder if liberal policymakers—for all their confidence and expertise—knew enough to fix problems of such magnitude and complexity.

By the spring of 1965, the War on Poverty, having been authorized in August 1964, was rounding into shape. Its head, Sargent Shriver, was a Kennedy brother-in-law who also directed the Peace Corps. Energetic and almost evangelically enthusiastic, he was a generally effective lobbyist for congressional approval of the $1.5 billion appropriation—nearly double the amount provided in 1964—that LBJ had called for in January. Shriver was also adept at circulating press releases celebrating the achievements of the Office of Economic Opportunity (OEO), which had been created to run the War on Poverty. In March, he proudly announced the graduation of the first class that had signed up for Volunteers in Service to America, or VISTA, which was billed as a sort of domestic Peace Corps. By the end of June, Shriver proclaimed, there would be two thousand VISTA volunteers either in training or working to help poor people in communities throughout the nation.

At the same time, Shriver announced the opening of the first Job Corps training camp—in the Catoctin Mountains of Maryland. It was the forerunner, he pledged, of some one hundred camps that would be under construction or up and running by the end of June. These would be home to some twenty-five thousand young men age sixteen through twenty who would receive remedial education and vocational training enabling them to find employment. By the end of 1966, Shriver said, there would be one hundred thousand trainees.[12]

Because the much-hyped War on Poverty was channeling politically attractive sums of money into congressional districts, it was almost certain to receive additional funding in 1965. But even as the effort was being devised in 1964, consensus had eluded the sociologists, economists, and government officials who were drafting the bill to create its programs. Poverty, after all, was a vast and complex phenomenon. Among the thirty-three million Americans (some 17 percent of the population) who were classified by the government as living in households with incomes under "poverty lines" in 1964 were large and varied numbers of people—among them the elderly, the disabled, minorities, the unskilled and ill-educated, farm workers, women and children in fatherless families—who were disadvantaged in different ways and needed different forms of help.[13]

Johnson, characteristically impatient, had pushed hard in 1964 for rapid passage of a large-scale program he could call his own during the presidential campaign. What emerged—and was signed in August 1964—was not a welfare measure or radical initiative to endow poor people with "special" rights or guaranteed incomes. Nor was it directed primarily against the poverty of blacks. Instead, it was a characteristically Johnsonian effort—a liberal effort—to promote greater equality of opportunity. Government programs, he believed, would enable poor people to help themselves and in time to become self-sufficient.[14]

The law—grandiosely and unfortunately sold as a war—set up a variety of programs including not only the Job Corps and VISTA but also a Neighborhood Youth Corps, which offered part-time jobs to school dropouts, and work-study, which did the same for needy college students. Other programs—Head Start, Upward Bound for high school students hoping to go to college, Legal Services to aid poor people in their quests for justice—were being developed in 1965.

The legislation also authorized creation of community action agencies, which were intended to operate as local programs funding community-wide efforts to promote economic opportunity. Some advocates hoped local poverty boards—aided if necessary by Legal Services—would challenge what activists believed to be the crony-ridden and paternalistic practices of mayors, city bureaucrats, and social workers who had run programs affecting low-income people in the past. The poor, the statute said, were to have "maximum feasible participation" in the design and management of the community action plans.[15]

By April 1965, community action plans, arising in hundreds of cities and towns, had become a central focus of the War on Poverty. Even then, however, the OEO, a new bureaucracy, was encountering difficulties. Some of these featured turf fights with established government departments, such as Labor (which ran the Neighborhood Youth Corps) and Health, Education, and Welfare. Bureaucratic overlap and competition, rising amid the proliferation of Great Society programs, was to bedevil the agency. More generally, the OEO's troubles reflected the conceptual confusion that had marked establishment of the war. Should the focus of the program be to aid the unemployed, as had been the case with many of FDR's work relief programs in the 1930s, or should it concentrate on elevating the life chances of people—many were low-income women with children—who suffered from long-term poverty and dependency? How would living-wage jobs be created in the market economy for these varied groups of people, let alone for the millions of baby boomers, many of them unskilled and poorly educated, who were streaming into the work force?

When the poverty bill had gone to Congress, some observers had predicted such confusion. Assistant Secretary of Labor Daniel Moynihan, one of the planners, complained that the bill did not include a large-scale government jobs program and that it "represented not a choice among programs so much as a collection of them." When it passed, the economist Robert Theobald observed that it exposed a "lack of research. We don't know enough. We are flying blind." Shriver conceded later, "It's like we went down to Cape Kennedy and launched a half dozen rockets at once." Americans, he admitted, "are just plain confused about what the poverty program is all about. It's like giving an American sports page to an Englishman."[16]

Some OEO programs nonetheless enjoyed fairly good reputations in early 1965: the Neighborhood Youth Corps, for one. Others, however, were encountering considerable criticism. The Job Corps, which became a special target, was very expensive per trainee to run and enlisted many ill-educated and unskilled young men who needed far more help than the camps could provide. *Time* described trainees at the Catoctin camp as a "pathetic lot": some had never had enough to eat or a bed of their own to sleep in. Many could not read. (An estimated one-third of Job Corps trainees could not read a simple sentence.) Though *Time* did not make it explicit, its description exposed a frightening fact: many young people in America, an extraordinarily rich nation, suffered not only from poverty but also from malnutrition and little education. If larger numbers of living-wage and long-term jobs could somehow be made available—an enormously difficult objective in itself—how would these deprived young trainees manage to perform them?[17]

Salvos against the OEO came from many directions by the spring of 1965. From the Left, advocates for poor black women complained that the OEO ignored the needs of low-income mothers and their children. Mobilizing, they created a lobby, the revealingly named National Welfare Rights Organization (NWRO), which grew rapidly over the next few years and furiously demanded that the government provide generous entitlements for welfare mothers and their families. The rise of the NWRO revealed a significant development of the mid and late 1960s: the spread of social programs in the Johnson years, stimulating ever grander popular expectations, had the unintended consequence of intensifying the demands of a host of rights-conscious interest groups in America.

Other criticisms from the Left came from Saul Alinsky, a radical and a community organizer. Aiming his fire at community action programs, he charged that many of them were top-down efforts run by political machines, bureaucratic hacks, and social workers. The OEO, he exclaimed, was a "huge political pork barrel" and "history's greatest relief program for the benefit of the welfare industry." Social workers, he said, were "pimps of the poor."[18]

OEO programs also encountered heavy criticism in early 1965 from conservatives. The essence of many of these complaints was predictable: spending government funds on poor people, many of them (especially blacks) branded as "shiftless" and "irresponsible," would be a waste of the taxpayers' money. This was a familiar argument that had a long history in the United States, a nation whose citizens had traditionally celebrated the virtues of individual effort and where unflattering images of "undeserving" poor people had consistently helped to weaken or derail public programs aimed at relieving need.[19] A Gallup Poll in November 1964, for instance, had discovered widespread opposition to spending for "welfare mothers." More than half of respondents agreed with the statement that the government should "stop giving them relief money." When asked what should be done in the case of women who were on relief and "continue to have illegitimate children and get relief money for each new child born," roughly 20 percent of respondents said yes to the option "sterilize the women."[20]

Among the most vocal critics of community action was Moynihan, who in 1969 wrote a book whose title, *Maximum Feasible Misunderstanding: Community Action in the War on Poverty*, evoked the early controversies over aiding poor people. The poor, he argued, needed money (from jobs), not community organization. Like other critics, Moynihan believed that the word "community" was vague and a source of confusion. How was one to define a "community"? Urban neighborhoods, after all, often blended into one another. Many communities with large numbers of low-income people were politically weak, disorganized, or seriously divided along racial, ethnic, class, or religious lines. Organizing poor people in "communities" was hardly an easy task to accomplish.

Many critics of the OEO complained about the idea, which Shriver generally tried to support, that poor people should have "maximum feasible participation" in designing and managing community action plans. A number of these critics pointed out the obvious: the phrase was vague. Did it mean that poor people should actually run the plans? If so, which poor people? And on whose behalf? The unemployed? Welfare mothers (via the NWRO)? Black people? Other claimants? How would leaders of "the poor" in a "community" secure popular recognition (and certification by the OEO, which would then release the funds) as credible representatives?

As debate flared up over these issues in the spring of 1965, a number of mayors, governors, and other public officials began to complain that militant activists claiming to represent the poor were trying to seize control of the plans, thereby using the OEO's money to advance "radical" agendas of their own. Defending their turf, these officials insisted that most poor people lacked the time or management skills to play major roles in a community action program. As Chicago's Mayor Richard Daley was to put it, placing poor people in positions of influence in a community action agency "would be like telling the fellow who cleans up to be the city editor of the newspaper." The staff director of the New York antipoverty board added, "You can't go to a street corner with a pad and pencil and tell the poor to write you a poverty program. They wouldn't know how."[21]

Complaints such as these about the OEO, community action, and "maximum feasible participation" remained scattered in the spring of 1965. But they indicated that trouble was ahead for the War on Poverty, and they grew stronger during the next few months, during which time doubters, branding the effort as an example of the administration's hubristic social engineering, also demanded evidence that the War was actually reducing economic deprivation. Many advocates for the poor, meanwhile, continued to raise their demands, emphasizing that much more money would be needed to fight anything resembling a consequential assault on poverty. After all, they said, with thirty-three million poor people, the $1.5 billion that LBJ requested for fiscal 1966 would scarcely fund a skirmish, let alone an entire war.

The controversies surrounding the War on Poverty—a highly touted, highly visible Great Society effort—were revealing. On the one hand, they showed that impatient, ever more rights-conscious advocates for the poor were eager to take control of a far larger campaign against economic disadvantage, thereby challenging public officials. But they also revealed a slow but steady revival of conservative opposition even amid the liberal triumphs of the time. If something as formidable as the War on Poverty could be shown to have been ill-conceived, oversold, and divisive, as critics were increasingly arguing, conservatives might rise again to the fore in the United States, thereby undercutting the apparently powerful liberal mandate that LBJ had received in 1964. When the Sixties arrived in force, that is often what happened.

—

RACIAL TENSIONS ALSO CONTINUED TO SIMMER DURING THE SPRING. Much of the elation that had buoyed civil rights advocates after the triumphant march to Montgomery was fading. Hostilities dividing the SCLC and SNCC remained sharp. Many who had led the struggles in Selma dispersed, usually to organize elsewhere. Local advocates in the Selma area who persisted in their efforts to register voters ran up against the same relentless white opposition as in the past. Activists initiated a boycott of stores in Selma in April, but it generated little support from local consumers and collapsed. SNCC workers, including the militant activist Stokely Carmichael, struggled to register people in adjacent Lowndes County, but progress in that large and rural country, where many black people were isolated, destitute, and illiterate, was painfully slow.[22]

Impatient with Congress, Johnson worked hard to move the voting rights bill. As James Farmer of CORE later put it, he was "cracking the whip, he was cajoling, he was threatening."[23] But liberals in the Senate fought among themselves over whether to include an amendment, proposed by senators Robert and Edward Kennedy, that would have banned poll taxes as a requirement for voting in state and local elections. These taxes existed in only four Southern states—Mississippi, Alabama, Texas, and Virginia—and while they were considerably less important as obstacles to voting than literacy tests, which the bill would have outlawed, many liberals were following the Kennedy brothers' lead.[24]

Other liberals worried that the proposed poll tax amendment would be of dubious constitutionality. King, closely following the negotiations on Capitol Hill, feared that if it was included it might sink the whole bill. Johnson agreed. It was not until May 11 that the Senate—strongly lobbied by the president—finally defeated the amendment on a close vote, after which delaying tactics by Southern opponents further postponed a final reckoning. On May 25, a cloture vote of 70–30 ended debate, and the bill passed the next day with bipartisan backing, by a vote of 77–19.[25] This was ten weeks after Johnson had sent the measure to the Hill.

Considering how slowly important legislation moves through Congress, ten weeks was not a terribly long time. Still, the delay was frustrating. And the House, where advocates of the poll tax amendment were determined to prevail, still had to act. In early June, when the House finally took up the issue, it seemed all but certain that an effective voting rights bill would ultimately pass, giving civil rights advocates—and LBJ—a legislative triumph of great significance. But the House debates were only beginning. LBJ remained impatient, as were Southern black people who continued to agitate for their rights.

In April and May, racial divisions in the North, where blacks were increasingly restive, were if anything more troubling than in the South. Many black leaders, intensifying their quests for OEO funding, were redoubling their efforts to take control of community action programs. Bayard Rustin and other civil rights spokespeople, arguing that the War on Poverty had had little impact, voiced far more ambitious aspirations. The federal government, they argued, must spend many more billions for public works, job training, public housing, and other measures promoting socioeconomic justice. Poor blacks, they insisted, needed more than the "equal opportunity" promised by the War on Poverty. They had a right to a decent standard of living.

Most white Americans, however, still did not recognize the depth of black dissatisfaction in the North. The Gallup Poll, whose surveys continued to show large popular majorities in favor of a strong voting rights bill, made this fact clear in late April, when it released the answers to two questions about racial attitudes. The first asked, "If colored people came to live next door, would you move?" Thirteen percent answered, "Yes, definitely"; 22 percent replied, "Yes, maybe"; and 65 percent said, "No." Gallup then asked, "Would you move if colored people came to live in great numbers in your neighborhood?" To this question, 40 percent said, "Yes, definitely"; 29 percent replied, "Yes, might"; and 31 percent answered, "No."[26]

Events in Boston confirmed the persistence of such racial views. More than a century earlier, in 1855, it had been the first major

American city to outlaw school segregation. In April 1965, however, over 80 percent of Boston's black students attended public schools in which 80 percent or more of the student body was nonwhite. A blue ribbon committee, created in response to complaints from black leaders, recommended enlarging and reshaping school zones to promote integration. But Louise Day Hicks, a forty-eight-year-old lawyer-politician from the predominantly working-class and Irish-American area of South Boston and chair of the city's school committee, was a vociferous defender of neighborhood schools. She refused to budge from her view that racial imbalance in the city's schools stemmed from long-standing residential patterns, not from racism. "We have in our midst," she declared, "a small band of racial agitators, non-native to Boston, and a few college radicals who have joined in a conspiracy to tell the people of Boston how to run their schools."[27]

Then and into the 1970s, Hicks, who narrowly missed winning election as mayor in 1967 (her slogan: "You Know Where I Stand"), not only remained a highly popular politician in Boston but also became a nationally recognized foe of court-ordered busing and other liberal proposals aimed at combating school segregation.[28] Children who were being bused, she explained, were "pawns" of racial politics. And many Americans agreed with her: accelerating in 1965 and lasting for more than a decade, angry confrontations and court cases involving the desegregation of America's public schools bared sharp class, racial, ethnic, and religious divisions throughout the United States and magnified the polarization that characterized the Sixties and its aftermath.

In late May 1965, a month after the troubles in Boston had become national news, James Reston of the *New York Times* clearly laid out the terms of this inflammatory issue. The "major barriers" facing blacks in the North, he wrote, were not legal obstacles such as those Southern blacks were still hoping to overcome. Instead, they were "economic and social." In Reston's view, "the economic segregation of the American Negro is in some ways worse than it was eleven years ago" at the time of the *Brown v. Board* decision. Too many people, Reston avowed, think that the dissolution of legal barriers "seems to be an end in itself rather than merely a means to an end."[29]

Moynihan was one of a relatively small number of white federal officials who had already emphasized this point within the government. In

April and May he was busy firing off memos to Johnson and his top aides, urging them to read a seventy-eight-page report he had completed in March. Titled *The Negro Family: The Case for National Action*, the report documented the formidable social ills—notably poverty, joblessness, and out-of-wedlock childbearing—that were devastating inner-city, lower-class black families. Nearly 24 percent of black babies, Moynihan wrote, had been born out of wedlock in 1963—nearly eight times the percentage of white babies. The situation, he added, "may indeed have begun to feed on itself." His statistics were telling and his language vivid, emphasizing that many lower-class black families were snared in a "tangle of pathology" and that, if America did not seek "equality of results" for Negroes, "there will be no social peace in the United States for generations."[30]

Though Moynihan's report did not specify what government ought to do to combat these social maladies, it was evident that he sought bold measures, including large-scale government job programs that would amount to a form of what later became known as affirmative action to help black Americans. A year earlier he had argued at a scholarly conference, "If you were ever going to have anything like an equal Negro community, you are for the next thirty years going to have to give them unequal treatment."[31]

It is not clear whether LBJ read Moynihan's report, but aides apprised him of its conclusions. Eager to shape the future of civil rights efforts, he asked Moynihan to help draft a major address that he was to give at the commencement ceremonies of Howard University, a black institution, on June 4. The address, "To Fulfill These Rights," followed Moynihan's report in describing the miserable socioeconomic conditions of black people in the inner cities. It also promised to convene a White House conference, to be titled To Fulfill These Rights, in the fall, where "scholars and experts" would discuss the problems of American Negroes. That way, Johnson said, the nation could "shatter forever not only the barriers of law and public practice but the walls which bound the condition of man by the color of his skin."[32]

LBJ, again following Moynihan, emphasized a central point: blacks needed more than the legal freedoms the Civil Rights Act of 1964 had conferred and the voting rights bill, when passed, would expand. They must also enjoy social and economic justice. "Freedom is not enough," he insisted.

You do not wipe away the scars of centuries by saying: Now you are free to go where you want, do as you desire, and choose the leaders you please.

You do not take a person who, for years has been hobbled by chains and liberate him, bring him up to the starting line of a race and then say, 'you are free to compete with all the others,' and still justly believe that you have been completely fair. Thus it is not enough to open the gates of opportunity. All our citizens must have the ability to walk through those gates.

Johnson added, in his most memorable passage, "This is the next and more profound stage of the battle for civil rights. We seek not just freedom but opportunity—not just legal equity but human ability—not just equality as a right and a theory but equality as a fact and as a result."[33]

The Howard University address, which Johnson rightly called the best civil rights speech of his life, received prominent and mostly positive coverage in the press. Martin Luther King told him over the phone that it was "the greatest speech that any President has made on the question of civil rights."[34] But the racial problems the president had described—like those presented by poverty—were huge, complicated, and interrelated, and solutions would be far from simple to craft. Even as liberals were hailing Johnson's speech, it was not at all clear whether he would be able to steer mounting civil rights militancy into safe channels, let alone secure passage of far-reaching policies to cope with the myriad ills of the ghettos. If civil rights militants demanded more than he could deliver, his standing as a strong and sure-footed liberal champion would be undermined.

It also remained to be seen in June 1965 whether Johnson could figure out a way for the United States to prevail in Vietnam. Given the seriousness of the rapidly mounting troubles there, dealing effectively with domestic issues such as poverty and civil rights, urgent as they were, might very well have to wait. If that were to happen, liberal dreams of a Great Society—dreams that had seemed within reach earlier in the year—might die and the Golden Age optimists had foreseen at the start of 1965 might never appear.

8

A CREDIBILITY GAP

WHILE LBJ WAS COPING WITH DOMESTIC ISSUES IN APRIL AND MAY, the increasingly shaky situation in Vietnam gave him little rest. Rebellion in the Dominican Republic, moreover, led him to make military decisions that aroused ever-louder complaints about his handling of international affairs. By late May, critics, including larger crowds of antiwar protestors, were charging him with having fomented a "credibility gap"—that is, a disparity between what he said his administration was doing in the realm of foreign policy and what he actually was doing. This accusation infuriated him, but it clung to him and ultimately undermined his presidency.

——

AS HE WAS BUILDING HIS GREAT SOCIETY AND MANAGING A burgeoning conflict in Vietnam, antiwar demonstrations were spreading not only in the United States but also around the world. Some broke out in front of American embassies in Paris, London, and Mexico City. Like most protests at the time, they focused on condemning the bombing raids of Operation Rolling Thunder, which had been devastating since their launch in early March.[1] Closer to home, Dr. Benjamin Spock, one of America's most visible antiwar activists, led a three-thousand-person-strong protest at the United Nations in New York City in early April. At the same time, a persistent antiwar group, Women Strike for Peace, mounted a nationwide Get Out of Vietnam campaign. Some twenty-five hundred members of the clergy took out a full-page ad in the *New York Times* that read, "In the name of God, STOP IT!"[2]

Teach-ins had proliferated since late March, fading from prominence only after summer vacations dispersed students. The largest, lasting thirty-six hours and attracting more than ten thousand people, took place at the University of California's Berkeley campus in late May.[3] Some of those attending burned LBJ in effigy. Among the many well-known speakers and participants were Dr. Spock, veteran socialist-pacifist Norman Thomas, Norman Mailer, the comedian Dick Gregory, Bob Moses of SNCC, Paul Potter (head of the Students for a Democratic Society), and the Berkeley activist Mario Savio.

This mammoth turnout included considerable numbers of adult nonstudents—then, as later, young people were by no means the only Americans who demonstrated against the war. But students and other young people made up most of the crowds at Berkeley and elsewhere. The Berkeley teach-in also made it unmistakably clear that the student restiveness that had prompted creation of the Free Speech Movement of late 1964 had seized on an especially urgent cause.

In early April, however, antiwar activists still seemed to be ineffectual. As was the case earlier in the year, few media accounts took student protestors seriously. Nor did many members of what was identified at the time as the Old Left. Experienced radicals, such as Irving Howe and Michael Harrington, were among the many stalwarts of the Old Left who believed that student protestors representing the New Left were far too disorganized to promote serious social change.[4] Many in the Old Left, having developed a loathing of Soviet-style communism during the Stalinist era, also thought that the younger leftists lacked a sophisticated understanding of Cold War history. Neither then nor later in the year was there close collaboration in antiwar activities between the two generations of Americans on the Left. Nor was there any overarching organization in the spring of 1965 to coordinate the activities of the various peace-oriented groups or to direct an overall strategy.[5]

SDS was, of course, student-led. By April, thanks primarily to LBJ's escalation of the war, it was enlisting an unsigned following that was larger than the two thousand or so who were formal members.[6] A minority of those who joined were first-generation college students from blue-collar homes. Most, however, were middle-class and male, often raised by liberal parents. Many attended or had attended private universities such as Harvard and Columbia or large and prestigious state universities such as Michigan and Wisconsin. Some who joined SDS in 1965 that spring and summer—mainly Westerners and Midwesterners from lesser-known public universities—further swelled the size of the organization. Labeled within SDS as partisans of an ardently antiwar "prairie power" faction, they were not much interested in other left-wing causes. The convergence in 1965 of these different strains around opposition to the war galvanized the once-tiny SDS, which later in the decade exploded in size to become the largest radical student organization in American history. At its peak in 1968, its membership was estimated at eighty thousand.[7]

In the spring of 1965, however, SDS continued to face divisions within its ranks. Some of its old guard (in their mid-twenties or older) argued that it should concentrate on organizing poor people in the inner cities. Those who were focusing on the agonies of Vietnam differed among themselves: some were absolute pacifists, while others backed a variety of tactics to bring about de-escalation or negotiations with the enemy. In 1965, SDS in fact had no official position on the war.[8]

Though many SDS members had cut their teeth in civil rights protesting in the South, the organization was also slow in early 1965 to appeal to blacks. Several civil rights leaders—John Lewis, Bayard Rustin, and James Farmer of CORE, for instance—were well known as pacifists. Many others, including King, openly opposed the bombing and called for serious negotiations with Hanoi. And a goodly number of younger blacks were enlisting in SDS, becoming perhaps 10 percent of the organization's membership by mid-1965. But in the spring of 1965 many black militants, with the violence at Selma very much on their minds, believed passionately that the major cause of the era was racial justice. Lewis, who strongly opposed the war, exclaimed at a Mississippi Freedom Democratic Party conference in late April, "if we can call for free elections in . . . Saigon, we can call for free elections in Greenwood and Jackson, Mississippi."[9] Though many individual civil rights activists, like Lewis and Bob Moses, were active in demonstrating against the war, none of the best-known civil rights organizations—CORE, SNCC, NAACP, SCLC, the Urban League, or the MFDP—came out formally against it in 1965. It was not until January 1966 that SNCC became the first to do so.

Antiwar students also differed in their understanding and assessment of American society and culture. Some who joined SDS self-identified as radicals—as people who had developed a broad, critical understanding of what they deemed to be the corporate and imperialistic nature of America's political and economic system. Escalation of the war, they believed, manifested a larger dehumanization of American life. But many other SDS members, like the large majority of nonmembers who opposed the war, did not regard themselves as radical in this sense. Even in the later 1960s, surveys of higher education tended to show that very small minorities of America's college and university students (who would grow from 5.2 million in 1965 to 8 million by 1970), considered themselves to be part of the Left.

As former SDS president Todd Gitlin pointed out later, it was this broader critique of America's sociopolitical order that the American media made especially little effort to understand. Continuing to trivialize the ideas of demonstrators, reporters often focused instead on their beards and long hair—or, as time passed, on the protestors' alleged propensity for violence.[10] Still, as the war expanded, rising numbers of antiwar students, radicals included, managed to be heard. On a large campus such as Berkeley's, which had an enrollment of twenty-seven thousand students in late 1965, even a relatively small minority of radical students could (and did) rally nonradical antiwar students and stage sizeable demonstrations.

Many American opponents of the war in 1965 and later did have one important thing in common: they were young. Unless they managed (like roughly 40 percent of high school graduates at the time) to go to college, in which case they would enjoy deferments from military service, they were old enough, from age eighteen through twenty-six, to be drafted for two years. In 1964, a calmer time, few had worried greatly about such a prospect. And even after escalation in 1965, many in that age cohort supported the war. As always, any "generation" contains a huge variety of people and opinions. (Thousands of students joined Young Americans for Freedom and supported the war.) But escalation greatly alarmed millions of young people of draft age. Though they might be deferred until they finished college, they would then have to qualify for grad school or find some other way to evade the draft.

Baby boomers, having been born after the Depression and World War II, were not raised with the historical context that infused the foreign policies of men such as Johnson, who (remembering the rise of the Nazis and the failure of Western democracies to resist it vigorously) frequently spoke out against such long-ago sins as "appeasement." Growing up during the early Cold War years, the boomers were well aware of tensions with the Soviet Union—the Cuban missile crisis, after all, had been terrifying in 1962—but many had trouble understanding the fierce hostility that older Americans, remembering Stalin, continued to direct against communism. To fight or die in a war to save South Vietnam from communism seemed senseless.

GIVEN THE WIDESPREAD PERCEPTION THAT ANTIWAR SENTIMENT was weak in April 1965, what happened on April 17 in Washington, DC, was astonishing. Back in December, when SDS leaders were planning an antiwar rally, they had hoped that the presence of speakers such as Senator Ernest Gruening of Alaska—one of the two senators who had opposed the Tonkin Gulf Resolution of August 1964— would attract a decent-sized crowd.[11] Women Strike for Peace also drummed up support for the protest. But until just days before the demonstration, few people expected that anything like a massive crowd would gather.

But it did. On April 17, the day before Easter, a vociferous crowd variously estimated as between fifteen thousand and twenty-five thousand swarmed Washington for the protest. Reporters estimated that three-fourths of the demonstrators were students but that many college faculty members, labor unionists, and clergy also were on hand. Perhaps 10 percent were African Americans. As the *New York Times* reported, "Beards and blue jeans mixed with Ivy tweeds and an occasional collar in the crowd."[12]

Early during the daylong demonstrations, protestors picketed the White House, carrying signs with slogans such as "War on Poverty Not on People" and "End the War in Vietnam Now." They chanted, "No More War!" (LBJ, at his ranch, heard none of this.) Many high points of the demonstration then took place at the Washington Monument, where the protestors marched at midday. There, during a long afternoon, they applauded not only Gruening but also other antiwar speakers, including Bob Moses and I. F. Stone, a radical journalist. Joan Baez and Judy Collins led the crowd in songs—among them "We Shall Overcome" and "The Times They Are A-Changin'."

Paul Potter, the twenty-six-year-old president of SDS and the last to speak, gave a memorable address that for the first time provided a big audience with an agenda that situated antiwar protest within a larger, radical critique of racism and the US economic and political system. "We must name that system," Potter declared. "We must name it, describe it, analyze it, understand it and change it. For it is only when that system is changed and brought under control that there can be any hope for stopping the forces that create a war in Vietnam today or a murder in the South tomorrow."[13]

Because the administration had released very little information on the ground war, many of the speakers focused on denouncing Operation Rolling Thunder. The media remained more intent on describing the crowds than relaying the content of speeches. The *New York Times* account did not mention Potter's address. Still, the demonstration of April 17, 1965, received front-page coverage in many papers. It was the largest peace demonstration up to that time in United States history.[14]

⸺

THOUGH THE APRIL 17 RALLY ENERGIZED THE FLEDGLING ANTIWAR movement in the United States, the demonstrators would have been delusional if they imagined that they would induce LBJ to change his course. Neither then nor later did the president pay serious attention to the antiwar activities of students. "Why should I listen to all those student peaceniks marching up and down the streets?" he snapped later. "They were barely in their cradles in the dark days of World War II; they never experienced the ravages of Adolf Hitler; they were only in nursery school during the fall of China; they were sitting in grammar school during the Korean War; they wouldn't know a Communist if they tripped over one. They simply don't understand the world the way I do."[15]

Three days after the April 17 protest, LBJ made a major decision that emphatically demonstrated his lack of concern about antiwar activists. Top aides, including Robert McNamara, Ambassador Taylor, General Wheeler (chair of the Joint Chiefs of Staff), and lesser administration officials met with General Westmoreland and other military brass in Honolulu. There they agreed that bombing could not "do the job alone" and recommended sending forty thousand reinforcements to Vietnam. This would be a staggering escalation of American military might.

The president quickly and secretly approved their recommendation.[16] These troops, when added by June to the roughly 40,000 already authorized to be there, were expected to enable maintenance of an "enclaves strategy" aimed at protecting major US military bases and at preventing the enemy from scoring a knockout blow against the sagging ARVN.[17] Some of Johnson's advisers admitted privately that "it might be necessary" to increase even further the total number of American servicemen in Vietnam by the end of the summer—to as many as 123,000.[18]

A telephone conversation LBJ had that day with McNamara revealed the combination of uncertainty and wishful thinking that characterized the stance of America's leading foreign policy advisers at the time. McNamara told the president:

There's still a little disagreement as to how many [more troops] there should be ultimately, but no disagreement as to how many there should be in the next ninety or a hundred and twenty days—they [the American military in Vietnam] feel that they can sufficiently stiffen the South Vietnamese and strengthen their forces to show Hanoi that Hanoi cannot win in the South. It won't be that the South Vietnamese can win. But it will be clear to Hanoi that Hanoi can't win. And this is one of the objectives we're driving for.

LBJ then asked, "Are they pretty encouraged by what's happened in the last few weeks out there in South Vietnam?" McNamara replied: "I wouldn't say very encouraged, but it's a change from a sharp downward trend to a bottoming out or a leveling off, with potential for some slight upward movement."[19]

—

FOUR DAYS LATER, ON APRIL 24, EVENTS IN THE CARIBBEAN FURTHER revealed LBJ's aggressiveness as an anticommunist manager of America's foreign relations, thereby prompting renewed complaints that his behavior was creating a "credibility gap." Rebels in the Dominican Republic revolted against a ruling junta whose leaders in late 1963 had overthrown a democratically elected government presided over by Juan Bosch, a noncommunist leftist. The junta, one of many authoritarian, militarily backed governments that the United States supported in Latin America, had received some $100 million in American loans during its eighteen-month control of the island.

Though the rebels quickly managed to oust the junta—its leader resigned—fighting continued, especially in the capital city of Santo Domingo.[20] America's ambassador, William Tapley Bennett, soon reported to the White House that the rebels had taken over the national palace in Santo Domingo and that the battling had become a struggle "between Castro-type elements and those who oppose." Warning that the situation was deteriorating rapidly, he recommended "immediate landings" of American marines to help evacuate foreign nationals, including Americans, who might wish to leave. Johnson responded quickly, sending more than four hundred marines on April 27 to handle the task.[21] Some one thousand people, protected by the marines, quickly left the island for the safety of nearby American warships.

Bennett had mentioned the involvement of "Castro-type elements," but he had stopped short of maintaining that communists

controlled the rebellion. Indeed, the ambassador, who had not anticipated that a coup would occur, had been visiting his family in Georgia
when the uprising began, and he was not well informed. Still, his agitated message was one of the many developments in those frenzied
days that propelled LBJ into large-scale intervention.

Johnson's director of the CIA evinced no uncertainty whatever.
He was Admiral William "Red" Raborn, whom LBJ had just named to
head the agency. Joining a high-level meeting on the subject at the
White House, Raborn asserted without qualification or verification
that Cuba was controlling the rebellion. In a phone conversation with
Johnson the next day Raborn added, "In my opinion this is a real
struggle mounted by Mr. Castro. . . . There is no question in my mind
that this is the start of Castro's expansion."[22]

While the president correctly harbored private doubts that communist elements or Castroites were behind the rebellion, he was
highly sensitive to the views of hawkish congressional leaders, such as
Speaker McCormack and Senator Dirksen, who perceived a communist threat in the Dominican Republic. General Wheeler advocated
large-scale military intervention. Johnson, deciding on a stronger
show of American power, responded by exclaiming at one point,
"How can we send troops 10,000 miles away [to Vietnam] and let Castro take over right under our nose?"[23]

The president then proceeded to order more marines to Santo
Domingo. In doing so, he acted unilaterally, thereby endangering
whatever small improvement in hemispheric relations the United
States had secured as a result of FDR's Good Neighbor Policy and
Kennedy's Alliance for Progress. He was contemptuous of the efficacy
of the Organization of American States (OAS), which was supposed to
approve of such interventions. The OAS, he sneered, "couldn't pour
piss out of a boot if the instructions were written on the heel."[24]

Some of LBJ's advisers nonetheless questioned Raborn's reliabil-
ity on the subject. Bundy reminded the president that the CIA had
sent no advance warnings concerning the role of communists in the
rebellion. "There was nothing," he said. McNamara, too, was skeptical about assertions of communist involvement. Johnson asked him,
"You don't think the CIA can document it?" McNamara replied, "I
don't think so," and added, "You don't know that Castro is trying to

do anything. You would have a hard time proving to any group that Castro has done more than train these people, and we have trained a lot of people."[25]

But McNamara could not restrain the president. Hearing that rebels had fired at marines in Santo Domingo, LBJ quickly dispatched twenty-five hundred troops from the Eighty-Second Airborne Division. Two days later he rushed in another sixty-five hundred marines. Speaking to a nationwide television audience on April 30, he indicated that the United States was cooperating with the OAS in efforts to establish a cease-fire, but he also insisted, "People trained outside the Dominican Republic are seeking to gain control." Two days later, preempting *Candid Camera* on TV, he exclaimed that a "popular democratic revolution"—the junta's—had been hijacked by a "band of Communist conspirators."[26] By mid-May, he had sent an astonishing number of American troops—more than twenty-three thousand—to quell the rebellion.[27]

Almost nothing, it seemed, could curb America's headstrong commander in chief. Continuing to debate with McNamara, Johnson talked with him again on May 12:

> LBJ: I think the time's going to come before very long when we have to kind of make up our choice to either let Castro have it [the Dominican Republic] or take [the island by force]. . . .
> McNamara: We just have to get a political [settlement] here.
> LBJ: Well, if [the rebels] are controlled by the Castroites, they're not going to give it to you.
> McNamara: I don't think they are. . . . I just don't believe the story that Bosch . . . [is] controlled by the Castroites.[28]

By then, American troops had ousted the rebels from control, and prodding from the United States and the OAS had managed to establish a cease-fire. Though it was unstable—fighting continued sporadically for the rest of the year—an Inter-American Peace Force, which included US troops, was formally established on May 23 and gradually assumed command of the situation. LBJ then began reducing America's military presence on the island: most marines were home by mid-June, leaving some twelve thousand American troops in the Dominican Republic. A provisional government was put in place, with promises of free elections within nine months. It lasted until June 1, 1966, when a largely fraud-free election was held, in which a moderate conservative, Joaquin Balaguer, outpolled Bosch by a substantial margin. Only then did a surprising degree of stability return to the Dominican Republic. The last American troops finally departed in September 1966.

Johnson's intervention in the Dominican Republic, like many previous American military actions in the Caribbean, proved popular with the American people. The Gallup Poll reported in mid-May that 76 percent approved of his actions and only 17 percent disapproved.[29] Most of those among the 76 percent presumably believed that LBJ's stated goal—to protect the Dominican Republic from communism—was honorable and that it had been achieved.

The president's Dominican enterprise, however, unleashed popular protests in many Latin American capitals against US "imperialism." Some Americans, especially those who were already critical of his escalation in Vietnam, denounced him as a liar. A number of leading political figures, including Mansfield and Fulbright, had resisted his adventurism from the start. Robert Kennedy publicly assailed him for not consulting the OAS in advance. Johnson, still hating Kennedy, moaned that he had become "the most denounced man in the world."[30]

LBJ's critics were clearly on target. Johnson's gunboat diplomacy, motivated both by his own fervent anticommunism and by his sensitivity to hawkish pressure, was a major overreaction—one that killed 24 US servicemen and wounded 156.[31] Bosch was not a communist, and neither Castro nor other communist figures had incited the revolt. Once fighting broke out, for the United States to dispatch a small contingent of marines to help evacuate foreign nationals was probably a prudent thing to do. But LBJ's initial dismissal of the OAS, and America's subsequent invasion of the Dominican Republic by a large military force, solidified the belief of critics that his reflexive anticommunism had opened up a credibility gap.

JUST AS MARINES AND AIRBORNE FORCES WERE LANDING IN THE Dominican Republic, large numbers of American troops, authorized by LBJ following the Honolulu conference on April 20, were also beginning to descend upon South Vietnam. The first combat units of the US Army, part of an airborne brigade, arrived on May 5. Additional thousands of combat troops landed during the next few weeks.

On April 20, Johnson had assured Westmoreland that American troops might venture out as far as fifty miles from the enclaves they were supposed to protect.[32] But Westmoreland, an aggressive, World War II–style commander, continued to chafe at limitations on the movements of his troops. The function of infantry, he insisted, was to locate, pursue, and kill enemy forces. Then and later he pressed Johnson to back and publicly announce a bolder strategy, which would authorize his ever-expanding forces to embark regularly on offensive combat missions.[33]

By late May, some American troops were already engaged in such missions, normally in command of demoralized and disorganized ARVN forces.[34] But the Vietcong, pummeling the ARVN, were clearly winning. Reporters on the ground in Vietnam picked up information that penetrated the veil of administration secrecy, revealing the dismal results of some of these military engagements. On April 23, the *New York Times* displayed photos of wounded US Marines on its front page. In late May, *Newsweek* reported that 376 American servicemen had been killed during the slightly more than nine weeks between March 8, when the marines had landed at Danang, and May 15.[35] News reports at that time also disclosed that the Vietcong, bolstered by infusions of soldiers from the North, were opening major offensives in the highlands and north of Saigon.

But Johnson remained secretive, for he continued to fear that thorough (and unavoidably critical) media coverage of the escalation would threaten the passage of Great Society measures in Congress. During these weeks he did not publicly acknowledge that more aggressive military strategies were being undertaken. Only in early June did the administration state that American ground forces were in combat "in defense of key installations," and that they would continue to engage in combat if so requested by the ARVN. Only in late June did it confirm that American combat troops had been authorized to undertake offensive actions of their own.[36] Evasions such as these further poisoned his relations with the press—so much so that Emmett Hughes, a *Newsweek* columnist, wrote in late May of a "climate more acrid than any since the sulphurous days of McCarthyism."[37] A joke circulated, "How do you know when Lyndon Johnson is lying?" The answer: "When he pulls his ear lobe, scratches his chin, he's telling the truth. When he begins to move his lips, you know he's lying."[38]

Art Buchwald, known as a humorist, famously echoed criticisms such as these in his syndicated column at the time:

> Every once in a while, when I have nothing better to do, I wonder what the country would be like if Barry Goldwater had been elected President of the United States. . . . Based on his campaign and his speeches, it is a frightening thing to imagine. The mind boggles when you think of it. For one thing, we would probably be bombing North Vietnam now.

Buchwald then described Goldwater's likely Vietnam strategy, which would have involved "sending in a battalion of Marines with Hawk missiles to protect our airfields." He concluded, "Fortunately, with President Johnson at the helm, we don't have to think about it."[39]

Concealing vital information about the war nonetheless enabled Johnson to leave an impression that America's involvement in ground combat was fairly small—even in May, many antiwar protests still focused on the more widely publicized bombing. His subterfuge may also have helped him maintain his standing in the polls. Though just 52 percent of Americans told Gallup pollsters in late May that Johnson was handling Vietnam policies "as well as could be expected" (about the same as the percentage in late April), only 27 percent replied that he was handling them "badly," and 21 percent had no opinion. In a mid-May Gallup Poll, two-thirds of American still thought he was doing a good overall job as president.[40]

Poll numbers such as these persisted in June and early July. They reveal an important fact about the history of America's involvement in the Vietnam War: contrary to later impressions (after the North won the war, many Americans did not admit to having supported it), anti-war opinion in the early months of the struggle remained relatively weak. Like Johnson, most people believed that "appeasement" would be disastrous, that the United States must keep its commitments, and that international communism had to be stopped. So long as "our boys" were in danger, they would continue to back their commander in chief.

LBJ, TRYING TO QUIET OUTCRIES AGAINST THE WAR FROM MANY parts of the world, called a bombing halt on May 13—one of several that he ordered over the next few years. But in no way did this move suggest that he would alter his course, and the respite lasted for only five days. Hanoi dismissed his gesture as a "hoax" and held fast to its political and military goals.

Antiwar forces in America, denouncing the credibility gap that Johnson had opened, were equally unimpressed by the suspension of bombing. On May 15, a large number of academics, including Hans Morgenthau, Harvard professor David Riesman, and former University of Chicago president Robert Hutchins, led a twelve-hour "national teach-in" at Washington's Sheraton Park Hotel. Some five thousand people attended. Another hundred thousand followed the proceedings over radio hookups connected to more than one hundred college and university campuses.

A few political insiders also tried to show Johnson the folly of his ways. Clark Clifford, an influential Washington lawyer and occasional presidential adviser (in early 1968 he replaced McNamara as secretary of defense), wrote LBJ in May 17, "Our ground war should be kept to a minimum. Consistent with the protection of our installations and property in that country." Otherwise, he wrote, "This could become a quagmire . . . an open end commitment on our part that would take more and more ground troops, without a realistic hope of ultimate victory."[41]

Westmoreland, far away in Vietnam, did not receive letters like that, and if he had, they would not have weakened his resolve. He continued to call for more support and for a more aggressive, offensive strategy on the ground. Meanwhile, the bombing, having resumed with all its previous ferocity, was devastating villages and increasing the flow of refugees, many to already overcrowded and overburdened cities such as Saigon. The enemy surge that began in mid-May also threatened to disintegrate the ARVN and topple the South Vietnamese government.

Especially frightening to ARVN and American forces were the guerrilla tactics of the enemy. These featured nighttime raids, trip-wired booby traps, and sniping. American soldiers, spooked by such tactics, raged that that there was no visible "front" to the war. "Victory," impossible to measure by conquest of territory, was instead being defined according to "body counts." Virtually the only measure of progress was the number of enemy combatants classified as killed.

There was no way, American troops complained, to tell who among the Vietnamese people were friendly and who might slit your throat in the night. As an American general, E. J. Banks, recalled:

> You never knew who was the enemy and who was the friend. They all looked alike. They all dressed alike. They were all Vietnamese. Some of them were Vietcong. Here's a woman of twenty-two or twenty-three. She is pregnant, and she tells an interrogator that her husband works in Danang and isn't a Vietcong. But she watches your men walk down a trail and get killed or wounded by a booby trap. She knows the booby trap is there, but she doesn't warn them. Maybe she's planted it herself. It wasn't like the San Francisco Forty-Niners on one side of the field and the Cincinnati Bengals on the other. The enemy was all around you.[42]

Philip Caputo, who had landed at Danang full of swagger and purpose, was among the American fighting men who by then were becoming battle-hardened. He and his comrades now recognized that the Vietcong (the VC) and their allies were brave and resourceful opponents. Because both enemy and ally in Vietnam were of the same race, and a race different from that of most US troops—not white or black but Asian—he also understood why his skipper had ordered his men to kill Vietnamese who were running away. In the heat of action, American and ARVN troops began to resort to the slaughter of livestock and the torching of villagers' huts. Burning huts, Caputo later explained, "was more than an act of madness in the heat of battle. It was an act of retribution as well. These villagers aided the VC. We are all learning to hate." For Caputo, Vietnam was "an ethical as well as a geographical wilderness. Out there, lacking restraints, sanctioned to kill, confronted by a hostile country and a relentless enemy, we sank into a brutish state."[43]

9

"THE TIMES THEY ARE A-CHANGIN'"

Technology, Music, and Fights for Rights in Mid-1965

ON THE AFTERNOON OF JUNE 3, MAJOR EDWARD WHITE II, A NASA astronaut, opened the hatch of *Gemini IV* while in space. Holding an oxygen jet-propulsion gun that would allow him to move around outside, he maneuvered himself at the end of a twenty-five-foot, golden-hued tether to enjoy the first "space walk" ever undertaken by an American. Ordered to return to the capsule, he reluctantly complied after twenty-two minutes. "This is the saddest moment of my life," he lamented.

Shortly after the space walk, *Life* ran a celebratory sixteen-page cover story that featured dazzling photographs taken from the capsule by White's fellow astronaut.[1] The story exulted that *Gemini IV* had completed the first multiday space mission in American history. Millions of Americans, lingering over the photos, rejoiced at the success of the venture, which was said to have advanced the United States toward the Kennedy-inspired goal of landing a man on the moon.

Though no event during the months of June and July 1965 was more exciting than White's walk in space, Americans continued to have other reasons to push Vietnam and domestic uncertainties to the back of their minds and anticipate progress on a host of fronts. News about the economy was especially gratifying. Unemployment for adult men, at 3.2 percent, had plunged to an extraordinary low.[2] In early July, General Motors, responding to pressure from auto-safety advocates, advertised that standard equipment in its 1966 models would include rear seat belts, padded instrument panels, backup lights, left-hand rearview mirrors, dual-speed windshield wipers, and padded sun visors.[3]

Other technological and scientific advances also aroused optimism. "Mechanisms by which the genetic code is transcribed," an editorial in *Science* explained, "are finally well understood." Researchers "sense the possibility that methods might conceivably be developed some day for intentional meddling, in the laboratory, with an individual's deoxyribonucleic acid (DNA)." Dr. Rollin Hotchkiss of the Rockefeller Institute commented, "It will surely be done or attempted. The pathway will be built from a combination of altruism, private profit, and ignorance."[4]

CULTURAL DEVELOPMENTS DURING LATE SPRING AND SUMMER indicated increasing mainstream curiosity about emerging American subcultures that would help to define the decade and in several cases transform the terms of their genres. Admirers of the novelist and short story writer J. D. Salinger, lauded for his *Catcher in the Rye* (1951), had the opportunity to read—if not always to comprehend— the last story he ever published, "Hapworth 16, 1924," in the *New Yorker* on June 19.[5] Other readers immersed themselves in Tom Wolfe's *The Kandy-Kolored Tangerine-Flake Streamline Baby*, a collection of essays that he had published during the previous year. Many of Wolfe's colorful characters—mobsters in Las Vegas, artists, hot-rodders, auto racers, dance-clubbers—were fascinating. Devotees of Wolfe hailed him as a pioneer of "New Journalism," a genre in which (among other things) feature writers use the first person and make no claim to objective, disinterested reportage. Over the next few years, New Journalism was to become one of the main narrative strategies writers would employ to capture the Zeitgeist of the Sixties.

While many movies of the time were standard-issue Hollywood, others introduced new and wry sensibilities at work, notably *What's New Pussycat?*, which premiered in early June. It marked the film debut of the comedian Woody Allen, as well as his first produced script. In the movie Peter O'Toole, cast as a notorious womanizer, refuses to settle down with his true love, played by Romy Schneider. Peter Sellers, playing a demented psychoanalyst, adds zest to the plot, which ultimately takes the characters to a hideaway hotel in the French countryside.[6]

The world of pop music, booming as ever, continued to feature familiar performers. In June these included the Beatles with "Ticket to Ride," the Beach Boys ("Help Me Rhonda"), the Byrds ("Mr. Tambourine Man"), and the Supremes ("Back in My Arms Again"). All four songs rose to the top of the singles charts. Though the jangly sound of singer Jim McGuinn's twelve-string electric guitar helped "Mr. Tambourine Man" to popularize the ascendant genre of folk rock, the lyrics were familiar, having been written and released by Bob Dylan three months earlier. As of early June, most of America's Top 40 tunes continued to be upbeat, melodic, and intelligible, and had not changed in these respects since the Beatles had reinvigorated the popular music scene in early 1964.

Within the next few weeks, however, startling performances began to revolutionize the world of American popular music. The Rolling Stones did perhaps the most to touch off these changes. The exhibitionist athleticism of their twenty-two-year-old lead singer and songwriter, Mick Jagger, and the skill of their lead guitar player, Keith Richards, also twenty-two, had attracted a sizeable number of admirers by 1965. But the song they wrote and introduced in early June, "(I Can't Get No) Satisfaction," was like no other they had released. An immediate hit, it shot upward in the charts, emerging as a number 1 single in early July and remaining at the top for four weeks—a long time for a pop tune. As Jagger later said, "It was the song that really made The Rolling Stones, changed us from just another band into a huge, monster band."[7]

"(I Can't Get No) Satisfaction" was rock music with a catchy title. It also had a compelling beat, which famously opened (and closed) with a three-note electric guitar riff by Richards. ("It sounded like a sour buzz saw," Todd Gitlin later wrote, "and never stopped snarling."[8]) What really made "Satisfaction" a pop music sensation, however, was the lyrics, as well as the cynical, harsh, sneering tone in which Jagger delivered them, sometimes by shouting. As the title suggested, many of the words—"tryin' to make some girl," "girlie action," "can't get no satisfaction"—expressed sexual yearning.

Though mild by later standards, the lyrics were considerably more explicit than those of the exuberant but only mildly irreverent Beatles, whose saccharine "I Want to Hold Your Hand" (1964) had become their first number 1 hit in the United States. Indeed, "Satisfaction" imparted a candor about sexuality that jolted some listeners. When the Stones performed it on television's *Shindig!* in September, the line "tryin' to make some girl" was censored.

Sex, moreover, was not the only notable theme of "Satisfaction." Other verses bewailed the ubiquity of advertising and materialism in America. In a contemptuous tone, Jagger sang of the "useless information" offered by radio commercials and of ads about the virtues of cigarette brands and about "how white my shirts can be."

It is sometimes argued that "Satisfaction," more than any other tune, redirected the course of American pop music. This remains open to debate. After all, performers such as the Beatles, the Beach Boys, and the Supremes, who continued to produce top hits, did not emulate the Stones' loud and angry tone. Other pop vocalists, continuing to sing about dreams and love, had little or nothing to say about sexual dissatisfaction or commercialization. Still, the claim is plausible. The popularity of "Satisfaction" was extraordinary. Both the lyrics and the tone of the song—loud and harsh—were breakthroughs of sorts for a tune of such wide appeal. It seemed that a significant new trend might be underway.

No star performer advanced this trend more brazenly than Bob Dylan. In the early 1960s, he had become an idol of folk song fans for writing and singing songs with political messages—"Masters of War" on Cold War arms dealers, "A Hard Rain's A-Gonna Fall" about the Cuban missile crisis, and "The Times They Are A-Changin'." But

Malcolm X and Martin Luther King met only once, in March 1964. When Malcolm was assassinated in February 1965, it appeared to some people that he was modifying his Black Nationalist critique of interracial civil rights activism. (LIBRARY OF CONGRESS)

Fannie Lou Hamer, the twentieth child of Mississippi sharecroppers, emerged in late 1964 as an eloquent spokeswoman for the Mississippi Freedom Democratic Party, which challenged LBJ's slate of delegates for the party's national convention. (LIBRARY OF CONGRESS)

"Bloody Sunday": A state trooper beats SNCC leader John Lewis at the start of an attempted civil rights march from Selma to Montgomery, March 7, 1965. (LIBRARY OF CONGRESS)

A marcher from Selma to Montgomery, March 1965. (LIBRARY OF CONGRESS)

Martin Luther King and Ralph Abernathy, his top associate, marching to Montgomery. (LIBRARY OF CONGRESS)

An aerial view of the procession to Montgomery. Some twenty-five thousand reached the state capitol. (LIBRARY OF CONGRESS)

LBJ, after signing the historic Voting Rights Act (August 1965), gives a pen to Martin Luther King. Abernathy is behind King. Representative Claude Pepper of Florida (with glasses) is in the middle. (LIBRARY OF CONGRESS)

Five days after LBJ signed the Voting Rights Act, the Watts area of Los Angeles exploded in violent protest, thereby transforming American race relations. Here a policeman drags a black man from a looted store. (LIBRARY OF CONGRESS)

Watts, where the responses of Los Angeles police infuriated many blacks. (THE EVERETT COLLECTION)

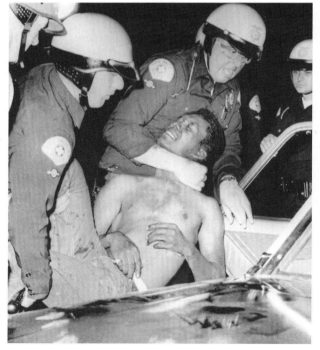

Defense Secretary Robert
McNamara, LBJ's most trusted
foreign policy adviser in 1965.
(THE EVERETT COLLECTION)

Maxwell Taylor, ambassador
to South Vietnam (left), and
General William Westmore-
land, commanding general in
Vietnam, conferring in Saigon
on February 11, 1965, four
days after a Vietcong attack
near Pleiku led LBJ to order
sustained bombing of the
North. (NATIONAL ARCHIVES)

Senate Foreign Relations
chairman J. William Fulbright of
Arkansas seems to be questioning
LBJ's military intervention in the
Dominican Republic, April 1965.
(LIBRARY OF CONGRESS)

Johnson and a skeptical Fulbright, on the eve of LBJ's pivotal announcement of large-scale escalation in Vietnam, July 27, 1965. (YOICHI OKAMOTO, LBJ LIBRARY)

An American corporal guards a Vietcong soldier, October 1965. (NATIONAL ARCHIVES)

Looking out for snipers, November 1965. (LIBRARY OF CONGRESS)

LBJ meets with South Vietnam Premier Nguyen Cao Ky, a flamboyant leader, at a hastily called conference in Honolulu, February 1966. (YOICHI OKAMOTO, LBJ LIBRARY)

LBJ joins Lady Bird Johnson as she starts her eight-day, sixteen-hundred-mile campaign train trip from Alexandria, Virginia, to New Orleans, October 1964. (LIBRARY OF CONGRESS)

Ronald Reagan emerged as a star Republican speaker for GOP presidential nominee Barry Goldwater (left) in 1964. To no avail: LBJ trounced Goldwater, setting the stage for liberal triumphs in 1965. (RONALD REAGAN PRESIDENTIAL LIBRARY)

LBJ arranged a spectacular set of events for his inaugural in January 1965. Chief Justice Earl Warren administers the oath as Lady Bird and newly installed Vice President Hubert Humphrey watch. (LIBRARY OF CONGRESS)

LBJ, a dominating personality, tangled with Harlem congressman Adam Clayton Powell in early 1965. Here, in June, they talk in the Oval Office. (YOICHI OKAMOTO, LBJ LIBRARY)

Senior citizens demonstrate for Medicare, June 1965. (LIBRARY OF CONGRESS)

Johnson, fond of grand political theater, journeyed to Missouri in July 1965 to sign Medicare into law in the presence of former president Harry Truman, who had backed national health insurance. Behind Truman are Lady Bird, Humphrey, and Bess Truman. (LBJ LIBRARY)

LBJ presents a pen to Robert Weaver, head of the Housing and Home Finance Agency, following passage of a bill creating a new Cabinet office, Housing and Urban Development (HUD), September 1965. In early 1966, LBJ named Weaver head of the department. Weaver was America's first black Cabinet secretary. (LIBRARY OF CONGRESS)

Johnson the gesticulator: speaking to Senate Majority Leader Mike Mansfield, with GOP Senate leader Everett Dirksen (right). (YOICHI OKAMOTO, LBJ LIBRARY)

Liberalism in decline: Ronald Reagan as newly elected governor of California, December 1966. (LIBRARY OF CONGRESS)

Heavyweight champ Muhammad Ali stands over Sonny Liston after knocking him out in the first round, May 1965. Fans shouted, "Fix!" (LIBRARY OF CONGRESS)

Though a blackout darkened New York City and much of the Northeast on November 8, 1965, citizens reacted cooperatively and peacefully. (LIBRARY OF CONGRESS)

Bill Cosby, the first African American to star as a hero in a prime-time television show (*I Spy*), with co-star Robert Culp, 1965. (PHOTOFEST)

The Beatles with Ed Sullivan on *The Ed Sullivan Show*. The Beatles had ten number 1 hits in 1964–1965. (LIBRARY OF CONGRESS)

The Supremes had six top
tunes in 1964–1965.
(PHOTOFEST)

The Rolling Stones, pioneers of an edgier rock music, became famous with
their controversial "(I Can't Get No) Satisfaction" in mid-1965. (PHOTOFEST)

Barry McGuire, singing "Eve of Destruction," the most popular protest rock song of the year. (PHOTOFEST)

when he sang his folk-style tunes, he had performed alone; he did not have a backup group. A good deal of folk music in the early 1960s, moreover, had tended to be affirmative ("We Shall Overcome") or to adapt spirituals (Dylan's "Blowin' in the Wind"). Especially as performed by Peter, Paul, and Mary, many of Dylan's most popular songs had appealed to universal sentiments for peace and understanding. Far from being loud or abrasive, these tended to be hopeful, even wistful, and had encouraged folk-music listeners—most of them well educated and middle class—to sing along.

But Dylan, having first released electrically amplified songs in his album *Bringing It All Back Home* in March, changed course even more dramatically in the summer of 1965, amazing and in some cases disgruntling his fans. On July 20, he released "Like a Rolling Stone," which he had recorded a month earlier. Like "Satisfaction," it climbed in the singles charts, reaching number 2 (behind "Help!" by the Beatles) in early September. The title, however, had nothing to do with the band by that name. Rather, "Like a Rolling Stone" was a sour, vengeful, and (some said) misogynist song in which Dylan appeared to gloat over the misfortunes of a highfalutin former girl-friend.[9] He sang it, moreover, with an electric backup band, which included a riff from an organ. Noise from the band made the lyrics, delivered in Dylan's rasping growl, difficult for some listeners to understand. Though "Like a Rolling Stone" has many admirers, years later it evokes hostile responses from some historians of popular music. One has dismissed it as "not just negative but nihilistic, even plain nasty." He adds, "It was in no way, shape, or form a folk song."[10] A far more receptive listener, cultural historian Morris Dickstein, nonetheless wrote of the "increasing violence and intensity of Dylan's work" at the time.[11]

On July 25, five days after the song's release, Dylan appeared at the Newport Folk Festival, an annual event that since 1959 had attracted many thousands of folk-music fans. (A total of seventy-five thousand appeared over the course of the four days of music in 1965—thirty thousand more than had attended a jazz festival at Newport three weeks earlier.) Dylan had performed there in 1963 and 1964, along with Joan Baez, Phil Ochs, and others, and was the headliner for the Sunday night concert in 1965. When Peter Yarrow, of Peter, Paul, and

Mary fame, introduced him, most people in the crowd of twenty thousand probably expected another moving performance of folk music. Instead, Dylan, wearing high-heeled boots and a black leather jacket, brandished an electric guitar. Behind him was a five-man electric rock 'n' roll/blues band he had pulled together the previous day. It accompanied him for three songs, the second of which was "Like a Rolling Stone."

What happened as they were playing became a subject of long-lasting dispute, both among the fans who were there and among later writers. Many recall that a sizeable segment of the audience, horrified to hear their folk-music favorite "going electric" and "selling out to the commercial sound," all but booed him off the stage. Some have said that folk idol Pete Seeger, outraged as he listened backstage, threatened to cut the electric cable. Others at the scene, however, retort that while many people booed, others clapped and cheered. Some of those who jeered, it is said, were mainly registering their dissatisfaction with the sound mix, which was ill equipped to transmit the music, drowning out some of the lyrics.[12]

What followed is also debated. After the third number, some accounts maintain, Dylan told the band, "Let's go, man. That's all." Whatever may have been said, they quickly left the stage. Though Dylan soon reappeared, this time alone with acoustic guitar, he stayed to perform only two songs, one of which was "Mr. Tambourine Man." The crowd, delighted, cheered him enthusiastically, only to be deeply disappointed when he abruptly ended his set. His overall time on stage was very brief (around fifteen minutes) for a headliner.

Characteristically, Dylan made light of the controversies. "It's all music, no more, no less," he said in November.[13] Still later, he protested that he had never intended to become known as a folk singer. But taking Dylan at his word has always been a perilous act. In fact, the booing may have hurt his feelings. Not until 2002, thirty-seven years later, did he return to perform at the festival.[14]

More important, it was evident that Dylan's highly public adoption of electrified rock was a consequential declaration of aesthetic independence: because of his high standing as songwriter and singer, his conversion was threatening the future of folk music, which was soon to be overtaken by the commercial gold of folk rock. As Dickstein explained, "When Dylan plugged in to an electric guitar at the Newport Folk Festival in 1965 to the anger of much of his audience, in effect the folk era ended and the rock era began."[15]

How much did the new music from the Stones, Dylan, and others matter in the larger dynamic of American life? Historians and music critics have suggested that powerful forces unsettling Americans at the time—notably racial tensions and popular fears associated with the Vietnam War—help to explain the increasing popularity of loud and often harsh music such as that of the Stones and Dylan. Gitlin, an SDS leader in the early 1960s, later wrote that "Satisfaction" was a "cross-class yelp of resentment that could appeal to waitresses and mechanics and students, all stomping in unison." Its sales showed "just how vast was the market for *badness*."[16] Jagger agreed, complacently observing that the song "captures a spirit of the times . . . which was alienation." Dylan's music, Dickstein later wrote, "mirrored the expanding violence in the country."[17]

Dickstein's statement needs a little elaboration. Neither the Stones nor Dylan nor other performers on the Top 40 charts were singing out against the war or against racism during the early summer of 1965. The Beatles, still relying on bouncy and melodic tunes, opened a sensationally successful two-week American tour in mid-August with an outdoor concert at Shea Stadium, the home of the New York Mets. A capacity crowd of 55,600, the biggest for a pop concert in global history, cheered them on.[18] The release in August of Frank Sinatra's album *The September of My Years* included a song, "It Was a Very Good Year," that later won him a Grammy for best male vocal performance of 1965.[19] Sinatra remained an extraordinarily popular performer throughout the late 1960s.

Tom Lehrer, a satirical songwriter/singer/piano player, was another musical performer who began to attract notice in mid-1965, with compositions that comically and directly needled orthodoxies of the time. In late July, appearing at a night club in San Francisco, Lehrer arranged to have some of his songs recorded in live performance and released in an album titled *That Was the Year That Was*. Though Lehrer did not claim to be a crusader—his touch was mostly carefree and light—many of his songs contained memorable zingers. "National Brotherhood Week," one of his best, drew huge if uneasy laughter when he dropped the reminder that it was during that week, in February, that Malcolm X was assassinated.

That Was the Year That Was included many other clever songs that enabled it to rise to *Billboard*'s Top 40 (and stay there for eighteen weeks) later in the year.[20] One title, "Pollution," spoke for itself, as did "New Math," which skewered the pretensions of a contemporary fad in mathematics teaching. "Whatever Became of Hubert?" mocked Vice President Humphrey, whom President Johnson appeared to have forgotten about. Several songs dwelled on American militarism and nuclear war, including "So Long, Mom (A Song for World War III)" and "MLF Lullaby," which concerned America's Multilateral Nuclear Force. Perhaps his most famous song was "Wernher von Braun," mocking the cavalier militarism of the World War II German rocket scientist whose expertise had since been relied on by the US government.

Lehrer's style was too sophisticated for many people—he was in no way a pop star. But his satires earned him a devoted following. As was true of songs such as "Satisfaction" and "Like a Rolling Stone," they revealed that large numbers of people, especially young people, were becoming increasingly receptive to topical and confrontational music. Millions, moreover, were gravitating toward electrically amplified and sometimes contentious rock music, perhaps because it reflected their own mounting fears and frustrations, because it legitimized their energy, or because it helped them to express rebelliousness against their elders. Later, many rock music fans would identify "Satisfaction" as "an anthem for a generation."

———

THE POLITICAL SCENE DURING JUNE AND JULY 1965, largely unaffected by cultural developments, continued to reveal the contagious power of rights-oriented political causes as well as LBJ's impatient but effective management of domestic objectives. Johnson worked hard during this time to advance the interests of black Americans. On June 2, the Senate confirmed his nomination of Patricia Harris, a civil rights activist, attorney, and Howard University law professor, as America's first black ambassador (to Luxembourg). A few weeks later, LBJ made a bolder move, picking Thurgood Marshall, the renowned litigator who had led the fight against mandated school segregation, to be the first African American solicitor general of the United States. The Senate, after overcoming delaying tactics from Southerners, confirmed Marshall's appointment in early August, thereby positioning him to become the nation's first black Supreme Court justice in 1967.

The Court, a stalwart supporter of liberal goals under Chief Justice Earl Warren since the mid-1950s, also continued to establish the extension of rights. In April, it had declared that earlier convictions of 1961 Freedom Riders could not stand.[21] And on June 7, the last day of its session, it announced its decision in *Griswold v. Connecticut*, which overturned an 1879 Connecticut law that had forbidden the use, even by married couples, of contraception. Though unenforced (and unenforceable), the statute was one of a number of similar state laws that had long dismayed advocates of contraceptive rights.

In announcing the decision, Justice William Douglas stressed that married couples must have the right to make their own decisions concerning birth control. "Would we allow the police to search the sacred precincts of marital bedrooms for telltale signs of the use of contraceptives?" he asked. "The very idea is repulsive to the notions of privacy surrounding the marital relationship." Conceding that the Constitution offered no guidance on the subject, he declared that "specific guarantees in the Bill of Rights have penumbras"—shadows—"formed by emanations from those guarantees that help give them life and substance." Various of these guarantees, he said, created "zones of privacy." Citing the First, Third, Fourth, Fifth, Ninth, and Fourteenth Amendments, Douglas maintained that there was a constitutional "right to privacy" that the Connecticut law violated.[22]

Two of Douglas's fellow justices, Potter Stewart and Hugo Black, dissented. Stewart, while observing that Connecticut's law was "uncommonly silly," could discover no constitutional basis for ruling against it. Black, who prided himself on his defense of the First Amendment, which among other things guarantees the right of peaceable assembly, commented, "the right of a husband and wife to assemble in bed is a new right for me." Six of Douglas's colleagues, however, supported him, citing varying constitutional provisions in the course of doing so. By a vote of 7 to 2, the Connecticut law was overturned.

Like Black and Stewart, critics of the ruling have since insisted that Douglas and his defenders, seeking rationales to justify their preconceived conclusions, had read their personal preferences into the Constitution. The critics were particularly dubious about the "penumbras" and "emanations" Douglas discovered in the nation's founding document. But the majority had spoken. *Griswold v. Connecticut* not only marked an important new direction in constitutional law but also served as precedent for a number of rights-based later decisions. In *Eisenstadt v. Baird* (1972) the Court, citing the Equal Protection Clause of the Fourteenth Amendment, ruled against a Massachusetts law that had prohibited unmarried individuals from possessing contraceptives. In *Roe v. Wade* (1973), it relied explicitly on *Griswold* in striking down state laws banning abortion. This was a very considerable enlargement of a woman's right to privacy.

Developments on the state level, also reflecting the era's pervasive rights-consciousness, further raised the spirits of liberals. On June 1, Governor Nelson Rockefeller of New York signed into law a bill banning capital punishment, except in cases involving the premeditated murder of police officers or involving guards killed by prisoners serving life sentences. New York was one of four states (Iowa, Vermont, and West Virginia were the others) to approve such a law in 1965, bringing to thirteen the total with such measures in place. Foes of the death penalty began to hope (incorrectly, as it happened) that a national trend was under way.[23]

Above all, liberals in the summer of 1965 rejoiced over the actions of Congress, which with rare exceptions continued to vote heavily for LBJ's ambitious agenda. On June 30, the House approved the president's housing and urban redevelopment bill. An extension of earlier laws, it authorized funding for low- and middle-income housing and sought to improve urban renewal projects and community facilities.[24] A House vote on the way to passage of the bill briefly suggested that some of LBJ's otherwise loyal liberals might be starting to balk. The issue concerned a heatedly debated provision authorizing the payment of rent subsidies to the poor, notably to people who had already qualified for public housing and to those who were physically disabled and elderly. As usual, however, the president exerted pressure, and the provision got through the House by a vote of 208 to 202.

LBJ drove his liberal followers to move even more quickly in July. On July 9, the Senate approved a Social Security Amendments bill, including Medicare and Medicaid, which in all significant respects resembled the measure that Wilbur Mills had steered to passage in the House in early April. The same day, the House supported the administration's voting rights bill, 333–85, with Democrats voting 221–61 and Republicans (with a larger percentage in favor) voting 112–24. A week later, the Senate approved the housing and urban re-development bill, including the provision for rent subsidies, 54–30. Thanks to minor differences between the House and Senate versions of these three measures, all would have to go to conference commit-tees. Still, final approval of the bills now seemed all but certain.[25]

Congress, though on its way to passing an unparalleled amount of progressive legislation, took a brief and embarrassing detour: bowing to the clout of tobacco lobbyists, it approved a hotly contested and greatly weakened Federal Cigarette Labeling and Advertising Act. Many antismoking advocates, appalled, urged LBJ to veto it. But in-stead he signed it on July 27. The act settled for an innocuous state-ment to be placed on cigarette packs in 1966: "Caution: Cigarette Smoking May Be Hazardous to Your Health." The label avoided use of the word "cancer" (and failed to prevent a rise in per capita cigarette smoking in 1966). Outraged, the *Atlantic* ran a story titled, "The Quiet Victory of the Cigarette Lobby: How It Found the Best Filter Yet—Congress."[26]

Having indicated that special interests could triumph once in a while, Congress then got back on its liberal track. On July 21, the Senate-House conference committee approved the Social Security Amendments bill, which included Medicare and Medicaid, and sent it to the two chambers for final votes. The next day, the House ap-proved the administration's antipoverty bill. On July 28, braced by strong labor union support, it voted 221–203 to repeal Section 14(b) of the Taft-Hartley Act of 1947.[27]

Within the next few days, Congress proceeded to pass two land-mark laws of its historic 1965 session. These were the Social Security Amendments Act of 1965 and the Voting Rights Act, from which a House-Senate conference committee—leaned on heavily by the administration—had removed the controversial poll tax ban that had earlier been inserted by the House. No laws more clearly revealed the still significant power of liberalism and of rights-conscious political advocacy in the United States.

The Social Security Amendments bill, which featured the creation of Medicare and Medicaid, had seemed almost certain to be enacted into law once the House had approved it in April. Although many members of the American Medical Association still opposed the measure in July, Johnson believed that the AMA and most doctors, fearful of damaging their public standing, would not dare to fight against it to the end. When the labor leader George Meany told him of his worries about the AMA, LBJ replied, "George, have you ever fed chickens?" "No," Meany replied. "Well," Johnson snorted, "Chickens are real dumb. They eat and eat and eat and never stop. . . . They start shitting at the time they're eating, and before you know it, they're knee-deep in their own shit. Well, the AMA's the same. They've been eating and eating nonstop and now they're knee-deep in their own shit and everybody knows it. They won't be able to stop anything."[28]

LBJ, as usual, was not only crude but also correct about the political chances for Medicare. The House-Senate conference bill passed easily, by 307–116 in the House and 70–24 in the Senate. Roughly half of the Republicans in each house, fearful of antagonizing the elderly, ultimately voted for it.[29] Victory, however, was achieved not because the AMA caved in, but because the bill was a moderate and therefore popular measure that did not significantly alter the structure of America's medical care system. As before, private physicians, hospitals, and insurance companies would enjoy free rein. HEW undersecretary Wilbur Cohen promised Congress "there would be no real controls over hospitals or physicians."[30]

The act, like most of LBJ's major domestic causes, broadened opportunity: in this instance by extending medical care to groups that needed it. Medicare promised to benefit some nineteen million elderly Americans, many of whom had had no coverage before. Medicaid would aid categories of needy people, especially the aged and disabled. All these health care provisions would begin to go into effect on July 1, 1966. The act also authorized generous Social Security benefits. Financed by higher Social Security taxes, the benefits would increase by at least 7 percent retroactively to January 1. Some of the checks would start reaching beneficiaries as early as September 1965.[31]

Medicare and Medicaid, it turned out, had large and unanticipated fiscal consequences. Medicare's costs rose far more rapidly than most people had imagined in 1965—from $3.5 billion in 1966–1967 to $144 billion in 1993.[32] A number of developments, including the adoption and use of expensive medical technology, accounted for the inflation, which had been occurring before passage of the law. Few framers of the act foresaw the leap in life expectancy that would later lead Medicare to spend a third of its budget on care provided during the last year of beneficiaries' lives and cause Medicaid to pump large sums into support of patients in nursing homes.

Even in the short run, the costs of Medicare and Medicaid rose rapidly. Most of these increases stemmed from the lack of cost controls in the law, which rewarded Medicare providers for the quantity of services extended, regardless of quality, outcome, or expense. Costs also rose from a surge in demand generated by the new programs. To help pay for the increased costs of Medicare, the Social Security Administration in the late 1960s had to raise Part B charges for beneficiaries by 25 percent.[33]

Yet in 1965 it was hard for the framers of reform to anticipate the magnitude of these developments, which later Congresses failed to address. Even if the framers, LBJ included, had been able to predict the high cost increases in medical care for older and needy Americans, they would likely have pressed for legislation similar to what Congress passed. As Johnson and his supporters knew, no measure that threatened to overturn the fee-for-service system stood a chance of enactment at that time. The framers also assumed that the robust economic growth of the early 1960s would continue, thereby enabling Medicare and Medicaid to function smoothly. They had no intention of reforming the structure of the system.

Indeed, advocates of the new law had every reason to rejoice when it passed, for it was one of the most significant acts of social legislation to be approved in the 1960s. The law, extending medical care to millions, probably affected more people directly than any other Great Society legislation. Medicare was very popular not only with the elderly, but also with Americans in general. After all, most people were paying into the Social Security system and expected to benefit from the provisions of the new program when they reached retirement age.

Southern blacks, too, benefited. Thanks to Title VI of the 1964 Civil Rights Act, which authorized the federal government to cut off aid to public institutions that segregated, they were able in time to take advantage of the new system to receive care in hospitals previously open only to whites. "White" and "Colored" signs gradually disappeared from hospitals in the South.

—

THE VOTING RIGHTS ACT, WHICH PASSED SHORTLY AFTER MEDICARE, was a historic achievement. To ensure the end of racial discrimination in voting, the measure authorized the government to suspend literacy tests and dispatch federal voting examiners to any states or counties where literacy tests or similar voter-qualification devices were used and where fewer than half of the eligible voting-age adults had been registered or voted in the 1964 presidential election. This provision, which took effect immediately, placed the burden of proof on local registrars to show that their procedures were nondiscriminatory.

A key part of the bill, often identified in later years as Section 5, was a clause calling for "preclearance." Government entities with a history of racial discrimination were required to secure permission from the Justice Department or from a special three-judge federal court in DC before they made substantial changes in their voting procedures, including the remapping of congressional districts that states undertake every ten years.[34] This was a significant and enduringly tough provision.[35]

A delighted LBJ made a characteristically elaborate production of celebrating the passage of both these major bills. On July 30, he flew with Lady Bird to the Truman presidential library in Missouri so that the former president, who had supported national health legislation, could be on hand for the signing of the Social Security Amendments Act. Humphrey, too, was among the dignitaries who attended the much-photographed scene, where LBJ announced that he was enrolling Truman, then eighty-one, as the first Medicare beneficiary. In a characteristically grandiose proclamation, LBJ proclaimed, "No longer will older Americans be denied the healing miracle of modern medicine."

LBJ planned a televised noontime ceremony on August 6 to showcase his signing of the Voting Rights Act. The date, however, also marked the twentieth anniversary of the dropping of the atomic bomb on Hiroshima, and antiwar protestors took to the streets in Washington. Led by David Dellinger, a well-known demonstrator for peace, some six hundred people gathered in front of the White House. Signs read, "WITHDRAW U.S. TROOPS FROM VIETNAM NOW!" and "JESUS CHRIST DID NOT CARRY A DRAFT CARD." Their agitation was a vivid reminder that amid the triumphalism surrounding enactment of Great Society measures, the war in Vietnam was arousing ever sharper tensions.[36]

Johnson did not let the antiwar protestors disrupt his ceremony. To emphasize the contribution of Congress to the legislation, he chose the Capitol rotunda as the site for a speech on the subject. Standing before a statue of a brooding Abraham Lincoln, he told a celebratory crowd of civil rights activists, representatives, senators, and others that the Justice Department was suspending literacy tests immediately in many areas of the South and that it would undertake court challenges to the constitutionality of state and local poll taxes.[37] He pleaded: "Let me now say to every Negro in this country: You *must* register. You *must* vote. . . . If you do this then you will find . . . that the vote is the most powerful instrument ever devised by man for breaking down injustice and destroying the terrible walls that imprison men because they are different from other men."[38]

Johnson then moved to the President's Room, an elegantly decorated space near the Senate chamber where 104 years earlier to the day, Lincoln had signed a Confiscation Act that aimed to free slaves who had been pressed into service by the Confederacy. LBJ, crediting civil rights workers and Congress with their dedication to the case of racial justice, signed the voting rights bill into law and gave pens to a number in attendance, including Martin Luther King, Ralph Abernathy, and Rosa Parks. John Lewis, echoing the sentiments of many at the ceremony, exulted that the Voting Rights Act was a "milestone and every bit as momentous . . . as the Emancipation Proclamation or the 1954 Supreme Court decision."[39]

Lewis, like Johnson, was correct to sing the praises of the law, which effectively outlawed literacy tests and, as periodically reauthorized by Congress, led to significant increases in black voter registration. Despite efforts by white racists to intimidate would-be black registrants, the percentage of registered blacks of voting age in the eleven states of the Old Confederacy jumped to 62 percent by 1968.[40] By the early 1980s, race-baiting had virtually disappeared, and some 2,500 blacks held elective office in the South. When George Wallace ran (successfully) for governor of Alabama in 1982, he eagerly courted black as well as white voters.[41]

Not for the first time, however, LBJ oversold his accomplishment, notably in his claim that the vote was "the most powerful instrument ever devised by man for breaking down injustice." Though the law increased black registration in the South, it could not attempt to address the inequality and poverty that had long submerged millions of black people in the region. These deeply set socioeconomic burdens, which victimized blacks in the North as well, persisted, thereby accentuating the more widespread income inequality that descended on the United States in later years.

Like Medicare, the Voting Rights Act had unforeseen consequences. Whites redoubled their efforts to enroll white people and to get them to the polls. Conservative Republicans, enlisting the majority of such voters, often won senatorial and presidential elections in the South after 1965. And gerrymandering—first by whites and then in retaliation by blacks—led in time to establishment of a number of predominantly black or white congressional voting districts. The Voting Rights Act, a measure that aimed to extend the rights of individuals, in some areas safeguarded the rights of groups. This was not the sort of democratic reform that framers of the act had anticipated.

The Voting Rights Act nonetheless went far to achieve its major objective: guaranteeing previously disfranchised black people the right to vote. It was a hard-won accomplishment that attested to the courage of rights-conscious activists in Selma and elsewhere, to the political skill of Lyndon Johnson, and to the unprecedented strength of liberalism in the United States in 1965, the peak year in the modern history of domestic reforms.

———

PASSAGE OF THE VOTING RIGHTS ACT, LIKE THAT OF MEDICARE/ Medicaid and other key measures by early August indicated that one of LBJ's nightmares—escalation in Vietnam would kill his dreams for a Great Society—had not materialized. Still, even as he was signing path-breaking laws, the Vietnam War continued to be the six-hundred-pound gorilla that millions of nervous Americans knew was there. By late July, as many of these Great Society bills were about to pass, he understood that he had to open up at last and tell an increasingly suspicious public at least a little more about what he planned to do in Southeast Asia.

10

BOMBSHELL FROM SAIGON

June 7, 1965, came three days after LBJ delivered his stirring speech "To Fulfill These Rights" at Howard University, in which he had called for consideration of measures to promote social and economic equality for black Americans. It was the same day the Supreme Court decision in *Griswold v. Connecticut* declared a right to privacy in striking down an anti-contraception law. It was a wonderful time for American liberalism.

But June 7 was also the day LBJ received an urgent message from General Westmoreland. "The South Vietnamese armed forces," he reported, "cannot stand up to this pressure [from the enemy] without substantial U.S. combat support on the ground." He beseeched the president to send forty-one thousand combat troops to Vietnam right away and another fifty-two thousand within the next few months. Still more men, the general indicated, would be required later if the United States hoped to prevent a "collapse" of the South Vietnamese effort. Westmoreland concluded bluntly, "We are in for the long pull. I see no likelihood of achieving a quick, favorable end to the war."[1]

If Johnson acceded to Westmoreland's pleas, by year end the number of American troops in Vietnam would more than double, from roughly 80,000 in early June to around 175,000. Approval would also officially endorse what some of Westmoreland's forces had already been doing: venturing beyond the enclaves they had been protecting and taking the offensive against the enemy.

Given the advances of the Vietcong since mid-May, it was hardly surprising that Westmoreland would seek more military muscle. The situation had become desperate by early June, not only for the ARVN but also for the South Vietnamese government in Saigon. As *Time* later reported, the Vietcong held "in thrall" 65 percent of South Vietnam's land and 55 percent of its people. It added, "The lethal little men in black pajamas roamed the length and breadth of South Vietnam, marauding, maiming and killing with impunity."[2]

The Joint Chiefs and McNamara strongly backed Westmoreland's requests for more combat troops and for an official go-ahead that would allow them to seize initiatives on the ground. General Wheeler, the chair, snapped, "You must take the fight to the enemy. No one ever won a battle sitting on his ass."[3] McNamara was especially hawkish. In a proposal that Bundy called "rash to the point of folly," he soon urged LBJ to call up the reserves to active duty—a step that was tantamount to an announcement of full-scale war—and, supported by the Joint Chiefs, advocated a massive offensive against North Vietnam that would include mining its harbors, destroying its airfields, and wiping out its rail and road bridges.[4]

LBJ, agonizing, knew that he had to make one of the biggest decisions of his presidency. If he rejected his commander's requests, South Vietnam would fall to the enemy. If he agreed to them, as from the start he suspected he would have to do, he would be taking an irreversible step toward all-out war. Not for nothing did McNamara later call Westmoreland's message a "bombshell."[5]

ONE OF LBJ'S FIRST RESPONSES WAS TO CALL SENATE MAJORITY leader Mike Mansfield on June 8 to inquire if Congress would update the Tonkin Gulf Resolution so as to give him authority to "dispatch additional elements of the United States armed forces" to Vietnam. Mansfield told him that Congress would refuse to do that. LBJ, as commander in chief, then acted on his own, bypassing Congress, to give Westmoreland official authorization to deploy American forces on offensive combat missions, with or without the ARVN.[6] Like missions that Westmoreland had already undertaken, this now officially authorized strategy would lead to more fighting against guerillas on their own familiar terrain. American casualties were certain to increase.

Johnson was otherwise deliberate in responding to Westmoreland's message—and to subsequent appeals from him within the next few weeks that would have raised the total number of troops by the end of the year to two hundred thousand.[7] Because he worried about bringing China into the war, he did not support McNamara's recommendation for heavy bombing of industrial areas near Hanoi or of land or sea routes connecting China to North Vietnam. In part because he feared that he might have a constitutional obligation to seek congressional permission, he also rejected the idea of calling the reserves onto active duty.[8] Temporizing, he accepted as an expedient McNamara's idea of sending slightly smaller numbers of additional troops. McNamara announced on June 16 that twenty-one thousand more combat soldiers were on their way to Vietnam. These were expected to bring the total to somewhere around a hundred thousand.[9]

Johnson then became deeply absorbed in deciding on a longer-run strategy. Though he continued to ride herd on Congress in support of his Great Society programs, he otherwise focused on the situation in Vietnam, an effort that resulted in what one historian later called "mountains of memorandums and hours of dialogue" within his administration.[10] Among the domestic efforts that became casualties of his preoccupation were those that might have given substance to his address at Howard. Civil rights leaders, discovering that his mind was elsewhere, grew ever more edgy and impatient.

Johnson also found, though not to his surprise, that he had to cope with opposition to further escalation from leading political figures. Worried especially that Robert Kennedy might openly criticize him, he urged McNamara, a friend of Bobby, to tone him down.[11] Kennedy did not speak out, but other doubters—mostly in private sessions—consistently did. A firm dissenter was Mansfield, one of the few members of Congress with whom Johnson seriously discussed the situation during the next few weeks. During his telephone conversation with LBJ on June 8, Mansfield warned against trying to bomb Hanoi or Haiphong. "You bomb them, you get nothing," he said. "You just build up more hatred. You get these people tied more closely together because they are tied by blood, whether from the North or the South." Mansfield added, "If you make [an] approach to Congress, I really think the roof will blow off this time, because people who have remained quiet will no longer remain silent."[12]

Undersecretary of State Ball remained the only high-ranking administration adviser to oppose major escalation. All the others—Rusk, Bundy, Taylor, and the Joint Chiefs—came around in one way or another to support it. Ball expressed his profound doubt that the United States could defeat the Vietcong "or even force them to the conference table on our terms, no matter how many hundred thousand *white, foreign* troops we deploy." Approval of Westmoreland's requests, he added, would lead to a "protracted war involving an open-ended commitment of U.S. forces, mounting U.S. casualties, no assurances of a satisfactory solution, and a serious danger of escalation at the end of the road."[13]

Ball had normally been even-tempered when dissenting from the pro-escalation consensus that had developed among top advisers since the start of the year. Westmoreland's request, however, was hard for him to take. When LBJ assembled a gathering of "wise men" to advise him in early July, he found to his satisfaction (as he had expected) that all of them—even Clark Clifford—favored escalation. But Ball was furious at the ill-informed, offhand way in which the "wise men," including former secretary of state Dean Acheson, had rendered their opinions. "You goddamned old bastards," he snapped at Acheson and another member of the group after the meeting. "You remind me of nothing so much as a bunch of buzzards sitting on a fence and letting the young men die. You don't know a goddamned thing about what you're talking about. . . . You just sit there and say these irresponsible things."[14]

While coping with opposition (relatively slight though it was) from the inside, LBJ also had to deal with controversy, all of it stemming from opposition to his policies in Vietnam, surrounding a White House Festival of the Arts. Although a relatively minor flap, it revealed the intensity of antiwar feeling that had developed among leading American intellectuals. Eric Goldman, a Princeton history professor who was serving the president as a special consultant, organized the event to highlight what he later called the "cultural renaissance" occurring in many American communities.[15] Invitations went to leading American writers, musicians, and artists to attend a variety of events at the White House beginning on June 14.

Three days before the festival was due to start, one of the most distinguished invitees, the poet Robert Lowell, sent LBJ a letter in which he rescinded his earlier acceptance and declined to attend. Though politely phrased, the letter bluntly laid out his hatred of the war. "We are in danger," Lowell wrote, "of imperceptibly becoming an explosive and suddenly chauvinistic nation, and may even be drifting on our way to the last nuclear ruin." Lowell sent a copy of his letter to the *New York Times*, which published it on its front page the next morning—five days after LBJ had received the bombshell message from Vietnam.[16]

Friends of Lowell immediately widened the controversy by circulating a statement in support of his position. Twenty well-known intellectuals signed it, including Lillian Hellman, Alfred Kazin, Bernard Malamud, Mary McCarthy, William Styron, and Robert Penn Warren. Three others who added their signatures were on the list of invitees to the festival: critic Dwight Macdonald and artists Larry Rivers and Mark Rothko, whose paintings had been selected for exhibition at the gathering.

When the festival started, Goldman was gratified by the turnout. Despite Lowell's stand, most of the distinguished invitees showed up, along with other special guests, for a total of some four hundred. Many who attended—poet Phyllis McGinley, actor Charlton Heston, historian George Kennan, novelist Saul Bellow, biographer Catherine Drinker Bowen, singers Roberta Peters and Marian Anderson, and jazz maestro Duke Ellington—gave readings or performed. Though Macdonald circulated a pro-Lowell petition at the event, only a few people agreed to sign it. Other guests (who included Chief Justice Earl Warren) enjoyed surveying the paintings and sculptures, listening to the

Louisville Symphony Orchestra, watching the Joffrey Ballet, and viewing excerpts from films and from the plays *Death of a Salesman* by Arthur Miller and *The Glass Menagerie* by Tennessee Williams.

Still, Goldman later characterized the festival as "an unmitigated disaster." This was because it enraged the president.[17] LBJ ad-libbed a brief talk before an evening event, but he did not attend performances or mingle with most of the artists and writers in attendance. It was obvious to him that many among America's intellectual elite despised him. John Hersey, for instance, had been invited in his role as a novelist but insisted on reading from *Hiroshima*, a nonfiction work about the aftermath of the atomic bomb the United States dropped on Japan during World War II. While reading he raised his eyes from the pages to stare pointedly at Lady Bird Johnson in the audience. LBJ left no doubt about his resentment, muttering within earshot of the press, "Some of them insult me by staying away and some of them insult me by coming." In private he added, "Don't they know I'm the only President they've got and a war is on?" The intellectuals, he said, were "sonsofbitches," "fools," and close to being "traitors."[18]

Though the festival embittered the president, it was far less significant to him than the political upheaval afflicting South Vietnam. On June 12, the civilian government in Saigon, having been on the rocks for several weeks, cracked apart and was replaced by a military junta. The backgrounds of the two men who took charge indicated how intensively the United States had been propping up South Vietnam in the past. The new premier, Air Vice Marshal Nguyen Cao Ky, had been trained as a pilot by the French and had later operated under CIA cover while flying secret agents to North Vietnam. Ky's co-leader was General Nguyen Van Thieu, who became chief of state and commander in chief. Thieu was a graduate of the United States Command and General Staff College at Fort Leavenworth, Kansas. In late 1963, he had led troops in an assault on the presidential palace of Ngo Dinh Diem, who was assassinated during the coup.[19]

Ky and Thieu, aided immeasurably by American troop increases that were soon to follow, managed in time to establish greater political stability in Saigon. In June 1965, however, they struck American observers as a totally unpromising pair. William Bundy, assistant secretary of state for East Asia (and McGeorge Bundy's brother), thought they were "absolutely the bottom of the barrel."[20]

Thieu, crafty and self-effacing, had what one historian has called the "personality of a political survivor"—a style that enabled him to stay in power during innumerable changes of South Vietnamese officialdom and to remain a leader in Saigon throughout America's involvement in the war.[21] Ky, a womanizer whose hero was Adolf Hitler, was a flamboyant character who strutted about in a flashy flying suit, a bright purple scarf wrapped around his neck and an ivory-handled pistol protruding ostentatiously from his hip. One American diplomat likened him to a character from a comic opera. "A Hollywood central casting bureau," he said, "would have grabbed him for a role as a sax player in a second-rate Manila night club."[22]

ALL THESE DEVELOPMENTS—THE DETERIORATING MILITARY SITUATION in Vietnam, the unwelcome advice from Mansfield and Ball, the rejection by intellectuals, the ascent to power of Thieu and Ky, and, above all, the need to respond completely to Westmoreland's bombshell message—took a toll on President Johnson. Some people close to him in June and July 1965 worried that his nerves might be cracking. As Tom Wicker, a columnist for the *New York Times*, phrased it in mid-July, "The news out of Washington these days is that Mr. Johnson is irascible, moody, high-handed, peeved at his critics, and generally hard to deal with."[23]

Richard Goodwin, LBJ's chief speechwriter, later (after having broken with Johnson) maintained that the president seemed at that time to be losing his grip. Attacks on Johnson's foreign policy, he recalled, were making him "paranoiac." Goodwin added, "Johnson began to hint privately . . . that he was the target of a gigantic communist conspiracy in which his domestic adversaries were only players—not conscious participants, perhaps, but unwitting dupes." Goodwin recalled how Johnson interrupted a conversation to blurt, "You know, Dick, the communists are taking over the country." On another occasion, LBJ declared to him, "I am not going to have anything more to do with the liberals. They won't have anything to do with me. They all just follow the communist line—liberals, intellectuals, communists. . . . I can't trust anybody any more. I tell you what I am going to do. I'm going to get rid of everybody who doesn't agree with my policies."[24]

Bill Moyers, a top presidential aide by that time, seconded Goodwin's reminiscences. Johnson, he remembered, told him, "The communists already control the three major networks and the forty major outlets of communication."[25] Moyers was convinced that being forced to make a decision about Westmoreland's appeals was provoking the president's outbursts. LBJ's agitated exclamations, he added, stemmed from his realization that "this was a road from which there was no turning back," one that might mark the "end of his presidency." Johnson had fallen into a "pronounced, prolonged depression. . . . He would just go within himself, just disappear—morose, self-pitying, angry. . . . He was a tormented man." One day, lying in bed with the covers almost over his head, he told Moyers that he felt as if he were in a Louisiana swamp "that's pulling me down."[26]

Lady Bird Johnson did not paint such an alarming picture. But she, too, remembered how the war often tormented her husband. "It was just a hell of a thorn stuck in his throat," she later told his biographer Robert Dallek. "It wouldn't come up; it wouldn't go down. . . . It was just pure hell and [he] did not have that reassuring, strong feeling that this is right, that he had when he was in a crunch with civil rights or poverty or education. . . . True, you can 'bear any burden, pay any price' if you're sure you're doing right. But if you do not know you're doing right"—her voice trailed off.[27]

At his most pessimistic, Johnson worried especially that even the huge troop buildups called for by Westmoreland might not be sufficient to pull the United States and South Vietnam out of the morass they were in. In late June he confided to McNamara, "It's going to be difficult for us to very long prosecute effectively a war that far away from home with the divisions we have here. . . . I'm very depressed about it. Because I see no program from either Defense or State that gives me much hope of doing anything, except just praying and grasping to hold on . . . and hope they'll quit. I don't believe they're *ever* going to quit. And I don't see . . . that we have any . . . plan for a victory—militarily or diplomatically."[28]

THOUGH JOHNSON WAS OBVIOUSLY TROUBLED DURING THIS TIME, four facts must be taken into consideration when evaluating his actions and the nature of the stress he felt. First, the choices he had to make would have tormented any president. Second, notwithstanding his outbursts, he was by no means losing his mind. As Moyers conceded, "He was erratic. One day he would be in a down mood and the next he would be quite upbeat."[29] Third, the strains he was undergoing solidified his secretiveness. They rendered him incapable of seriously engaging Congress in the decision-making process or of leveling with the American public. His refusal to tell the people what was at stake and thus to risk a great debate ultimately widened the credibility gap that had been growing since March.

Fourth, from the start Johnson was all but certain he would have to comply with Westmoreland's call for more troops. Appalled by the recent successes of the enemy, he believed that he could hardly refuse the appeal. He also believed, as he had from the start of his presidency, that his predecessors in the White House had committed the nation to the preservation of South Vietnamese independence. If the United States backed away from its commitments, it would forfeit its all-important credibility as leader of the Free World.

As he told McNamara as early as June 10, "They [the enemy] keep coming [into South Vietnam]. And . . . you've got to do something about it. . . . They're going to keep putting their stack in, and moving new chips into the pot. We've either got to do one of two things. We've got to tuck tail and run, or we've got to have somebody . . . tell us that 'the Indians are coming' and protect us."[30] That somebody, it was clear, was the commander in chief.

Still, into late July LBJ continued to postpone a final decision. Because the stakes were huge, he determined to give a hearing, however staged, to advisers who might disagree with him. Ball, for instance, was a regular at the many meetings that considered Westmoreland's appeal. Seeking more input, LBJ decided to replace Ambassador Taylor with Henry Cabot Lodge, Taylor's predecessor in Saigon, in early July. Shortly thereafter, he sent McNamara, Lodge, and General Wheeler to South Vietnam for an up-close look at the situation.

Johnson, still secretive, also held off deciding because he was afraid that announcement of further escalation would damage his political standing. Being candid with the American people about the dire situation, he thought, would touch off what he later called a "right-wing stampede," which would bull ahead to demand even more bellicose responses, perhaps including the invasion of North Vietnam, the bombing of Hanoi and Haiphong, and the mining of Haiphong's harbor.[31] Well aware of how McCarthyites had alleged that communists in the State Department had caused the United States to "lose" China, he worried that a virulent new Red Scare might sweep through the land.

The president also continued to fear that announcement of further escalation would threaten enactment of his most important Great Society bills, especially Medicare and voting rights, on track to be enacted within just a few weeks. If he postponed a decision on Vietnam until then, he need not worry so much about the political prospects for the most important pieces of his domestic program. As he said later,

> [I] could see and almost touch my youthful dream of improving life for more people and in more ways than any other political leader, including FDR. . . . I was determined to keep the war from shattering that dream, which meant I simply had no choice but to keep my foreign policy in the wings. I knew the Congress as well as I know Lady Bird, and I knew that the day it exploded into a major debate on the war, that day would be the beginning of the end of our Great Society.[32]

As LBJ was procrastinating, however, leaks and rumors led to ominous predictions about his intentions. As early as June 24, Senate Republican leader Everett Dirksen told the press that Johnson might soon commit as many as 200,000 men to Vietnam.[33] A few days later, *Newsweek* outdid Dirksen, reporting that the United States, aiming to seal off borders so as to stop infiltration from the North, would increase its troop strength to 225,000. *Time* anticipated that North Vietnam would more than match American manpower increases and predicted that the United States might need as many as 400,000 men in Vietnam in 1966.[34]

Opponents of the war—and others who deplored the credibility gap—reacted to stories like these by clamoring anew for Johnson to be open and honest about the situation in Vietnam and to press for negotiations to end the fighting. In early July, Martin Luther King reiterated his belief that "the war must be stopped. There must be a negotiated settlement even with the Vietcong."[35] *Time* reported a few days later that the fighting, having become savage, was leading to large numbers of casualties. As of early July, it noted, a total of 503 Americans had been killed and another 2,720 wounded since the marines had landed in early March. The South Vietnamese, it added, had lost 25,000, with another 48,000 wounded.[36]

Alarming reports like these didn't seem to affect poll numbers, which revealed in mid-July that some 60 percent of the American people continued to support the administration's course (what was known of it) in Vietnam.[37] Those kinds of numbers, which indicated that Americans were still backing their commander in chief—and the "boys" on the ground—offered some consolation to the president as he prepared to announce a final decision.

WHEN MCNAMARA RETURNED FROM VIETNAM ON JULY 20, HE TOLD the press that the military situation had deteriorated in recent months.[38] Efficient as always, he had prepared a memorandum, signed by Rusk, Bundy, Taylor, Westmoreland, and Wheeler, that set forth three options for the president to consider at a meeting on July 21. The first was: "Cut our losses and withdraw under the best of conditions that can be arranged." The second was: "Continue at about the present level, with the U.S. forces limited to say 75,000." The third was: "Expand promptly and substantially the U.S. military pressure against the Viet Cong in the South and maintain the military pressure against the North Vietnamese in the North while launching a vigorous effort on the political side to lay the groundwork for a favorable outcome by clarifying our objectives and establishing channels of communication."[39]

The presentation of these options and outcomes made it obvious that McNamara and the others favored the third. To "cut our losses and withdraw," the memo argued, would be to lead to "conditions almost certainly humiliating the United States and very damaging to our future effectiveness on the world scene." To "continue at about the present level" would amount to "holding on and playing for breaks." This would be a "course of action which, because our position would grow weaker, almost certainly would confront us later with a choice between withdrawal and an emergency expansion of forces, perhaps too late to do us any good." Option 3, on the other hand, was a way to "stave off defeat in the short run and offer a good chance of producing a favorable settlement in the longer run; at the same time, it would imply a commitment to see a fighting war clear through at considerable cost in casualties and materiel and would make any later decision to withdraw even more difficult and even more costly than would be the case today."

Johnson, as was his habit, encouraged discussion. Ball expressed his doubt that "an army of westerners can fight orientals in [an] Asian jungle and succeed." He recommended abandoning South Vietnam to its fate.[40] But it was obvious that LBJ had already made up his mind before McNamara's return, and he was quick to state his position. Though option 3 outlined long-run costs and dangers—and committed the United States to raise troop levels to close to two hundred thousand by the end of the year—he favored it. At the end of the meeting he said, "Withdrawal would be a disaster, a harsh bombing program would not win and could easily bring a wider war, and standing pat with existing forces was only slow defeat. Only doing what McNamara urged was left."

This meant, of course, that LBJ was prepared to commit the United States to far greater escalation on the ground. As William Bundy said later, "It was the end of debate on policy, and the beginning of a new debate on tactics and above all on presentation to the country." The president had decided, he said, to "put in his stack."[41]

As Bundy had observed, it still remained to be determined how LBJ would announce this decision to the nation. McNamara, continuing to call on LBJ to be candid, urged him to tell the American people that he would mobilize 235,000 reservists, call for a tax hike, authorize the sending of 100,000 to 125,000 more men, and declare a state of national emergency. This would put the nation on a war footing without a declaration of war. Otherwise, McNamara believed, Americans would not fully understand the seriousness of the situation and the need for sacrifice.

LBJ had problems with this advice. As earlier, he continued to fret that candor about the problems in Vietnam would unleash a "right-wing stampede" and "a mean and destructive debate." To go as far as McNamara suggested, he said later, would "shatter my presidency, kill my administration, and damage our democracy."[42] He also continued to fear that a declaration of national emergency and mobilization of reserves were warlike moves that would alarm the Russians and the Chinese, perhaps drawing them directly into the conflict. And he still worried that public announcement of major escalation might endanger his Medicare and voting rights bills, which remained to be passed. So he decided to wait a few more days, during which more meetings were held. He also planned to soft-pedal what he would say. He told his staff that he wished his decisions to be implemented in a "low-keyed manner in order (a) to avoid an abrupt challenge to the Communists and (b) to avoid undue concern and excitement in the Congress and in domestic public opinion."[43]

———

SIX DAYS LATER, ON JULY 27, THE HOUSE PASSED MEDICARE/ Medicaid, with the Senate scheduled to do so on the twenty-eighth. Enactment of the voting rights bill seemed assured as well. Johnson, having settled on what he was going to say to the American public about the escalation, concluded it was safe to announce his decision on July 28. This was more than seven weeks after he had received Westmoreland's cable on June 7. Instead of speaking before a television audience in prime time, he would announce his decision, as if it were a matter of no great consequence, at a routine press conference in the East Room of the White House at noon.

On the afternoon of July 27 Mansfield called LBJ to ask that he meet with a group of senators with expertise in foreign policy. Johnson did not want to talk with antagonists such as Fulbright and told

Mansfield that he would explain all that needed explaining at a meeting with congressional leaders later that day. He emphasized that he would be taking the "soft line of the deal" by not mobilizing the reserves. But, he added, "I can't run out. I'm not going to run in. I just can't sit there and let them be murdered. So I've got to put enough there to hold them and protect them. And . . . if we don't heat it up ourselves, and we don't dramatize it, we don't play it up and say we're appropriating billions and we're sending millions and all [those] men, I don't think you will get the Russians . . . or the Chinese worked up about it. That's what we're hoping."[44]

Later that day he met with his National Security Council and then with congressional leaders to confirm his decision to escalate. Though LBJ had assembled some of these congressmen from time to time that summer, Congress in general had been kept pretty much in the dark about his intentions. Instead, Johnson had made an extraordinarily important decision after seriously consulting only a handful of advisers, most of whom were military brass or "can-do" Kennedy appointees who had stayed on to serve the new president. It was a poor way to reach a historic decision.

As the hour approached to make his speech, Johnson grew tense. Three times in the early morning of July 28—at 1 AM, 3:30 AM, and 7:35 AM—he called the White House situation room to find out how the fighting was going.[45] But he had no intention of changing his mind, and at midday he finally told the press what he had determined to do.

As he had in his conversation with Mansfield, Johnson downplayed the seriousness of what he had decided. He would demand little in the way of sacrifices from the American people. Indeed, he acted as if Vietnam were only one of many items of business on his mind: he also informed the press that he was nominating Abe Fortas, a friend and adviser, to the Supreme Court and naming John Chancellor, a respected NBC newsman, to head the Voice of America. He did not declare a national emergency regarding Vietnam or request a hike in taxes. Nor did he say he would call up the reserves, though he would give the subject "most careful consideration" in the future.

His major revelation was that he was dispatching another 50,000 men to Vietnam, thereby hiking the total of Americans there to 125,000.

This was 50,000 to 75,000 fewer than McNamara had earlier urged him to send. "Additional forces will be needed later," LBJ explained, "and they will be sent as requested." Monthly draft calls, 17,000 in July, would increase "over a period of time" to 35,000. When a reporter asked if his announcement meant a change in America's Vietnam policy, the president answered, "It does not imply any change in policy whatever. It does not imply any change of objective."[46]

This was literally true—LBJ had consistently insisted on doing whatever it might take to sustain America's commitment to South Vietnam. But it was also misleading. Not only was the addition of 50,000 men the biggest escalation yet; it was also half the number he had privately agreed to send. LBJ knew that the American troop level in Vietnam by the end of the year would be at least 175,000 and that it might ultimately have to be in the range of 600,000.[47] His decision was the most significant in terms of manpower of any that he had made to that time. And it had huge implications: it committed the United States to take over much of the fighting from the demoralized South Vietnamese.

In retrospect, it is clear that LBJ's approval of escalation was badly flawed. One of his public arguments for escalation, as he declared at his press conference, was that the North Vietnamese, once battered by larger numbers of US forces, might sooner or later agree to bargain with him. As he had long recognized, however, any such outcome was highly unlikely: Ho Chi Minh, having struggled since the end of World War II for Vietnamese unification under his control, remained dedicated to the cause, no matter the consequences in casualties and destruction. When Johnson talked about getting the North to negotiate, he was deceiving his listeners.

LBJ was especially mistaken in hoping that the people of the United States would stay a long course with him. He was not delusional; after all, polls indicated that the majority of Americans were with him. But most people did not know what really lay ahead. In part because he did not level with the public about the seriousness of the situation, Johnson did not prepare them for sacrifices that would later be required. Imagining that Americans might tolerate ever-increasing costs and casualties, he overestimated the solidity of his popular support and the reverence of people for the presidency. As events were to demonstrate, Lyndon Johnson, master manipulator, was losing his political touch.

What is most remarkable about his decision to escalate is that it was not premised on a belief that sending in more troops would enable South Vietnam to win the war. Westmoreland, who emphasized that vast numbers of reinforcements would be needed even to prevent the North from winning, did not think escalation meant victory. Nor did McNamara, who said as much in his option 3. LBJ was also well aware that Hanoi had the will and the resources to match whatever the United States might do and that the best he might hope for would be stalemate. "I'm no military man at all," he had told Mansfield on June 8, "but . . . if they [Westmoreland's forces] get a hundred and fifty [thousand men], they'll have to have another hundred and fifty. And then they'll have to have *another* hundred and fifty."[48]

Johnson's awareness of the long-term military consequences of Westmoreland's proposals is what makes his readiness to escalate in July especially ill-advised. In February, when he had authorized bombing in response to the attack near Pleiku, he had not sent American soldiers into action on the ground. In March, when he dispatched two battalions of combat marines, he had hoped that they might suffice to protect the airfield at Danang. In April, when he approved a major escalation of combat troops, he still had some faith in an enclave strategy. In June and July, however, while recognizing that Hanoi's indomitable spirit would make far larger escalation a perilous step, he was nonetheless prepared to take it. That he did so, lacking a credible exit strategy, attests to his continuing determination to resist communist military advances in the world and to stand behind America's overseas commitments.

———

PROPONENTS OF THE MUSCULAR USE OF AMERICAN MILITARY POWER have maintained that the United States had to fight to preserve the freedom and independence of South Vietnam and that it was therefore right for LBJ to do so. As Ronald Reagan put the matter while running for president in 1980, "Ours was in truth a noble cause."[49] Other hawks have argued that the United States should have pursued still more vigorous military strategies in Southeast Asia. Some insist that Amercian forces should have invaded the North, bombed Hanoi and Haiphong, and destroyed the enemy's sanctuaries in Laos and Cambodia. Others maintain that the United States should have blockaded North Vietnamese ports and/or concentrated its armed forces along the borders with Laos, Cambodia, and North Vietnam. Moves such as these, hawks argue, would have deprived the Vietcong of supplies and of additional North Vietnamese manpower.

Because efforts of such magnitude—South Vietnam's borders with Cambodia, Laos, and North Vietnam were nearly a thousand miles long—were not seriously considered by the Johnson administration, let alone tried, it is impossible to prove that the hawks were wrong. But most historians have concluded that the American people, who increasingly turned against the war after 1966, would not have supported such vast ventures. Historians also agree that the odds for military victory, given the unyielding determination of the enemy, were extraordinarily dim. The United States escalated enormously during Johnson's presidency, until there were more than 550,000 American soldiers in Vietnam in early 1969, with nothing of substance to show for the bloodshed that they inflicted and which they suffered themselves.

Advocates of greater escalation sometimes tend to downplay another relevant problem: the sad state of South Vietnam. By June 1965, corruption and mismanagement had sapped the spirit of its government. Its military forces had been battered. Ky and Thieu, who took over thereafter, were far from popular. If massive military escalation were somehow to succeed in ousting the enemy from most of South Vietnam—an enormous "if"—substantial American occupation forces would presumably have had to remain to rebuild the country and preserve the peace. They would also have had to help millions of refugees who had been uprooted from their homes. How long would the American people have been willing to support the costly and complicated process of what in more recent years has been called "nation building"?[50]

Arguments about the answers to such questions may never end. Nor will debates over the wisdom of Johnson's handling of the war. Admittedly, his room for maneuver was far more limited by early 1965 than it had been for President Kennedy. Trapped by the course of events, LBJ had no easy options. But from the beginning of his presidency, he had made it clear to top advisers that he would not be the president to "lose" Vietnam. In 1964 he raised America's troop strength in South Vietnam from sixteen thousand to twenty-three thousand. From Pleiku onward, he chose to escalate, and in July 1965 he put in his "stack." From then on, it was Johnson's war. If Pleiku was one of the pivotal moments when the Sixties began, then July 28, 1965, was when some of the most divisive characteristics of that turbulent era—social fragmentation and political polarization—became all but inevitable.

11

VIOLENCE IN THE STREETS

Watts and the Undermining of Liberalism

AMERICANS WHO TUNED IN TO CBS ON THE EVENING OF AUGUST 5 had no reason to think they would see gripping footage of the Vietnam War. By then, the TV networks were devoting a fair amount of air time to coverage of the conflict. But most of the coverage had been brief, and it had hardly been hostile to the administration. The anchor for *CBS Evening News*, Walter Cronkite, maintaining a pose of impartiality on the air, was at that time privately sympathetic to the US effort. But viewers were in for a shock that evening. CBS correspondent Morley Safer and his camera crew featured footage in which a calm and collected American marine took out his Zippo cigarette lighter and, ignoring the pleas of an elderly and anguished peasant woman, set fire to thatched huts in the South Vietnamese village of Cam Ne. Fire from lighters and flamethrowers soon burned down some 150 dwellings, destroying the village. Safer, who was standing in front of the burning huts, stated, "This is what the war in Vietnam is all about."

The CBS correspondent explained that the marines, believing that the villagers had been aiding the Vietcong, had retaliated by wounding three women, killing one baby, and taking four old men as prisoners. "There is little doubt," Safer reported, "that American firepower can win a battle here. But to a Vietnamese peasant whose house has meant a life of backbreaking labor, it will take more than presidential promises to convince him that we are on his side."[1]

CBS received a barrage of calls from disbelieving viewers, some of whom, accusing CBS of lying, insisted that what they had seen could not possibly have taken place. But many others who saw the footage came to understand that it was a shockingly succinct visual depiction of why the United States would never "win" in Vietnam. As a Pentagon colonel explained, "The trouble is that in this kind of war you don't know the VC from the civilians. . . . You've got to drop grenades into caves or tunnels and you can't always know there are some babies in them."[2]

When Johnson heard about the footage, he was incensed. Privately he accused Safer, a Canadian, of being a communist. That night he woke up Frank Stanton, the president of CBS, to vent. "Frank," he roared, "are you trying to fuck me? . . . Your boys shat on the American flag." He demanded to know how CBS could "employ a Communist like Safer, how could they be so unpatriotic as to put on an enemy film like this?"[3]

This was classic Johnson—lightning quick to learn of media reports, to question the patriotism of people (like Safer) who annoyed him, and to think nothing of rousing a corporate executive from his sleep and berating him. His reaction showed how tense he continued to be following his announcement of escalation on July 28. Though the networks did not run reportage anywhere near as critical as Safer's later that year, LBJ's relations with the media, long since testy, continued to deteriorate.

Insofar as Vietnam was concerned, however, Johnson need not have worried too much in early August. Having announced his decision to escalate, he was pleased to note that the Dow Industrial Index, which had lagged a bit in recent weeks, did not fall. On the contrary, it gained thereafter. LBJ was especially gratified to learn from polls that some two-thirds of the American people were still behind him.[4]

The president also had defenders in the media. When Lippmann, still hammering away at him, criticized him for "pretending to profess that we can be the policeman of the world," a *New York Herald Tribune* editorial immediately rebutted him. "For better or worse," it said, "the U.S. is the 'policeman' on which the threatened people in China's expansionist path depend for whatever hope they have of independence and freedom."[5]

Johnson also knew that Congress, unwilling to "desert the boys," would support his requests for money to back the troops and that it would respond negatively to vehement antiwar protests. When antiwar protestors here and there began burning their draft cards that August (few had done so before then), he asked for a law to deter the practice. Congress responded immediately, approving a bill that made burning draft cards a federal offense punishable by fines of up to $10,000 and five years in prison. LBJ signed it on August 31.[6]

Congress also continued to support LBJ's domestic agenda. Having recently enacted Medicare and the Voting Rights Act, it pressed onward without protest. On August 3, the House Judiciary Committee approved LBJ's bill to liberalize the immigration system, 27–4. On August 10, the Senate confirmed his nomination of Thurgood Marshall as solicitor general. All indications were that Congress, providing butter as well as guns, would support Great Society bills still under consideration.

On August 11, the day after Marshall was confirmed, however, an especially damaging blow to liberal dreams occurred: a huge racial disturbance in Watts, a large black neighborhood in south central Los Angeles, broke out only five days after LBJ had signed the Voting Rights Act and lasted six days and nights. The destruction and its political aftershocks demoralized Johnson and left the once proud and luminously effective civil rights movement in a state of disarray from which it never recovered.

———

THE TROUBLE IN WATTS STARTED, AS IT OFTEN DID IN URBAN racial disturbances during the 1960s, with a confrontation between white police and black residents. At seven PM on August 11, a hot and humid evening, a twenty-one-year-old black man, Marquette Frye, was pulled over for drunk driving. His detainment was routine (he later pleaded guilty and paid a fine), but he resisted arrest. His brother, a passenger, and his mother, who lived nearby, rushed to help him. Additional police officers, having been called as backup, used batons to subdue and arrest all three.

Soon a rapidly growing crowd of Watts-area black people was surrounding the scene. As they watched the struggle, someone grumbled, "It's just like Selma." One of the policemen then felt someone spit on him; a seemingly pregnant black woman was identified as the culprit and dragged into a squad car. Infuriated, the crowd erupted by pelting the police with bricks, stones, and bottles.[7]

To avoid provoking more unrest, the Los Angeles police withdrew from the area. But that night and into the early morning angry blacks— mostly young men—set about looting and setting fires to buildings. Some chanted, "Burn, baby, burn!" The next day, violence escalated. Some blacks stoned white firefighters who were trying to douse fires. Others threw stones at white motorists, dragged them from their cars and beat them, or struggled physically with police.

Late on the morning of the thirteenth, Glenn Anderson, California's lieutenant governor (the governor, Pat Brown, was out of the country) authorized the dispatch of national guardsmen to reinforce the police. By early the next morning, more than three thousand were on hand, but by then the business district of Watts had become so devastated that onlookers called it "Charcoal Alley." It was not until August 16, by which time there were more than thirteen thousand guardsmen in Watts—an astonishingly high number—that the worst of the disturbances abated.

But the destruction that had occurred between August 11 and 16 was staggering. Thirty-four people were killed; some 1,000 were reported injured. A total of 3,438 adults and 524 youths were arrested. The damage, which affected nearly 1,000 buildings, was estimated at $40 million. On August 16, the *Los Angeles Times* described Watts as a "holocaust of rubble and ruins not unlike the aftermath in London when the Nazis struck, or Berlin after Allies forces finished their demolition."[8]

As MANY COMMENTATORS NOTED AT THE TIME, WATTS SEEMED AN unlikely place for a massive urban disturbance. *Newsweek* wrote, "To a Harlem Negro oppressed by moldering tenements, Watts might look like the promised land with its wide boulevards, grassy back yards, and single- and two-story houses."[9] Palm trees lined some of the streets; there were nine public swimming pools in the area. Black officeholders in Los Angeles included a congressman, two assemblymen, and three city councilors. African Americans held a quarter of the jobs in county government.[10]

And yet Watts was hardly a promised land. It was a black ghetto where some 250,000 people were forced to reside because whites would not tolerate them in their own neighborhoods. Four times as many people per square block lived in Watts as in the rest of the city. More than 30 percent of its black male adults were unemployed. Rising numbers of unmarried young women and their children were trying to make do on welfare. Because the mayor of Los Angeles, Sam Yorty, was feuding with the OEO over administration of antipoverty money, $20 million in federal funding had not reached the city. Los Angeles officials, ignoring complaints by black residents about the brutality of police, had admitted few blacks to the city's force of 8,000 officers. No black cop had a rank above sergeant. Of the 205 policemen assigned to Watts, 200 were white.[11]

All these problems fed the rage that gripped many residents of the area. Indeed, the rebelliousness of black city-dwellers, as the rising appeal of Malcolm X had shown, ran wide as well as deep throughout the United States. It stemmed not only from poverty, overcrowding, and racial discrimination but also from the higher expectations that the civil rights movement had helped to excite by 1965. As Johnson himself had pointed out in his address at Howard University in June, black Americans in the cities had become painfully aware of the ease of life that whites all around them were enjoying and therefore of their own relative deprivation. As LBJ had added, they were yearning for equality not just "as a right and a theory but equality as a fact and a result."[12]

So profound was the anger of blacks in Watts that peacemakers who tried to reason with the activists had little success. One was Martin Luther King, who interrupted a holiday to fly to Los Angeles.

Arriving when the troubles had subsided, he addressed a neighborhood association meeting, only to be greeted in part with derision. "Sending King down here ain't nuthin', man," an onlooker muttered. "But goddammit they better do something down here, brother, or next time it won't be a riot. It'll be a war." Another black man agreed, "Aw, they're just sending another nigger down here to tell us what we need." A third man mocked King, chanting, "'I had a dream, I had a dream'—hell, we don't need no dreams. We want jobs."[13]

Reactions such as these made it obvious to King that the rage of black Americans in the cities had reached a boiling point while he had been fighting against racism, Southern-style, in Selma. As he put the matter, "'I worked to get these people the right to eat hamburgers, and now I've got to do something . . . to help them get the money to buy [them].'"[14] James Farmer, national director of CORE, agreed with King. He conceded, "Civil rights organizations have failed. No one had any roots in the ghetto." Bayard Rustin added, "We must hold ourselves responsible for not reaching them. . . . We've done plenty to get votes in the South and seats in the lunchrooms, but we've had no programs for these youngsters."[15]

Johnson at first responded to the troubles in Watts with a mixture of disbelief, rage, and self-pity. On the second day of the disturbances, he had flown to his ranch in Texas for rest and relaxation. As the burning and looting escalated, Joseph Califano, a top aide for the coordination of domestic policies, called him from Washington for instructions. For more than two days, however, Johnson did not answer the phone. "He just wouldn't accept it," Califano recalled. "He refused to look at . . . the situation."[16] When LBJ at last answered one of Califano's calls, he showed that the disturbances had hurt him personally. "How is it possible? After all we've accomplished? How can it be?" Repeating an ugly rumor that had circulated among Southern whites during the Reconstruction era, he predicted that blacks were going to "end up pissing in the aisles of the Senate." Betraying his crisis-driven suspiciousness that communist elements were at work, he ordered an investigation into whether a "Communist conspiracy" was behind the rioting. He also told Califano to be sure that Governor Brown did not allow Ronald Reagan, then preparing to run against Brown for governor in 1966, to "make political hay out of the riots."[17]

A little later, Johnson calmed down enough to authorize $29 million in emergency aid for Watts residents.[18] But he recognized, as did civil rights leaders, that such a modest amount of money would do little to assuage the anger—or significantly improve the situation—of blacks in the area. And he remained furious. On August 19, he stated publicly, "A rioter with a Molotov cocktail in his hands is not fighting for civil rights any more than a Klansman with a sheet on his back and a mask on his face. They are both . . . lawbreakers, destroyers of constitutional rights and liberties, and ultimately destroyers of a free America."[19]

The next day, he engaged in a lengthy phone conversation with King, who—still shaken by what he had seen—spoke of the "risk of full-scale war." "So now what should we *do* about it?" LBJ demanded. King spoke of the need to "get this poverty program going in Los Angeles." "We'll get at it," Johnson promised. Conveying an understanding of ghetto life, he also told King, "There's no use giving lectures on the law as long as you've got rats eating on people's children, and unemployed, and no roof over their head, no job to go to, and maybe with a dope needle in one side and a cancer in the other."[20]

LBJ's anguish was understandable: after all, no twentieth-century American president had done more for civil rights. But his anger was visceral and, as in his reference to the KKK, extreme. As careful observers were to point out, neither outside agitators nor communists had caused the disturbances. Moreover, few of those who participated in the uprising were out of control. Even the burners and looters were for the most part selective, zeroing in on certain kinds of white-owned businesses and stores. Many structures—private homes, service stations, schools, libraries, and other public buildings—were left alone. And the blacks involved were not killers: of the thirty-four people who lost their lives, only five were white.[21]

Nevertheless, millions of white Americans shared Johnson's fury at the rebels. Thanks to nearly round-the-clock television coverage of the action, some of it filmed by helicopters, they had been mesmerized by the "orgies," as many commentators called them, of looting and burning. They had heard the cry "Burn, baby, burn!" Many whites wondered whether conspirators with a revolutionary political agenda were staging an insurrection. Others denounced the burners and looters as lowlifes. Governor Brown blamed the troubles on "a hoodlum gang element that took advantage of a situation." Oscar Handlin, a Pulitzer Prize–winning social historian at Harvard, echoed Brown, branding the rioters as "disorderly elements taking advantage of an occasion for looting."[22]

Many other white Americans, including liberals who had vigorously supported civil rights, rejected the idea that Watts was a left-wing conspiracy or that lowlifes had spearheaded the violence. They understood that blacks in ghettos such as Watts had legitimate grievances. But they also sensed that a pivotal change was taking place. As Charles Silberman, a perceptive observer of racial trends, was soon to observe, a "taboo" that had long restrained the rage of African Americans was disappearing. Silberman reminded his readers of a five-line poem penned twenty-three years earlier by the black writer Langston Hughes. Negroes, Hughes had written, were mostly docile and unthreatening. But Americans must beware the day when they change their minds and begin to fight for their rights.[23]

Silberman was correct. As Hughes had predicted, many black Americans were changing their minds, and they would no longer be docile. Outraged by the persistence of racism, they were also tiring of what they had come to identify as the patronizing stance of white liberals. They were losing faith in the nonviolent, interracial strategies that had dominated civil rights activism during the early 1960s. Some, as in Watts, were reacting violently. Others were determined to oust whites from major roles in civil rights organizations and to take control of fights for equality and justice.

Many of the rebels in Watts recognized that acts of violence would deprive them of the moral high ground that the nonviolent movement had so richly earned. But with their expectations whetted, they were eager, as Malcolm X had demanded, to be heard. One man boasted, "We won, because we made the whole world listen to us." Like many others in the freedom struggle, he believed that black people should take command of their own destinies. Moynihan later put the matter in a slightly different way, noting that long-suffering black people had ceased to act as "victims." He added, however, that after Watts, "the black urban population became, in effect, an aggressor."[24]

—

SUBSEQUENT SURVEYS CONCERNING WATTS MANAGED TO CONVEY the depth of urban black rebelliousness. Ramsey Clark, a liberal who was then LBJ's deputy attorney general, headed one of the investigations, a task force that reported back to LBJ. After talking at length to black people in Watts, Clark and others in his group told the president that poverty, unemployment, racial discrimination, and excesses by white police had caused the troubles. The government, Clark urged, should seek a massive public jobs program.[25] LBJ, however, rejected suggestions that whites were primarily to blame for what had happened; as during the formation of the War on Poverty in 1964, he rejected the idea of a large-scale federal employment effort. Instead, he looked forward to the report of a commission he had encouraged Governor Brown to set up in the immediate aftermath of the disturbances. Its head, as Johnson had urged, was John McCone, who had been director of the CIA until Raborn replaced him before the late-April rebellion in the Dominican Republic.

The 101-page McCone Commission report, issued in December, paid considerable attention to the disorienting results of mass migrations of blacks to the Los Angeles area over the previous several decades. Many Negroes who had arrived, it argued, had not adjusted satisfactorily to the difficult challenges of urban life. The commission also cited a number of socioeconomic woes: high unemployment, overcrowded housing, failing schools, and the like. It called for creation of a City Human Relations Commission that would fight against "prejudice and discrimination in employment, housing, education, and public accommodations." The report was prescient, warning that the troubles in Watts "may seem by comparison to be only a curtain raiser for what could blow up in the future."[26]

But the McCone Commission report also noted the destructive role of "riffraff," and it reprimanded black leaders who shouldered no personal responsibility for the outbreak. Critics complained that it paid more attention to poverty than to racism. Worst of all, many critics observed, the report avoided focusing on the LAPD, whose tough-minded chief, William Parker, had rejected charges of police brutality and had been outspoken in his denunciation of black participants in the disturbances.[27] For all these reasons, the McCone Commission report was hardly regarded by black Americans as the last word on a very controversial subject.

———

WELL BEFORE THE RELEASE OF THE McCONE REPORT IN DECEMBER, it had also become obvious that the rebellion in Watts had transformed the attitudes of millions of white Americans, thereby damaging chances for improvements in race relations. A Gallup poll in September showed that 88 percent of whites, asked how blacks might improve their situations, favored self-improvement, more education, and harder work, as opposed to help from the government.[28] More ominous was a rising white backlash, which was surging to the surface, especially in working-class areas close to black neighborhoods.[29] Hopes that large numbers of whites would continue to engage in interracial cooperation, such as the efforts that had led to the widely applauded Voting Rights Act, seemed doomed.

As Johnson had indicated in his conversation with King, he still hoped that governmental action might alleviate America's racial tensions. "It is not enough," he said in the aftermath of Watts, "simply to decry disorder. We must also strike at the unjust conditions from which disorder largely flows." But the rampaging in Watts continued to discourage him. He told an aide, "I have moved the Negro from D+ to C-. He's still nowhere. He knows it. And that's why he's out on the streets. Hell, I'd be there, too."[30]

Johnson nonetheless lowered his sights. Between mid-August and mid-September he made three moves to indicate he was following a more modest agenda. The first followed on leaks to the public in early August of snippets from Moynihan's in-house report, *The Negro Family: The Case for National Action*, which had been the basis for LBJ's inspirational talk at Howard University. Once leaked, the study became known as the Moynihan Report. Some of the civil rights leaders who read or heard about the document knew that Moynihan, having called for "National Action" to confront race-based economic injustice, was on their side. Others, however, were angry that he had written frankly and unflatteringly about a "tangle of pathology" ensnaring black families in the ghettos. By September many black leaders—and white liberals—were beginning to denounce the report.

LBJ, too, backed away from the report, fearing to associate himself with anything that would further damage his already deteriorating relationships with black leaders. In this spirit—and because he was absorbed by events in Vietnam—LBJ retreated from his promise at Howard University to call a large-scale White House conference in the fall to promote socioeconomic equality for black Americans.[31] Instead, he ordered that the conference be downgraded to a relatively small planning meeting. The larger convocation he had promised would not take place until June 1966. Moynihan, deeply upset, complained of Johnson's coolness: "If my head were sticking on a pike at the South-West Gate to the White House grounds, the impression [of LBJ's hostility] would hardly be greater."[32] Black leaders, worrying that LBJ was abandoning his quest to promote black equality, grew especially discouraged.

LBJ's second move was to humiliate Vice President Humphrey, who until then had served as chief administration liaison with civil rights leaders. Humphrey, he thought, had been too solicitous of black demands. So the president handed the management of important civil rights matters to the Department of Justice and other departments and agencies. He managed the switch with characteristic stealth and swiftness, informing Humphrey of his demotion only after it had been accomplished. He even managed to get Humphrey to sign a memo in which the vice president recommended his own removal. Califano, who had the task of overseeing the reassignment, wrote later that Humphrey was staggered at the news. "He knew he had just been castrated."[33]

The president's third move was to declare a "war on crime." In late September while signing a bill that Congress had just enthusiastically enacted, the Law Enforcement Assistance Act, Johnson declared, "I will not be satisfied until every woman and child in this nation can walk any street, enjoy any park, drive on any highway, and live in any community at any time of the day or night without fear of being harmed." The law resulted in creation of yet another Johnson-era bureaucracy, the Office of Law Enforcement and Assistance, which would gather data and recommend federal responses to the crime issue.

The anticrime act was not a direct result of Watts. Rates of violent crime (thanks in part to the coming-of-age of millions of boomers) had been slowly rising since 1964, and LBJ had called for such a statute in March 1965. But it was evident from the bellicose comments of congressmen, senators, and editorialists, as well as from LBJ's grandiloquent statement, that popular as well as presidential concerns about "crime on the streets" had expanded considerably since the explosion in Watts.[34]

—

IN 1967, MOYNIHAN PUBLISHED A WIDELY NOTED ARTICLE, "THE President and the Negro: The Moment Lost."[35] As the subtitle indicated, it bewailed the chain of events—highlighted by Watts and negative reactions to his report—that in the late summer of 1965 had transformed the politics of race in the United States. His melancholy was understandable, for the river of progress toward greater racial equality, which had seemed broad and smooth after Johnson's speech at Howard in June, had become choked with obstacles by the fall of 1965.

In hindsight, however, Moynihan's argument needs tweaking. It was far from clear, even before Watts, how America might surmount the barriers that blocked the path toward racial equality. Recognizing how little policymakers knew at the time, Moynihan himself had avoided making specific recommendations in his report. He had hoped that the late 1965 conference of experts and civil rights leaders might begin to come up with answers.

An especially strong barrier to progress for black Americans, of course, was the abiding strength of white racism, highly visible manifestations of which were de facto segregated schools and housing. Another barrier was the high incidence of black out-of-wedlock childbearing that the Moynihan report documented. This incidence skyrocketed within the next few years, rising from 23.6 percent of all black births in 1963 to 38 percent by 1970 and to 70 percent by the 1990s.

A third obstacle—the most widely discussed racial problem—was the high incidence of black unemployment, which continued to be more than twice that of whites, and the level of poverty, which was more than three times as high. In 1965, 45.4 percent of blacks were still living in poverty (compared to 13.2 percent of whites).[36] The linkage of high rates of black poverty and unemployment to a host of social problems afflicting African Americans—fatherless families, dropping out of school, juvenile delinquency, crime, and drug abuse—had a long history, and the connections would persist into the twenty-first century: forty-five years after the Moynihan report, in 2010, the official poverty rate for blacks was 27 percent, roughly three times the 9.9 percent rate for non-Hispanic whites. The black unemployment rate in 2011 was 16.7 percent, for whites 8 percent.

This is a familiar litany of miseries. But as Moynihan and others recognized, the sources of racial inequality were not only deep and enduring but also interrelated in tangled and complicated ways that needed careful and concentrated study. Moreover, neither then nor later have solutions to these ills secured reliable political support.

One solution, often favored by Moynihan, was to establish massive government jobs programs. But these are necessarily very expensive and difficult to set up, and skeptics, including some liberals, have consistently challenged their potential effectiveness. What sort of jobs might be created? Would government-sponsored job training programs, which have also been described as expensive and unproductive, enable ill-educated young people—often school dropouts—to qualify for them? What effect would federal employment programs have on workers and employers in the private marketplace? Many white Americans, having little confidence in the work ethic of low-income black people, wonder why taxpayers should finance programs for a particular group of people they believe were just "sitting around."

Even in 1965, an extraordinarily prosperous year, it was unclear whether the economy was robust enough to enable every able-bodied, decently educated, and ambitious American to secure living-wage work, especially because huge numbers of boomers were coming of age and moving into the workforce. By the 1970s, when the economy began to slump, it became ever more obvious that the marketplace could not be relied on to provide a good job to everyone who needed one. Troubles besetting America's manufacturing sector, which had historically offered the best-paying jobs for blue-collar folk, became increasingly serious after the mid-1960s.[37]

Efforts to improve the welfare system, another goal on the list of reformers, have also encountered formidable political difficulties. Many Americans have blanched at the thought of using tax money to aid large numbers of women who have one or more children out of wedlock. If the mothers are required to work in order to qualify for assistance (as has normally been the case since a federal welfare "reform" bill that passed in 1996), they are likely, even with training, to be unqualified for anything but very low-paying jobs. And who would pay for child care? For these and other reasons, Califano later grumbled that welfare reform was the "Middle East of domestic politics" in the United States.

A frequently stated answer to the plight of low-income people, including blacks, has been to improve public education. That is why Johnson, a passionate advocate of better schooling, had pushed through the Elementary and Secondary Education Act in April 1965. But it has long since become evident that the cognitive difficulties of lower-class black children—millions of whom grow up in fatherless, poverty-stricken homes and crime-ridden neighborhoods—are large, compared to those of most white children, even before they enter kindergarten. Narrowing the test-score gap between blacks and whites has regularly frustrated reformers.

In short, Moynihan's argument that a "moment" for seriously addressing black problems was "lost" in the summer of 1965 is unverifiable. Still, Watts was a disastrously consequential event in American history. Aside from the escalation in Vietnam, no occurrence that year did more to damage American race relations or to undermine the power of Johnsonian liberalism in the United States. The angry, contentious Sixties were surely arriving.

12

EVE OF DESTRUCTION
The Rise of Unease

IT HAD BEEN A HISTORIC THREE WEEKS. ON JULY 28, LBJ HAD announced a large and irrevocable escalation in Vietnam. On the thirtieth, he signed the Medicare/Medicaid act. On August 6, the voting rights bill became law. On the eleventh, rebellion erupted in Watts, lasting until the sixteenth. These were the most consequential days of 1965, the inaugural year of the Sixties.

No event during the next two and a half months set off such turmoil. Signs of cultural discord, however, were appearing in popular music. The nation's politics was beginning to polarize. The liberal consensus that had been impregnable at the start of the year mostly held together in Congress but seemed a little more fragile than it had been. America's "Golden Era," predicted by *Time* at the start of 1965, was fading away.

——

UNTIL MID-SEPTEMBER, THERE SEEMED TO BE LITTLE TO INDICATE that military escalation and Watts were dramatically affecting American cultural life. Summertime readers, for instance, were still buying big-selling books published earlier in the year, as well as some (like Saul Bellow's *Herzog*) that had first appeared in late 1964. Easy (though lengthy) reads like James Michener's *The Source* and Arthur Hailey's *Hotel* continued to ride high on fiction best-seller lists.

Joining them by late August were many popular works of non-fiction, notably Theodore White's widely praised *The Making of the President, 1964*. Offering a positive account of Johnson's defeat of Goldwater, it especially appealed to liberals. Well-regarded new fiction included John le Carré's spy novel *The Looking Glass War*. Most notable, however, was Robin Moore's best-selling *The Green Berets*, a book of fiction that celebrated the derring-do of America's Green Beret soldiers in Vietnam. Moore, who had taken Special Forces guerrilla warfare courses, had gone to Vietnam in 1963 as an accredited correspondent. Action-packed heroism no doubt accounted for the book's popularity—it was one of the top five fiction sellers of the year in the United States. But the success of *The Green Berets* may also have been a sign that many Americans, having become uneasy with the course of events in Vietnam, were looking for reasons to be reassured about the war.

Moviegoers and television watchers, as earlier in the year, encountered little that was in any way startling or avant-garde. Feel-good films that had premiered earlier in the year, notably *The Sound of Music*, continued to pack theaters. Young people flocked to watch the Beatles' movie *Help!* as well as *How to Stuff a Wild Bikini*, which was yet another in a series of "beach party" films starring Frankie Avalon and Annette Funicello. Many widely watched television shows from 1964—*Bonanza* (still the top-drawing show), *Gilligan's Island*, *The Beverly Hillbillies*, *Bewitched*—returned for the coming season. *The Ed Sullivan Show* and *The Dick Van Dyke Show* continued to captivate millions of viewers.

A record number of new prime-time programs struggled to compete with these standbys, but the only one to break new ground was *I Spy*, which featured Robert Culp playing a talented traveling tennis player and Bill Cosby acting as his trainer. In fact, the duo were undercover government agents who globe-trotted to exotic locales, exchanging hip banter as they solved cases. Cosby was the first African American actor to have a leading role in a prime-time show, and his character was a far cry from the standard stereotypes of the past. A Rhodes scholar, he was master of many languages. He did not smoke, drink, or chase women. None of his banter concerned race. As a talented actor and nonthreatening African American, Cosby was a success, and the program, highly regarded by critics, lasted for three seasons.[1]

The popular music scene, having embraced electric rock in a major way by July, continued to feature stars such as Bob Dylan ("Like a Rolling Stone") and the Rolling Stones, whose "(I Can't Get No) Satisfaction" remained a hit in August and September. Meanwhile, at the Matrix nightclub in San Francisco, a new group, Jefferson Airplane, received local notice. Though they were far from headliners at that time, later in the decade they became famous as pioneers of a psychedelic rock movement that captivated many young people.[2]

Stars such as Dylan and Mick Jagger shared the spotlight with pop singers who were considerably less ground-breaking. Starting on August 14, "I Got You Babe" by the newcomers Sonny (age twenty-five) and his wife, Cher (age nineteen), topped the charts for three weeks. One critic praised them as "the reigning sweethearts of folk rock."[3] Other hit tunes like "I'm Henry VIII, I Am," by Herman's Hermits, and "California Girls," by the Beach Boys, beguiled devoted followings.

In mid-September, however, a breakthrough rock song, "Eve of Destruction," shook up the popular music scene, thereby suggesting that the cultural unease intensified by escalation and Watts was spreading among the young. Written primarily by P. F. Sloan, a nineteen-year-old admirer of Dylan's "Like a Rolling Stone," the song featured vocalist Barry McGuire, who had previously been a lead singer for the New Christy Minstrels. McGuire, recording hurriedly, did not even finish the vocals on the instrumental track, and "Eve of Destruction," only three minutes long, was a rough mix when it appeared on the radio. Still, it became a mini-sensation, zooming up the Top 40 singles charts in late summer and peaking at number 1 on September 25. Sung in a raspy, brooding manner, it had none of the good cheer of a Beatles ballad. On the contrary, its lyrics, accompanied by sounds of bombs going off, were bitter, blunt, and devastatingly bleak about contemporary events, predicting that all manner of terrible developments—war in Vietnam, racial tensions, nuclear weapons—were propelling the United States (and "the whole crazy world") toward the apocalypse. How, McGuire asked, could people be so naïve as to believe that they were not on the "eve of destruction?"

Reactions to the song varied. The United States, after all, remained a nation in which pop music fans, like the population at large, were divided along lines of age, race, ethnicity, religion, region, and social class: sweeping generalizations about the impact of Top 40 music and about the "Boomer Generation" were often inapt. *Time*'s response was nonetheless characteristic of many. "Eve of Destruction," it wrote, was "big-beat music with big-message lyrics" that heralded a very different genre: "the rallying cry is no longer, 'I wanna hold your hand,' but 'I wanna change the world.'"[4]

Other listeners, outraged, reacted with hostility. Many stations banned the song, and others played it only infrequently. The Christian Anti-Communist Crusade, a right-wing student group, announced that "Eve of Destruction" was "obviously aimed at instilling fear in our teenagers as well as a sense of hopelessness," thereby helping to "induce the American public to surrender to atheistic international Communism."[5]

"Eve of Destruction" remained high on the singles charts for a substantial time—for eight weeks within the top twenty.[6] Thereafter it competed with apolitical fare, notably "Yesterday" by the Beatles, "Get Off My Cloud" by the Rolling Stones, and "I Hear a Symphony" by the Supremes, all of which rose to number 1 soon afterward. It probably did not change many opinions—rather, like many protest songs, it likely reinforced the views of listeners who were already prepared to endorse its politics. And a number of music critics dismissed it. One observed later that it is best remembered for its "easy beat and puerile discontent." Another wrote of its "bathetic pastiche."[7]

Fans of the song, of course, could not have cared less about critical reviews. And even while it was slowly slipping down the list of top tunes, "Eve of Destruction" prompted emulation: Phil Ochs and Judy Collins soon brought out electrically amplified versions of protest songs. "Eve" continued to appeal to millions of Americans, especially youth, who (remembering Selma, which was mentioned in the song) were angry about racism, worried about nuclear annihilation, and outraged by the escalation in Vietnam.

For these reasons, "Eve of Destruction" has continued to be accorded a significant place in the history of popular music in the 1960s. One historian later wrote that it was a marriage of rock and protest that extended the range of lyrical dissatisfaction beyond that of generational conflict and "exploded the 'art is a weapon' ethos upon the Top Forty." Todd Gitlin agreed, noting later that "Eve" "seemed to certify that a mass movement of American young was upon us."[8]

———

NONE OF THESE CULTURAL DEVELOPMENTS AFFECTED PRESIDENT Johnson, who rarely read a book, viewed a new movie, went to a sports event, listened to pop music, or watched much of anything on television aside from political news. He remained dismissive of just about everything that youthful protestors did. "Don't pay attention to what those little shits on the campuses do," he told George Ball. "The great beast is the reactionary elements in the country. Those are the people that we have to fear."[9]

But LBJ did have to tend to a few troublesome domestic developments in August and September 1965. For the first time that year, he had to pay serious attention to the state of the economy. In almost all respects, it was continuing to thrive. The Dow Industrial Index climbed to 942.5, a record high, in mid-October. Inflationary pressures, however, were slowly mounting. Most of these stemmed from the rise in government spending, especially for the war. But pressures also arose from below, where rights-conscious yearnings were continuing to lift popular expectations among different sectors of working people. Even as the disturbances in Watts were quieting down, steel workers threatened to strike unless they received a significant raise in pay. Company executives balked, arguing that for some time they had been facing intense price competition from overseas producers.

Johnson hoped to avoid a strike as well as a settlement that would lead to increases in steel prices. Such a result, he knew, would snowball and affect the economy at large. When neither side budged, he directly intervened in late August, ordering negotiations to move to the Executive Office Building next to the White House. Thanks in large part to LBJ's "jawboning," as reporters called his subsequent efforts, the pact that resulted on September 3 was noninflationary. But pressures for wage and price increases persisted, as did the threat of inflation in the longer run.[10] How long, uneasy economists were wondering, would the booming economy last?

Labor-management conflict led to strikes in two other areas of the economy in September. These, too, revealed the presence of economic antagonisms. The first broke out in Delano, California, on September 8, when Filipino grape pickers struck, demanding wages of $1.40 per hour. (They were then working ten-hour days and earning $1.25 an hour.) A week later, Cesar Chavez, a thirty-eight-year-old farmworker, labor leader, and civil rights activist who headed the predominantly Mexican American National Farm Workers Association, enthusiastically backed the strike action.[11]

"La Huelga," as Mexican Americans called the strike, gradually spread, dramatizing the hitherto little-noticed miseries of farm laborers. Protests in October resulted in the arrest of workers seeking union recognition. By December, some five thousand grape pickers were out on strike.[12] CORE and others urged a boycott of table grapes—a call that some Americans eventually heeded. The struggles of farmworkers lasted for years, helping to make Chavez, a charismatic figure, a nationally recognized spokesman for civil rights.[13]

The second strike in September hit the *New York Times* on the sixteenth, eight days after the grape pickers' walkout in Delano. The key dispute, which exposed the flip-side ramifications of technological progress in the 1960s, concerned automation. This was the same issue that had provoked a 114-day strike of typographers at six New York City papers, including the *New York Times*, in 1962–1963. The fight in 1965 broke out following computerization of some of the paper's departments. The New York Newspaper Guild, representing journalists, demanded assurances from management that the workers who would operate the computers would do so under Guild jurisdiction. But the *New York Times*, like other American newspapers, was facing worrisome developments, notably television and suburbanization, which were threatening its advertising revenue and circulation. When its owners refused to give in, the Guild unit at the paper called a strike. Journalists at nine other New York City newspapers—all but the *New York*

Post—refused to cross picket lines and joined in the action. Starting on September 17, millions of people (the daily circulation of the *Times* was 730,000) had to make do without their newspapers.[14]

When a settlement was reached more then three weeks later, the newspapers resumed publication. But no one was happy with the outcome. The Guild secured its short-term goal of gaining jurisdiction over newly automated workers, but its members were well aware that serious economic problems still confronted American newspapers. Nothing made this fact more clear than the collapse of the once proud *New York Herald Tribune* in 1966.

—

EXCEPT FOR THE STEEL INDUSTRY CONFLICT, THESE LABOR-management issues did not distract the administration. As earlier, President Johnson worried more at the time about other matters, notably reactions to his escalation of the war and fallout from the rebellion in Watts. Racial violence in the South, moreover, further angered civil rights activists. In late August, a white deputy sheriff shot-gunned to death a white Episcopal theology student, Jonathan Daniels, and seriously wounded a white Catholic priest, Richard Morrisroe, in Lowndes County near Selma. Daniels was helping with voter registration efforts at the time. An all-white jury that "deliberated" for an hour and nineteen minutes found the deputy sheriff not guilty.[15]

LBJ was relieved to discover, however, that Congress, though restive about events in Vietnam, would continue to support his domestic as well as his military agenda. In late August, the House approved a higher education bill that promised to provide $624.5 million a year for the next five years to help students needing financial aid to go to college. As passed in October by the full Congress—and as reauthorized in later years—it helped to promote enormous growth in college and university enrollments.[16] In late August, lawmakers also approved a measure that over the next five years would send $3.3 billion, a large sum, to so-called depressed areas.[17]

Congress continued to be cooperative in September. On the ninth LBJ signed into law a bill authorizing a new cabinet department, Housing and Urban Development. Twenty days later he approved a measure enabling the creation of the National Endowment for the Arts and National Endowment for the Humanities. It was the first time since the arts and writing projects of the New Deal that the federal government had intervened on a significant scale to enrich American cultural life.

No congressional action of the time, however, gave Johnson more pleasure than the late-September passage (by overwhelming margins in both houses of Congress) of immigration reform. Delighted, he once again resolved to make a big ceremony out of signing a bill into law. Standing in the shadow of the Statue of Liberty on October 3, he denounced America's existing immigration system, which since the 1920s had discriminated flagrantly and shamefully against Southern and Eastern Europeans and had virtually excluded Asians. That system, LBJ thundered, was "un-American in the highest sense . . . [and] untrue to the faith that brought thousands to these shores even before we were a country." "Today," he declared, "this system is abolished. We can now believe that it will never again shadow the gate to the American nation with the twin barriers of prejudice and privilege."[18]

Approval of immigration reform, a signal achievement that had long eluded Congress, demonstrated yet again the power of rights-based activism in American politics in 1965. Supporters of the law repeatedly hailed the civil rights movement as their inspiration for abolishing a racist system and for creating in its stead procedures that promised to be fair to would-be Americans throughout the world. Johnson's words, though characteristically high-flown, were accurate in placing the reform in the context of America's egalitarian values.

In hindsight, it is abundantly clear that the immigration act did not work out as anticipated. The framers of the 1965 bill, who established quotas for newcomers from the Eastern and Western hemispheres, did not think they were opening wide the gates. On the contrary, they estimated that the total number to be admitted in the future would be roughly 350,000 per year—or slightly more than the 270,000 who had arrived in 1964. But primarily because they did not foresee the way that would-be immigrants would manipulate complicated but permissive "family reunification" provisions of the law, they badly miscalculated. During the 1980s, by which time the flow of newcomers had surged, 7.26 million immigrants—an average of 726,000 per year—were accepted. A total of 9.1 million arrived in the 1990s. By then, immigration (made more controversial by illegal immigration) had become a hotly contested political issue in the United States.

It is easy to chastise the framers of the statute, the history of which has demonstrated with special clarity a truism of political science: many laws have large unintended consequences.[19] It is worth remembering, however, that the immigration act, by reflecting the equal-rights spirit of the mid-1960s, succeeded in accomplishing its primary goal: scuttling the racist and discriminatory policies that had existed for years.

It was therefore no wonder that LBJ exulted at the Statue of Liberty or that he continued to compare himself to FDR and boast of his successes with Congress. Roosevelt, he said a year later, "passed five major bills the first hundred days. We [Congress, under his guidance] passed 200 in the last two years. It is unbelievable. We must dramatize that."[20]

Many scholars and activists, then and later, have largely agreed with Johnson's own highly positive assessment of his domestic policy accomplishments, especially those in the unprecedentedly productive legislative year of 1965. Tom Wicker, a columnist for the *New York Times*, wrote at the time that the 1965 congressional session was "one of the most remarkable of this century."[21] William Leuchtenburg, a leading scholar of Roosevelt's New Deal, later compared Johnson's domestic policy record favorably with FDR's and concluded, "The country did not properly appreciate Lyndon Johnson."[22]

LBJ's legislative record in the vital area of civil rights is particularly strong. The historic acts of 1964 and 1965 not only transformed American race relations, but also avoided—unlike Great Society measures such as Medicare and immigration reform—major unforeseen consequences. Charles Mitchell, the NAACP's chief legislative lobbyist, observed later that LBJ "made a greater contribution to giving a dignified and hopeful status to Negroes in the United States than any President including Lincoln, Roosevelt, and Kennedy." According to Bayard Rustin, "The Johnson administration [did] more than any other group, any other administration. . . . I think Johnson was the best we've ever had."[23]

—

IN OCTOBER 1965 LBJ EXPERIENCED HEALTH PROBLEMS. FIVE DAYS after signing the immigration law, he entered Bethesda Naval Hospital to have his gall bladder removed. He told reporters, "A thorough examination showed this to be the only trouble." Following the operation, however, it was disclosed that physicians had also removed a kidney stone. After more questioning, doctors indicated that he had still another stone in his kidney, the existence of which had been known "for some years." Critics pointed to LBJ's less-than-candid description of his health as yet another example of his passion for secrecy and desire to deceive the press—traits that had already expanded the credibility gap afflicting his presidency.[24]

Recovering slowly, LBJ remained in the hospital for almost two weeks, leading to rumors that he had suffered a heart attack. To prove to reporters and photographers in front of the hospital that he was all right, he lifted his shirt to display his incision. When the photo appeared in the papers, however, it revived criticisms that he was crude. The incision later became famous. In May 1966, the caricaturist David Levine published a pen-and-ink drawing depicting a Pinocchio-nosed, long-eared, beady-eyed LBJ displaying his scar, the outline of which matched the boundaries of Vietnam. The drawing, widely reproduced, became an iconic symbol of LBJ's obsession with bombing maps and more broadly of his badly misguided Vietnam policies.[25]

Johnson, still depressed after leaving the hospital, grumbled privately, "What do they want—what *really* do they want? I'm giving them boom times and more good legislation than anybody else did, and what do they do?—attack and sneer! Could FDR do better? Could anybody do better? What do they want?"[26]

Worse, LBJ's magic touch with Congress was beginning to lose a little of its power. His hospitalization distracted him during the final two weeks of the session, but presidential aides also recognized that some legislators, tiring of executive pressure, were exhibiting greater independence. Though Congress approved clean-water and air-quality bill, these marked only the start of federal efforts to deal with serious national problems.[27] Following a successful filibuster by conservatives in the Senate, Congress refused to repeal Section 14(b) of the Taft-

Harley Act. Congress also failed to enact an increase in the federal minimum wage or to approve Johnson's request for a law that would advance the prospects for Home Rule for the citizens of the District of Columbia. Though it had earlier authorized federal rent subsidies enabling poor people to afford better housing, it rejected an appropriation bill that would have financed them.

Conservatives even weakened his proposal for highway beautification (described as "Lady Bird's bill"). The original legislation had proposed to slash federal highway funds in states that did not ban roadside billboards and exposed junkyards, but lobbying by billboard interests helped to frustrate the president's hopes. The final bill authorized the Commerce Department to cut only 10 percent of federal funding from states that did not cooperate with the guidelines.[28]

When Congress finally adjourned on October 23, LBJ wrote Mansfield to praise him for his leadership on the Hill but also to point to "23 major items of legislation" that remained to be enacted. Mansfield responded by cautioning the chief executive to concentrate on implementing the many laws that had been passed.[29] The majority leader was correct to believe that Congress was henceforth unlikely to respond with anything like the alacrity that it had displayed during the session of 1965. The high-water mark for postwar liberalism had crested in early August, never to rise again during Johnson's presidency. It was not long before a considerably more divided and disputatious politics—a hallmark of the Sixties—would surge into view.

Mansfield was also correct to call for careful implementation of the many laws that had been enacted. As Tom Wicker observed at the time, Congress had "poured more money, power, administrative responsibility, and opportunity into the hands of the already overburdened and over-muscled executive."[30] *Time* seconded Wicker. LBJ, it claimed, was a "box-score president": a man who excelled at pushing large quantities of measures through Congress but who was not so good at providing for their careful administration.[31] And Walter Lippmann, assessing "Johnson's 89th Congress" in the *Washington Post*, cautioned that the president's "dazzling record"—one that had "revolutionized [America's] domestic political life"—was as yet only a "series of promissory notes" that might or might not realize the "hopes of progressives in this century."[32]

Many later descriptions of LBJ's leadership have echoed these evaluations, correctly praising his energetic and skillful handling of Congress but lamenting the lofty rhetoric he used to get his programs through. In part because of his haste to outdo FDR, they emphasize, Johnson often resorted to oversell, thereby exciting expectations that could not be fulfilled. Pressing for the Elementary and Secondary Education Act, he had exclaimed that aid to education was the "only valid passport from poverty." To fight against poverty he had launched a "war"—one that Sargent Shriver proclaimed would wipe out destitution within ten years. Medicare/Medicaid, LBJ had said, would advance the "healing miracle of modern medicine." Voting rights represented the "most powerful instrument ever devised by men for breaking down injustice."

As the persistence after 1965 of social, educational, and racial problems was to demonstrate, these statements oversimplified the daunting complexity of key social issues, such as school reform and poverty, and underestimated the stubborn power of self-interested pressure groups and of attitudes, such as racism and popular distrust of Big Government. By 1965, many of America's domestic problems, having long been neglected, had worsened over time and had become resistant to idealistic social engineering—some of it hastily enacted—from Washington.

LBJ's oversell, combined with the extraordinary affluence of the country in the 1960s, also fed popular hopes and pressures—much of it from a proliferation of well-organized groups—for new and bigger governmental promises to be made and fulfilled. Millions of people, especially the young, were demanding more and more freedoms, rights, and entitlements. Many of these aspirations, as it turned out, were beyond the ability of policymakers to satisfy. As a result, even as rights-conscious advocates on the Left—notably blacks—were seeking more from government, others, mostly on the Right, were more loudly beginning to question the capacity of Washington to accomplish great and wonderful things. The political center, slowly being squeezed, was one of the many stabilizing forces that were to lose strength in the Sixties that followed.

13

FROM CRISIS TO CRISIS

The Great Society and the
Challenge of Government

THOUGH LBJ WAS BEGINNING TO EXPERIENCE PROBLEMS WITH Congress in late 1965, rising criticisms of programs he had already established revealed signs of larger troubles ahead. The institution of the Great Society led to serious questions: Was the growth of the federal government leading to bureaucratic deadlock and confusion, thereby calling into question the effectiveness of democratic government? And with Vietnam straining the nation's treasury, could America afford both guns and butter? Controversy in late 1965 over three such programs centered on questions such as these.

———

THE FIRST OF THE GREAT SOCIETY EFFORTS TO BECOME A MAJOR target of critics in late 1965 was the War on Poverty. Its director, Sargent Shriver, remained an evangelical spokesman for community action, the Job Corps, Head Start, Legal Services, VISTA, and other activities of the OEO. Keenly attuned to the desperation of many poor people in Watts, he urged LBJ in late October to support a mammoth increase in OEO funding—from $1.5 billion in fiscal 1966 to $9 billion for fiscal 1967, which would begin in July 1966. Much of the new money, he said, should support a public jobs program. If Johnson were to follow this route, America's skirmish against poverty might truly become a war.[1]

By late 1965, however, criticisms of the OEO that had spread during the spring had intensified. Many of these, as earlier, came from conservatives who renewed their argument that the OEO was incompetent.[2] *US News & World Report*, for instance, had headlined a story in late August, "Poverty War Out of Hand?" The OEO, it charged, was guilty of "administrative chaos, bureaucratic bungling, waste, extravagance, costly duplication of existing services, and internal squabbling." A photograph depicted a bunch of black workers lounging about at a Job Corps center.[3]

A cover story three weeks later in *Newsweek* was almost as harsh. It conceded that Shriver, renowned for his political skills with Congress, was adept at lobbying for money. But *Newsweek* asked a question that had already bothered others: Would the OEO succeed in actually creating jobs? Or reducing poverty? It also described the OEO's bureaucratic overlap, confusion, and lack of direction. "This place is an administrative shambles," an unnamed OEO official in Washington complained. "We operate from crisis to crisis. We're always in perpetual motion, but I'm not sure where we're going."[4]

As is often the case in politics, an especially contentious issue troubling the OEO by September 1965 involved the apportioning of power: Who would have ultimate control over how the money would be used? Shriver, of course, insisted that the OEO in Washington should. Many mayors and governors, however, sought this control for themselves. Elected officials, they argued, should have the right to run the programs and to veto OEO projects in their states.

A number of local officeholders also believed that Shriver, who continued to take seriously the ill-defined guideline that poor people should have "maximum feasible participation," was bankrolling militant groups—some of them led by radical black people—that were seeking to direct antipoverty programs in their cities. Sam Yorty, mayor of Los Angeles, was one of the most vocal critics. Leaders of antipoverty efforts, he insisted, should be "responsible to the electorate," by which he meant responsible to elected officials such as himself. His contention had led him in July to wage a political struggle with Shriver, who had retaliated by withholding funding for antipoverty efforts in LA. It was not until early September, after Watts had exploded, that a rough compromise (one that satisfied neither side) led to release of the money.[5]

This issue of how to direct the poverty effort also sparked a nasty struggle between Shriver and LBJ's budget director, Charles Schultze. Eager to ease tensions between the OEO and mayors, Schultze sent Johnson a memo. "*We ought not,*" he wrote on September 18, "*to be in the business of organizing the poor politically.*"[6] The OEO, he argued, should stop sponsoring so many local elections to poverty boards. Johnson penciled at the bottom of the memo, "O.K. I agree."

When Shriver heard about this, he vociferously objected. Soon the spat became public. Within a few weeks, the dispute died down, but LBJ had become so tired of the bickering—and unflattering publicity—that he directed Joseph Califano to look into dismantling OEO and moving its responsibilities to other departments and agencies within the government. These—notably Labor, HEW, Agriculture—would be delighted to expand their own operations. In December, Califano showed LBJ such a plan, along with a warning that it could be "the most politically explosive act the Administration could take, even though it makes administrative sense."[7]

After reflecting on the political perils of reorganization—Califano was right about these—LBJ did not follow up on the matter. Moreover, the official poverty rate was slowly declining, and though the decline stemmed mainly from growth in the overall economy, it offered the OEO some political cover. But the brawling between Schultze and Shriver was yet one more example of the political and bureaucratic infighting that was bedeviling the War on Poverty.

Infighting also did not help Shriver's case for a vast expansion of OEO activities in 1966. Johnson, never a fan of large and expensive public jobs programs, did not heed his pleas. Moreover, LBJ knew that spending for the Vietnam War would swallow up ever-larger sums of federal money, leaving little for expansion of the Great Society. Whether the government could support increasing domestic and military expenditures would become an increasingly divisive issue in the months to come.

All these struggles over OEO exposed to public scrutiny that fact that Johnson and Congress, in creating the War on Poverty, had been considerably less careful about establishing clear policy guidelines about how to fight it. As LBJ hurried ambitious Great Society programs into existence, he was expanding the bureaucracy of the federal government, adding to what Califano later described as the already "bewildering number of agencies" that had begun to proliferate in the earlier 1960s.[8] Such expansion increased the potential for overlap, the likelihood of battles over turf, and the development of policy goals that could be confusing and unfocused.

Worse, by late 1965 high-flown promises about a "war" had excited large popular expectations, leading rights-oriented spokespeople for the poor—the National Welfare Rights Organization, for instance—to ratchet up their demands for ever more generous entitlements, including guaranteed annual incomes. By the late 1960s and early 1970s, demands like these, raised by a variety of interest groups, had become extraordinarily ambitious—none more so than a (politically hopeless) "Demogrant" proposal espoused by Democratic presidential candidate George McGovern in 1972. It would have guaranteed every man, woman, and child in the United States $1,000 per year.[9]

LBJ, a New Deal–style liberal who dreamed that his Great Society programs—by helping people to help themselves—would advance equality of opportunity, was cool to grandiose demands such as these. Still, the promise of a "war" on poverty, like other high-sounding appeals of his administration, excited such pressures. As Daniel Moynihan observed in 1968, "The great liberal failing of this time," was "constantly to overpromise and to overstate, and thereby constantly to appear to under-perform."

Finally, the War on Poverty aroused the ire of anti–Big Government conservatives like Ronald Reagan, who was clearly aiming to run for governor of California in 1966. Not only Johnson but also his successors in the White House were to discover that rapid governmental growth—and overblown rhetoric—would incite opposition from the Right as well as from the Left. Bigger government could and did help people in need, but it could also be a mixed political blessing.

THE SECOND GREAT SOCIETY EFFORT TO PROVOKE CONTROVERSY IN late 1965 was the Equal Employment Opportunity Commission (EEOC). Confrontations over the agency, revealing the bitterness of bureaucratic infighting within the government, also exposed a still larger problem: the power of sexism in American life in 1965.

The EEOC, authorized by Title VII of the Civil Rights Act of 1964, was supposed to prohibit businesses and labor unions from discrimination based on "race, color, religion, sex, or national origin." The statute called for the commission to begin its work at the beginning of July 1965. In late May, LBJ had named five commissioners, of whom two were black and one was a woman. Its new chair, Franklin D. Roosevelt Jr., the son of the president, had been a Democratic congressman from New York from 1949 to 1954 and was serving as LBJ's undersecretary of commerce.[10]

Well before Johnson's appointments, however, there were signs that the EEOC would encounter problems. The overriding purpose of the Civil Rights Act of 1964, approved after enormous controversy on Capitol Hill, had been to end the massive Jim Crow system of state-mandated racial segregation in public accommodations—not to fight against various forms of job discrimination. Indeed, congressional discussion in 1964 of Title VII and of the role to be played by an EEOC had been perfunctory.

Johnson acknowledged his uncertainty about the EEOC's reach in late 1964 and early 1965, when he sought clarification from aides about what the commission was empowered to accomplish. His uncertainty about the commission's mandate was one reason—along with the press of other civil rights business, notably his effort for a voting rights law—why he was slow to name the commissioners. Roosevelt, a cavalier figure who seemed more interested in yachting than in running the EEOC, and his colleagues had only a month following their appointment to secure office space, assemble a staff, and establish procedures. Congress had yet to appropriate funds for the commission's operations.[11]

As if these were not problems enough for the new commissioners, advocates of vigorous enforcement of nondiscrimination worried that Title VII lacked teeth. The civil rights law stipulated that the EEOC would hear complaints by employees. But Congress did not empower the agency to issue "cease and desist" orders to employers or unions believed to be discriminating. Instead, the EEOC would be expected to rely on "informal methods of conference, conciliation, and persuasion." If these failed to accomplish a satisfactory settlement, the commission could refer a dispute to the Justice Department, which might or might not agree to litigate. If it did not, the complainant could file suit in a federal court. As the *New York Times* observed on July 2, 1965, the day the EEOC started its work, the law was "cumbersome" and "riddled with loopholes."[12]

The language of Title VII, it turned out, proved problematic for the EEOC in yet another, more fundamental way. When the title was being considered in 1964, many congressmen and senators worried that enforcement of nondiscrimination might lead to the establishment of racial quotas in hiring or promotions. Responding to such fears, they inserted a key sentence: "Nothing contained in this title shall be interpreted to require any employer . . . to grant preferential treatment to any individual or to any group . . . on account of an imbalance which may exist." Senator Joseph Clark of Pennsylvania, a liberal who managed the bill on the floor, declared, "Quotas are themselves discriminatory."

What this meant was that while the EEOC was authorized to investigate on a case-by-case method whether the treatment of an individual had been discriminatory, the commission and the courts would not be expected to go beyond the "intent standard" of the common law toward a standard that demanded equal results of decisions concerning hiring, promotions, and the like. To take that step would be to switch from an individual to a group-based concept of rights. That, in turn, would require establishment of a credible statistical demonstration of unequal impact in the distribution of jobs and rewards.

But no such comprehensive national database existed in 1964–1965. It was only later, as discriminatory practices persisted, that the limitations inherent in the EEOC's case-by-case approach became increasingly obvious and advocates lobbied for ways to establish justice for groups. Many pressed for various versions of affirmative action, which ultimately became a means by which the EEOC sought to accomplish equality in employment.[13] The evolution of the EEOC toward such an approach after 1965—one unintended by LBJ or

Congress in 1964—is a case study of the ways in which the reach of governmental bureaucracies can expand over time. The commission, established as a characteristically Great Society quest to expand opportunity, evolved into an agency that also concerned itself with equal results.

It was also clear from the start of its operations that the EEOC would not have the field to itself in contending against discrimination in employment. Like the OEO, which fought jurisdictional battles with other government bureaucracies, it would have to find its niche amid an array of federal agencies and departments, including Labor, Justice, HEW, the Women's Bureau, and the US Civil Rights Commission. To further complicate matters, Title VI of the 1964 Civil Rights Act had authorized the Justice Department to cut off federal funding from public institutions (mainly school systems and hospitals) that continued to practice racial discrimination. The competition between overlapping agencies concerned with employment discrimination, like those that dealt with poverty, indicated that the proliferation of federal bureaucracies could be a problem in itself.

Insofar as racial issues were concerned, the EEOC commissioners quickly discovered that they would have plenty to do. The NAACP flooded the commission's staff with complaints—476 right away and nearly 1,400 by mid-December. Roosevelt, who quit in May 1966, moaned that he was stuck with an "uncontrollable complaint workload" and begged for more funding.[14] In time, the commission received it: EEOC, armed with subsequent executive orders and court decisions that supported affirmative action, was to become an important though controversial federal agency in the complicated legal fights against racial discrimination in employment.

Many of the most controversial issues to embroil the EEOC in late 1965 revolved around sex, not racial discrimination. This came as a considerable surprise to many people, LBJ included, who in backing the civil rights bill of 1964 had focused on race. The House sponsor of the sex discrimination clause in the bill had been Howard Smith of Virginia, a vigorous foe of civil rights legislation, who called during debate on the floor for an amendment that would add "sex" as a category in the language of Title VII. Smith's amendment, approved after brief and sometimes jocular debate that revealed a lack of seriousness among congressmen about sex discrimination, became part of the bill as finally enacted in June 1964.

This was a source of great satisfaction to legislators on Capitol Hill who had concerned themselves with women's issues in that patriarchal age. Some of these advocates, notably Representative Martha Griffiths of Michigan, had collaborated quietly but effectively with Smith in getting the amendment included in 1964. It was by no means a joke. But the existence of "sex" in the language of Title VII still received little notice in the media. When the bill was signed at an enthusiastically attended and widely reported White House ceremony, no women were present, and the *New York Times* story about the event did not even mention that the new law prohibited sex discrimination.

LBJ's appointment in late May 1965 of the commissioners, which brought greater attention to what the EEOC might accomplish, began to change this picture—but not in a way that pleased Griffiths and others who championed women's rights. On the contrary, news stories and comments concerned with the commission's role tended to treat the inclusion of "sex" in Title VII either as a ploy by Smith to encumber the bill in the hope of defeating it or as a joke. The nervous levity with which many people discussed the issue exposed an important continuity in American thinking to that time: despite the rising rights-consciousness of the era, women's rights had yet to secure a place on the agenda of the Great Society or to result in anything resembling an organized feminist movement.

Comments by male executives in mid-1965 revealed the existence of considerable alarm about how the category of sex in Title VII might affect their companies. A personnel officer of a large airline asked what he should do "when a gal walks into our office, demands a job as a pilot and has the credentials to qualify." A manager of an electronics components company lamented, "I suppose we'll have to advertise for people with small, nimble fingers and hire the first male midget with unusual dexterity [who] shows up."[15]

Other responses from men were equally dismissive of the notion that the EEOC should concern itself with sex discrimination. A widely noted *Wall Street Journal* article in late June called on readers to imagine a "shapeless, knobby-kneed male 'bunny' serving drinks to a group of astonished businessmen or a 'matronly vice-president' lusting after her male secretary." Taking their cue from this story, other articles referred to Title VII as the "bunny law." An editorial in the *New York Times*, engaging in speculation about what the EEOC might do, asked what would happen if a woman sought a job in a Turkish bathhouse, a man looked for work in a corset shop, or a woman applied to become a deckhand on a tugboat.[16]

Unfortunately for women, attitudes such as these pervaded the EEOC itself. No one made this more obvious than Roosevelt, who was hardly an advocate of women's rights. When the commission was about to start its work, he was asked at a press conference, "What about sex?" Roosevelt smirked, "Don't get me started. I'm all for it." The *New York Times*, reporting his remark, added that no one seemed to have thought much about the issue of sex discrimination or to know the extent to which women might wish to move into new areas of work.[17]

As the commission set about its business, it focused almost exclusively on complaints—notably those from the NAACP—concerning racial discrimination. Many of these called for the commission to outlaw race-segregated want ads published in newspapers and magazines. When the EEOC in mid-August agreed to prohibit such segregation, it was a sign that the commission, though limited in its power, could nonetheless make a difference.[18] The prohibition was a highlight of its activity during the early months of its existence.

Ignoring the complaints of women's rights activists, who remained politically weak in 1965, the commission refused to do the same regarding sex-segregated want ads. As earlier, ads were allowed to run headed by "Help Wanted—Male," and "Help Wanted—Female." The EEOC was also slow to address the complaints of stewardesses who objected to airline policies that required them to be single, set limits on their age, and subjected them to endless measurements to check for weight gain.[19]

On September 24, LBJ issued an executive order, No. 11246, which addressed employment policies within the federal government. Henceforth, it stated, executive departments and agencies were expected to "establish and maintain a positive program of equal employment opportunity" consistent with a prohibition of discrimination. The EEOC would be partly responsible for monitoring and enforcing these programs as they affected contractors and subcontractors with fifty or more employees. This was a step along the road that broadened the reach of EEOC in American life.

But Johnson's order, in specifying the varieties of nondiscrimination that government agencies must practice, listed only race, creed, color, and national origin, thus omitting the category of "sex," even though the Civil Rights Act of 1964 had included it. His omission, which was unexplained, did not attract widespread attention or complaint from liberals, including leaders of the NAACP and the AFL-CIO. Their leaders like most Americans in 1965 clung to paternalistic views of relations between the sexes. But the omission of "sex" in Executive Order 11246 further angered Griffiths and others who already had been complaining about the failure of the OEO to develop job training programs for women.

As of October 1965, most American women still seemed to tolerate the patriarchal world they had known all their lives. Then, as earlier, few people could have predicted that a broad women's movement might soon gain momentum. Nor would it be accurate to argue that anger at the male-oriented policies of the Johnson administration and the EEOC was to become the only source of such a movement. Still, the EEOC had ignored the complaints of women's rights advocates, and executive order 11246 had been obtuse. By late 1965, policies such as these were leading increasing numbers of activists to resent the administration. When a group of them, including Betty Friedan, met in the summer of 1966 to discuss their grievances, many expressed their bitterness about the failure of the EEOC to ban sex-segregated want ads. Before they finished their meeting, they agreed to form the National Organization for Women, or NOW.

—

THE THIRD GREAT SOCIETY EFFORT TO RUN INTO POLITICALLY unwelcome flak in the late summer and early fall of 1965 involved efforts to advance desegregation of the public schools. As of early October, by which time an especially glaring example of political conflict exposed serious divisions within LBJ's liberal Democratic coalition, many advocates of civil rights were despairing about the administration.

The issue of racially segregated schools, along with segregated housing, had always been especially difficult to resolve. Though the Supreme Court's *Brown v. Board of Education* decision of 1954 had struck a judicial blow against state-mandated segregation in the public schools, massive white resistance in the South had succeeded in negating its effect. In the 1964–1965 school year, only around 1 percent of black children in the Deep South attended schools with white children.[20] Outside the South, de facto residential and school segregation—supported by deliberately racist zoning and housing policies—remained widespread.[21]

Johnson, a man of the South who had briefly been a teacher in his youth, needed no prompting to fight against school segregation. Nor did Francis Keppel, a committed integrationist whom Kennedy had plucked from the deanship of the Harvard Education School and named as commissioner of education within the Department of Health, Education, and Welfare. In the spring of 1965, Keppel had issued guidelines to be followed by school districts in the South as of the start of the 1965–1966 school year. These were expected to desegregate at the rate of four grades per year over the course of the next three years. Schools that failed to comply, Keppel warned, would forfeit their claim to federal funding as decreed by Title VI of the Civil Rights Act of 1964.[22]

By midsummer, scattered evidence seemed to indicate that a fair number of Southern school officials might heed Keppel's instructions. In July, his Office of Education claimed to have collected plans for or promises of compliance from 2,429 of the 2,929 school districts in eleven states of the South.[23] As the opening of the school year approached, LBJ gave the issue his personal attention, ordering an aide to call Keppel daily. "How many more [students] have you brought in?" he demanded to know. "What's the count?" With characteristic imperiousness he would wander into the aide's office periodically to say, "Get 'em! Get 'em! Get the last ones!"[24]

Scattered signs of change were also appearing in the North. In August, Massachusetts passed what was described as the first state law to ban de facto school segregation. A school would be identified as racially unbalanced, the statute decreed, if an annual review were to show that more than 50 percent of its enrollment was nonwhite. Local officials must then devise plans—redraw district lines, build new schools, bus students around the district—to correct the situation. If they failed to do so, the state would cut off aid to the district involved. Edward Brooke, who as attorney general of the state was often identified by the media as the highest-ranking elected black state official in the United States, called passage of the law "dramatic and heartening."[25]

When the new school year started, however, it was obvious that changes would be minimal. In the South, there were a few encouraging developments: two of Martin Luther King's children and three of Ralph Abernathy's children, for instance, would be attending a previously all-white school in Atlanta. But this was token integration. In the South as a whole, the *New York Times* estimated on August 31, only 2.3 percent of black children would be going to schools with whites. While this was slightly more than two times the pathetically small percentage during the 1964–1965 school year, it was hardly a dramatic step forward. In the Deep South states of South Carolina, Alabama, Mississippi, and Louisiana, virtually nothing had changed.

The optimism of officials such as Brooke in Massachusetts also proved to be misplaced. In September, it was reported that at least twenty-five Boston schools had enrollments that were less than 20 percent white. But as in the past, Louise Day Hicks, chair of the Boston school committee, refused to press for racial desegregation in the city. "Racial imbalance in itself," she said, "is not educationally harmful." Continuing to defend neighborhood schools, she declared that Boston would do without state aid rather than bus students for the purpose of racial balance.[26] Boston voters soon endorsed Hicks's stand, electing her as the top vote-getter to a third term as school committee chair and thereby strengthening her stature as a national symbol of resistance to governmentally imposed school desegregation. The voters also chose three like-minded opponents of busing to Boston's five-person committee, thus ensuring that her views would continue to prevail in the city.[27]

Hicks was by no means the only white official in the North to resist change. *Newsweek* reported in late September that municipal officials had devised ruses that would leave more than 65 percent of black students outside the South in predominantly black schools in 1965–1966. In cities like Chicago and Philadelphia, with large black populations, the percentages were 90 percent or more. Kenneth Clark, a nationally recognized black advocate of desegregation, observed mordantly, "By following the example of the North, it would be possible for the South to follow the law without desegregating a single school."[28]

With numbers such as these, it was hardly surprising that civil rights advocates grew angry. And with reason, for the obstacles to change remained formidable. In many areas of the South, for instance, Keppel's threat to withhold federal school aid did not greatly concern school officials. Though passage of Title I of the Elementary and Secondary Education Act in April entitled them to receive federal aid for students from low-income families, the amount of money was not expected to be large enough in many districts to prompt worries about a cutoff. Other school officials believed that Keppel would have to think twice before using Title VI: withholding funding was, after all, a blunt instrument that would deprive needy children of federal assistance. Still other Southern officials, having done without federal funding in the past, were willing to do so in the future rather than take steps to desegregate. By October, Keppel had withheld aid from sixty districts without weakening the doggedness of white Southern opponents.[29]

Civil rights activists from CORE and SNCC, though angry about the persistence of school segregation in the South, had focused so intensely on voting rights issues that they were not yet well prepared to deal with the problem, which was huge. Black community leaders in the South, moreover, included many who were teachers, coaches, and administrators in the separate black school systems of the region. Like many black parents, they were proud of their institutions and harbored doubts about the wisdom of sending black children to schools with whites. Some also worried (correctly as it turned out) that desegregation, were it ever to occur, would lead to the closing of black schools and loss of their jobs. For all these reasons, they were not quick to demand change. It was not until 1969, when a combination of developments—notably, decisions by impatient federal judges ordering that *Brown* be immediately carried out—that substantial desegregation of schools began to occur at last in the Deep South.

Keppel, closely monitoring these discouraging developments in 1965, grew increasingly anxious and upset. He was especially irritated, as were leaders of CORE, the NAACP, and the National Urban League, with Chicago school officials, who refused to take action against school segregation in the city. He was also impulsive. On October 1, and without consulting President Johnson, he suspended $30 million in federal school aid that had been designated for Chicago.

His sudden move set off a storm of protest from white leaders in Chicago and in the state. The superintendent of the city's schools, Benjamin Willis, denounced Keppel's action as "illegal, despotic, alarming and threatening." Everett Dirksen threatened to call for a Senate investigation. Richard Daley, the city's mayor, contacted Johnson to demand that he reverse Keppel's decision.[30] These reactions, which pitted Daley, the nation's most powerful political boss, against the federal government, received sensational coverage in the media and landed Keppel on the cover of *Time* magazine.[31]

When LBJ learned what Keppel had done, he was preparing for the signing ceremony at the Statue of Liberty that would highlight the rights-enhancing wonders of immigration reform. He quickly confronted his education commissioner and ascertained that the suspension of funds had not followed procedures as required by the civil rights law. Keppel had not advised Willis or Daley of their failure to comply with the statute or given them a chance to desegregate, and he had not notified the appropriate congressional committees thirty days prior to his decision.

Johnson then moved quickly to resolve the conflict. Arriving in New York on October 3 for the Statue of Liberty ceremony, he met with Daley and assured him that Keppel's suspension of funds would be revoked. He also sent HEW Undersecretary Wilbur Cohen, a skilled mediator, to Chicago to talk with Willis and work out a plan of voluntary compliance with federal guidelines. The city subsequently agreed to set up a committee to examine the situation. Keppel was relieved of his post. In late October, Daley received the federal education money, and in November, LBJ instructed the Civil Rights Commission to do a major study of de facto segregation in the North.[32]

By acting swiftly, Johnson managed to limit the severe political hammering that would have battered him had he tried to stand up to Daley. (The mayor, a Democrat, was said to be powerful enough to tell fourteen Chicago-area congressmen how to vote). But spats over school segregation continued to break out within the federal bureaucracy, in part because high officials in HEW believed, as Keppel had, in using Title VI to fight against racial segregation in the schools. As one such official observed at the time, "The difficulty is that the instrument we're wielding is a rather shaky one. Perhaps we weren't as clever wielding it as we could have been, but we're still trying to use it as firmly as we know how."[33]

Johnson often supported HEW activists after 1965: his commitment to desegregation was serious. But the highly public fracas with Chicago suggested that he had buckled under pressure from a mayor and party boss who had refused to comply with federal guidelines. The fracas also confirmed that advancement of educational desegregation in cities with substantial black populations would continue to be an extraordinarily difficult task. That so powerful and determined a leader as Johnson would give way to a mayor showed how difficult it could be for advocates of racial justice in Washington (and elsewhere) to impose their will on recalcitrant political leaders at the state and local level.

———

As LBJ WAS COPING WITH THE BUREAUCRATIC, FISCAL, AND POLITICAL problems that were bringing the OEO, EEOC, and Office of Education into the headlines, conservative politicians, taking heart, were gearing up to challenge liberal Democrats in 1966. Reagan, a highly popular figure, was by far the most prominent of these challengers. By December, pundits were predicting that he would defeat Governor Pat Brown, the incumbent, in 1966 and take control of the nation's most populous state.[34]

Moreover, a number of America's leading political and social thinkers—some of whom had been known as liberals—were then arriving at increasingly skeptical views about the capacity of the federal government to undertake grand (or grandiose) visions of a Great Society. Many of these—the sociologist Daniel Bell, the political scientist James Q. Wilson, Daniel Moynihan—were articulate academics and intellectuals who began writing essays for a new journal, the *Public Interest*, the first issue of which appeared in October.

In a remarkably quick time, the journal succeeded in appealing to a number of well-educated readers, many of whom swelled the ranks of a "neoconservative" movement, as it became called. Other readers of the journal included policymakers who, like the essayists, were coming to believe that the government was erecting a thicket of regulations, encumbrances, and torts that would baffle federal administrators and clog up the courts. More broadly, they wondered if LBJ and his liberal advisers possessed enough expertise to deal effectively with large and complex socioeconomic problems, such as poverty, inadequate schools, and racial discrimination, and whether the administration was promising more than the federal government—a maze of bureaucracies—could deliver. The success of the *Public Interest* was a warning sign, one among many as of late 1965, that more conservative approaches to governing were gaining favor in the country.[35]

The battles over Title VI and school segregation, like those over the OEO and EEOC, had their roots in LBJ's conviction in 1964 and early 1965 that he had to move quickly if he expected to push his vast vision of a Great Society through Congress. After all, he believed correctly, it would not be long before he would become "Lame Duck Lyndon." But his understandable quest for speed—and for so many new programs—had led to oversell and to administrative and programmatic difficulties that were frustrating ever more ambitious rights-conscious groups on the one hand and arousing criticism from conservatives on the other. By the end of the year it was evident that serious political trouble lay ahead for Johnson and his liberal followers.

14

AMERICA AT THE END OF 1965

WHEN THE *NEW YORK TIMES* SURVEYED THE STATE OF THE ECONOMY shortly after Thanksgiving, it highlighted the blessings of unparalleled economic expansion. "Shoppers," it added, "seem to be gobbling up everything in sight, at almost any price."[1] The paper was correct to be optimistic about the economy. Unemployment toward the end of the year reached extraordinarily low levels, sinking to 4.1 percent in December. By the end of 1965, the gross national product had grown by $34 billion over the course of the year to $675 billion, an increase of more than 5 percent.[2]

Technological triumphs remained another realm about which Americans could feel unbridled enthusiasm and optimism that fall. In October, construction of Eero Saarinen's 630-foot-high concrete and steel "Gateway to the West"—the Arch—was completed in St. Louis. On November 15, NBC's evening news program, *The Huntley-Brinkley Report*, became the first to be broadcast in color. In mid-December, excited news accounts reported that two manned American spaceships, *Gemini 6* and *7*, had achieved a rendezvous in space. It was the first such accomplishment in world history. Television provided the first live coverage of a spacecraft splashdown, that of *Gemini 6*.[3]

Americans especially welcomed the way people responded during a power outage that darkened much of the Northeast, including most of New York City, in early November. Though the blackout descended at dusk and lasted in places for more than thirteen hours, the thirty million or so Americans who were affected by it behaved in remarkably calm and cooperative ways. In New York City, where throngs were trapped in subways, the elevated railway, skyscrapers, and elevators, no one panicked. There was no looting and almost no crime on the streets. Marveling at the communitarian response (which some reporters contrasted with the "rampaging" that had devastated Watts), *Newsweek* observed, "All across the Megalopolis, the cliff dwellers—who had come to believe in their own folk image as so many encapsulated, private atoms—surprised themselves with their neighborly good spirit at an hour when everyone, at last, had something in common."[4]

Many aspects of America's cultural scene, too, continued to promote popular satisfactions while reinforcing ideas of American heroism and shared values. Readers of contemporary history, for instance, could immerse themselves in the events of the wondrous Kennedy years: Theodore Sorensen's *Kennedy* (number 1 on the nonfiction best-seller list), Arthur Schlesinger Jr.'s *1000 Days: John F. Kennedy in the White House* (number 2), and Evelyn Lincoln's *My Twelve Years with John F. Kennedy*.[5] The Kennedy era, it seemed, was becoming a defining myth of modern American life.

Two new books that appeared in November were among the most significant of the year. One was *Unsafe at Any Speed* by Ralph Nader, an unknown forty-one-year-old attorney. Nader's hard-hitting book indicted the American auto industry, which he argued valued comfort and style over safety. When General Motors retaliated with a campaign of personal harassment and intimidation, he fought back, ultimately forcing the head of GM to apologize before a Senate subcommittee. He also won a lawsuit charging the corporation with invasion of privacy. The book, and the controversy that followed, gave Nader a national reputation. It also pushed Congress into action. In 1966 it passed a National Traffic and Motor Vehicle Safety Act that required American auto manufacturers (by 1968) to include seat belts, padded instrument panels, sun visors, and arm rests in their new models. It was the first time that Congress had addressed the subject in a serious way.

The other important new book in November was *The Autobiography of Malcolm X*. The author, Alex Haley, based it heavily on his interpretation of interviews with Malcolm. It was a largely unsparing but in many ways inspiring account of Malcolm X's serial conversions from troubled youngster to convicted criminal to Nation of Islam organizer to leader of his own movement, the Organization of Afro-American Unity.

The *New York Times*, which at the time of his death had spoken of Malcolm as a "twisted man," now hailed his autobiography as a "brilliant, painful, important book." It added, "With his death American Negroes lost their most able, articulate, and compelling spokesman." Its praise of Malcolm—so different from its rejection of him in February—indicated that racial attitudes had changed dramatically during the year.

In a paperback edition, *The Autobiography of Malcolm X* later became extraordinarily popular, selling more than three million copies by 1992. In the process it further rejuvenated Malcolm's image. Far more revered in death than in life, he became an inspirational hero to many black people: a *Newsweek* poll in 1990 reported that 82 percent of African Americans regarded him as the quintessential "strong black man."[6]

Most other cultural developments of late 1965 followed conventional paths. Even at the end of the year *The Sound of Music* remained a great draw, finishing at number 2 at the box office. Number 1 was *Thunderball*, again featuring Sean Connery as James Bond. Even more than *Goldfinger*, which had been a hit at the end of 1964, it relied heavily on Cold War concerns, high-tech gadgetry, and suggestions of sex to draw in viewers.

Television producers, still concentrating on providing wholesome, commercially successful entertainment aimed primarily at white middle-class viewers, hit gold with a new offering that was savored by millions of viewers: *A Charlie Brown Christmas*. But NBC and CBS also ventured forth into more troubled waters, presenting hour-long documentaries on the situation in Vietnam during the Christmas season, bringing a bit of the war into American living rooms. *CBS*

Reports ran a program titled, "Watts: Riot or Revolt?" Features such as these were hardly as graphic as Morley Safer's focus on hut burning had been in August, but they indicated TV programmers' understanding that escalation of the war and deteriorating race relations were very much on the minds of viewers and could not be ignored.

As the sudden fame of "Eve of Destruction" had indicated, trends in popular music were far less predictable than those in the slower-to-change genres of film and TV, and in late 1965 three highly popular releases appeared whose lyrics were darker than those of most other tunes. All seemed to resonate with millions of Americans—especially young Americans—whose uneasiness, notably concerning race relations, social tensions, and Vietnam, was becoming more evident than ever.

One was the Beatles' sixth studio album, *Rubber Soul*, which was released in time for the Christmas sales. It included songs such as "I'm Looking Through You" and "Run for Your Life," whose sounds and lyrics differed from those of their feel-good hits in the past. Some of these lyrics revealed the influence of Bob Dylan's often blunt and unsentimental lines about relationships between the sexes. "Run for Your Life," about the possibility of betrayal, warned a "little girl" of the dire consequences of being "with another man."

The second release, "Turn! Turn! Turn!" by the Byrds, had been adapted from the biblical book Ecclesiastes and put to music by Pete Seeger in 1958. Though it was not a protest song, one of its lines, hoping for peace—"I swear it's not too late"—clearly resonated with listeners who were alarmed by escalation of the Vietnam War. The song topped the singles charts for three weeks between December 4 and 25.

The third release, "The Sounds of Silence" by Paul Simon and Art Garfunkel, dated to early 1964, when Simon had written it in response to the assassination of President Kennedy.[7] In mid-1965 it was overdubbed and released, now with electric guitar, bass, and drums, emerging as a spooky and spectral song.[8] After entering the pop charts in September, it moved steadily upward and peaked as the top single on New Year's Day, 1966. Its theme, a kind of downbeat "The Times They Are A-Changin'," centered on the failure of Americans to communicate with one another; alienation was spreading, especially in the post-Watts world of urban America, where people were "talking without speaking."

As evidenced by these songs and the TV specials on Vietnam, many Americans by late 1965 seemed to have become considerably less optimistic about the future than they had been a year earlier. And they were expressing their alarm. The president, who was well aware of popular concerns, especially about the war, was a little more careful than in the past about claiming too much in public speeches as the year wound down.

Back on December 18, 1964, when he lit the National Christmas Tree, he had declared, "These are the most hopeful times in all the years since Christ was born in Bethlehem." Now, when he turned on the lights on December 17, new, multicolored bulbs dazzled onlookers who had assembled. But he wisely eschewed the bombast of December 1964. With the British prime minister, Harold Wilson, and Vice President Humphrey at his side, he told the American people, "Our first and most compelling task is peace." He added,

> Our celebration this year is tempered by the absence of brave men from their homes and from their loved ones. We would not have it so. We have not sought the combat in which they are engaged. We have hungered for not one foot of another's territory, nor for the life of a single adversary. Our sons patrol the hills of Vietnam at this hour because we have learned that though men cry, "Peace, peace," there is no peace to be gained ever by yielding to aggression.

LBJ then announced that Prime Minister Wilson (who had steadfastly refused to engage British troops in the war) would help him look for ways to enter negotiations leading to peace. He concluded by insisting that as always he was searching for "an honorable peace in Vietnam" and "that nothing is to be gained by further delay in talking."[9]

—

BUT JOHNSON KNEW THAT SERIOUS TROUBLES LOOMED AHEAD. IF he had spoken with any frankness about the course of the war in his speech, he would have thoroughly depressed his listeners. Had he talked about race relations, he would likely have been equally as pessimistic.

Civil rights advocates, to be sure, were gratified in early December when an all-white, all-male jury convicted three Klansmen who had been arrested in connection with the killing of Viola Liuzzo toward the close of the Selma campaign in March. Each of the three, found guilty of a federal charge of conspiring to violate Liuzzo's civil rights, received prison sentences of ten years. Johnson issued a statement saying that "the whole nation can take heart" from the outcome.[10] A few days later, however, another all-white, all-male jury (one of the jurors was a Klansman who had once escorted a Nazi leader to assault Martin Luther King) delivered a very different verdict in a state court. It acquitted three white men who had been arrested for beating the Reverend James Reeb to death in Selma. When the verdict was announced, whites in the Dallas County courtroom erupted in applause.

Civil rights leaders were also becoming a little discouraged by the state of voter registration drives in the South. Though federal examiners and local volunteers had enabled these to go reasonably well—an estimated two hundred thousand blacks had been added to the rolls between mid-August and mid-November—the drives appeared to be losing steam, in part perhaps because the novelty of enrolling was wearing off and because whites, as ever, continued to resist.[11] Martin Luther King, who was taking part in voter registration demonstrations in rural Alabama at the time, knew that his ambition to register a million new voters by the end of the year would fall well short of success.

To accelerate the enrolling process, activists demanded that the Justice Department send more examiners, as well as federal workers, to help with the difficult task of sustaining their efforts. Attorney General Nicholas Katzenbach, however, refused them, explaining that he had already added examiners in violence-prone counties where they were most obviously needed, and that the Voting Rights Act had not specifically authorized the department to supply federal workers to help with the tasks of registration.[12]

Advocates of civil rights also criticized Johnson for not following up on his widely hailed speech, "To Fulfill These Rights," at the Howard University commencement in June.[13] The Washington conference he had promised during that speech finally convened in mid-November. But it was a small affair, which civil rights activists used as an occasion to demand $100 billion for what they called a Freedom

Budget to aid black America. This was an amount nearly equal to the entire budget of the federal government at the time.

Some Johnson administration representatives at the conference were disgusted with the antics of many of the black people—posturers, they complained—who attended. A Justice Department official snapped, "It [the conference] was a disaster—an outpouring of shabby campus style politicking, bickering, and talking for effect."[14] LBJ was especially irate. "They come right in," he fumed to McGeorge Bundy, "and while they still got their hors d'oeuvres going, and whisky in one hand and a wiener sausage in the other, they're just raisin' unshirted hell and say it's got to be a hundred *billion*."[15]

As all these developments demonstrated, a large divide by then separated the Johnson administration and the more militant leaders of civil rights organizations such as CORE and SNCC. Many of these leaders, increasingly impatient in the aftermath of Watts, had raged at LBJ's obeisance to Mayor Daley of Chicago. By December, they were openly questioning the virtues of nonviolence and interracial cooperation. Still other black leaders were speaking out against the Vietnam War and cooperating in antiwar demonstrations. The Lowndes County [Alabama] Freedom Organization announced in mid-December that it would henceforth operate as an "all-Negro third party." The *New York Times* reported that "It will operate in only one county and use a black panther as its party symbol."[16]

Moves such as this, while emboldening rights-conscious militants in CORE and SNCC, discouraged many Americans—black as well as white—who had supported the once luminously appealing nonviolent and interracial civil rights movement. As Charles Silberman had already lamented in November, "The civil rights movement is not dead. . . . [But] the movement is at a dreadful impasse; its leaders . . . are estranged from their rank and file and divided and uncertain where to turn."[17]

Few people in early 1965, when King had launched his inspirational drive in Selma, could have predicted such disappointment and discord. Though a black freedom struggle was to continue, the fracturing and enfeebling of the nonviolent, interracial civil rights movement was one of the most significant developments of a pivotal year in recent American history.

IN LATE 1965 JOHNSON HAD TO CONCENTRATE ABOVE ALL ON developments in Vietnam. In doing so, polls indicated that he continued to command support from a considerable majority of the American people, especially those of a conservative orientation. In September, some twenty-five thousand young people had assembled for the fifth annual convention of Young Americans for Freedom, still a considerably larger organization than any antiwar group on the political Left. Though some of the attendees were libertarians who opposed the war, most were enthusiastic supporters of it.[18]

A Gallup poll conducted between October 29 and November 2 asked whether the United States should have become militarily involved in Southeast Asia. Sixty-six percent of respondents answered yes, as opposed to only 21 percent who said no. The others voiced no opinion.[19] Then and later in 1965, between 62 and 65 percent of Americans replied yes to the question, "Do you approve of the way Lyndon Johnson is handling his job as President?"[20]

Johnson also continued to enjoy the backing of major shapers of public opinion, notably *Time* magazine. In many articles it hailed what it described as the successes of the air war, which had become ever more ferocious. News reports sometimes conceded that American bombing attacks killed civilians and unleashed floods of refugees. But many accounts nonetheless celebrated the might of American air power.[21] On October 22, *Time* outdid itself in a twelve-page cover story about the war. It expressed alarm about the fate in South Vietnam of "680,000 desperate refugees" as well as about "soaring inflation" and high desertion rates from the ARVN. But it praised the efforts of Prime Minister Nguyen Cao Ky to promote social reform in the South. His policies, it continued, "have so far kept the nation's fractious Buddhists and Catholics quiescent." The story reported that the nation's "political situation is the most stable it has been since 1960."[22]

The major source of such stability, *Time* explained, was what it described as the ever more promising military situation. By then, nearly three months following LBJ's decision to further escalate the war, there were roughly 145,000 American troops in South Vietnam. Reinforcements were pouring in on a regular basis and were expected to swell the American troop presence to more than 180,000 by the end of the year. The expansion of American military presence, *Time* insisted, had made a great difference, not only in helping to stabilize the South Vietnamese government but also in bloodying the enemy. Its description of America's fighting men was vivid: "Wave upon wave of combat-booted Americans—lean, laconic, and looking for a fight—pour ashore from armadas of troopships. . . . The VC's once-cocky hunters have become the cowering hunted as the cutting edge of U.S. fire power slashes into the thickets of communist strength." Citing an American officer, *Time* enthused, "We've stemmed the tide." It concluded, "Today South Viet Nam throbs with pride and power, above all with an *esprit* scarcely credible against the summer's somber vista."[23]

Newsweek, though less breathless in its coverage, also carried upbeat articles about the fighting. It even lauded the ability of the military to create a racially integrated combat force. Vietnam, a story explained in early December, was America's "first truly integrated war." It cited Pentagon estimates that nearly 8 percent of American troops in Vietnam, or 13,000 of the 165,000 men there, were black. The services, it added, were "far ahead" of the rest of the country concerning integration. An American captain said, "I see only one color. And that's olive drab."[24]

What *Time* and many other sources of opinion did not write as much about was the nature of the fighting on the ground, which was fierce. The Vietnam War continued to be less about gaining territory— it was as hard as ever to define a front—than about killing as many of the enemy as possible. *Time* said as much by regularly boasting, as did Defense Secretary Robert McNamara and other top officials, of "kill ratios." These, considerably inflated by the Pentagon, were said to be three-to-one or better in favor of the United States and its South Vietnamese allies.

Writing later of his experiences as a marine, Philip Caputo observed that by the fall of 1965 he and his mates were not fighting because they were anticommunist but because their friends had been killed or wounded. Furious, they yearned for retribution. He went on to write: "By autumn, what had been an adventurous expedition had turned into an exhausting, indecisive war of attrition in which we fought for no cause other than our own survival. . . . [The war had become] a murderous succession of ambushes and firefights . . . and vicious manhunts through jungles and swamps where snipers harassed us constantly and booby traps cut us down one by one." Caputo groused that the enemy rarely risked a "set-piece battle" and when it did, "weeks of bottled up tension would be released in a few minutes of orgiastic violence, men screaming and shouting obscenities above the explosion of grenades and the rapid, rippling bursts of automatic rifles." Indiscriminate killing and atrocities were common. "The unwritten rule," he wrote, "was, 'If he's dead, he's VC.'"[25]

Some of the heaviest fighting of the war to date—a "set-piece" battle such as Caputo was hoping for—took place over the course of five days in mid-November in the Ia Drang Valley, a remote area in the Central Highlands not far from Pleiku. It was a confrontation that for the first time pitted American combat forces against sizeable numbers of North Vietnamese regulars as well as the Vietcong. The fighting, which was sometimes hand-to-hand, was savage and sustained. Enemy forces impaled captured South Vietnamese soldiers on stakes and gunned down Americans who were wounded. Americans and ARVN troops killed some of their North Vietnamese and Vietcong prisoners.

The battle of Ia Drang Valley was significant, because although American and ARVN forces managed to thwart a sweep from the Central Highlands to the populated coast, the battling confirmed that the enemy was both brave and resourceful. Following five days of especially heavy combat, the Pentagon estimated that a record number of American soldiers, 240, had been killed. This was triple the previous weekly high. Another 470 were wounded. Though the Pentagon reported a sensationally positive "kill ratio" (the North Vietnamese and Vietcong, it said, lost 2,262), a "CBS Special News Report" on the fighting hosted by Walter Cronkite on November 30 helped viewers understand that it had been a ferocious and bloody experience for all.

Shaken, General Westmoreland, the Joint Chiefs of Staff, and Defense Secretary McNamara knew that while escalation had helped to stabilize the South Vietnamese government in Saigon and prevent military collapse, the situation remained perilous. The Joint Chiefs, determined to prevail, demanded a range of escalatory responses, including a bombing of Hanoi and a bombing and naval blockade and mining of Haiphong's harbor. But when McNamara returned from a trip to Vietnam after the battle—his seventh visit there—he seemed a bit subdued, and he was more candid than usual with reporters. He told them, "It will be a long war."[26]

———

WHILE THE VIETNAM WAR WAS HEATING UP IN LATE 1965, LEADERS of SDS and other oppositional groups continued to face organizational problems. Young people, after all, had left the campuses during the summer, and on their return they continued to be difficult to coordinate.[27] SDS was in disarray, with many in its national office still focusing on poverty and related issues. Todd Gitlin, later describing its situation, recalled that the organization was then "crawling around in the semi-dark."[28] Still, foes of the war were mobilizing. Higher draft calls, which were expected to rise to more than forty-five thousand in the month of December, especially alarmed young people.[29]

Seeking to make themselves heard, antiwar activists began staging newsworthy demonstrations, notably the International Days of Protest Against American Military Intervention in Vietnam on October 15 and 16 that featured marches, speeches, and demonstrations in some forty cities across the United States. Estimates were that as many as a hundred thousand people took part. Thousands of people, young as well as not so young, paraded from Berkeley to protest at the Oakland army supply depot. Ronald Reagan blasted the demonstrations—and the liberals who failed to quash them—as "the fruit of appeasement."[30] In Manhattan, David Miller, a twenty-two-year-old member of the pacifist Catholic Worker movement, was arrested in Manhattan under the federal law against draft card burning that Congress had approved at the end of August. Miller later served twenty-two months in a federal prison.

Though the protests of mid-October did not affect the prosecution of the war, they received an even more hostile reception in the media than in the spring. No longer were the demonstrators treated as trivial. Many stories now identified them as bearded, disheveled, and dangerous.[31] *Time* ran a feature story titled, "Vietniks:

Self-Defeating Dissent," in which it reported that "active, militant protestors" were a "ragtag collection of the unshaven and the un-
scrubbed." Some, the story continued, were communists, Marxists,
and "selective pacifists" who were promoting resistance to the draft.
Time concluded by informing readers that what the Vietniks were
achieving was "probably what they would least like: prolonging the
war and adding to the casualty lists on both sides."[32]

Newsweek chimed in on November 1 with a lengthy article, "The
Demonstrators: Why? How Many?" After identifying antiwar activists
as "young draftniks and Vietniks" wearing "faded dungarees and steel-
rimmed glasses," it went on to observe that the antiwar movement was
"marked by an unwillingness—especially where collaboration with the
Communists is concerned—to absorb the lessons of history, and by a
penchant for thinking the worst of their country and their leaders."
The protestors were a "highly fragmented collection of individuals
and groups with little in common beyond their distaste for what's hap-
pening in Vietnam. . . . They are the young radicals, often bearded
and sandaled, always verbose and earnest, who have made civil rights,
university reform, and a decentralized ideal called 'participatory democracy' their catchwords."[33]

Having described the protestors as fragmented, *Newsweek* proceeded
to argue that they nonetheless posed a threat. Some, it reported, were
"self-consciously unwashed, undisguised Viet Cong rooters." Others
(here the magazine cited FBI chief J. Edgar Hoover) were communists exploiting the young. *Newsweek* applauded a call by Johnson for
an investigation of the protestors, and quoted Thomas Dodd, a
prowar Democrat from Connecticut who headed the Senate's internal
security subcommittee: "The control of the anti-Vietnam movement
has clearly passed from the hands of moderate elements . . . [to those]
who are openly sympathetic to the Viet Cong and openly hostile to
the United States. . . . We have to draw a line, and draw it hard, between the right of free speech and assembly and the right to perpe-
trate treason."[34]

Other politicians seconded Dodd. California Senator Thomas
Kuchel, a Republican, denounced the "vicious, venomous, and vile
leaders of the infamous movement who attempt to influence young
people of this country to evade the draft by fraud and chicanery."

Dirksen called for quick punishment of "the wailing, quailing, protesting young men themselves." Democratic representative Hugh Carey of Brooklyn added, "The time has come not only to wave the flag but to wash from the toes of America this un-American case of athlete's foot which pretends to be part of the contagion of freedom."[35]

While news stories such as these grossly distorted the views and goals of antiwar protestors—SDS, for instance, had not endorsed draft resistance—the reports that drew attention to continuing disunity within antiwar forces were on target. Groups opposing the war were still not organized as a movement. They tried to accommodate pacifists—many of them religiously motivated opponents of all wars— as well as larger numbers who objected primarily to the war in Vietnam. Some protestors demanded, "Bring the GIs Home Now," while others urged the administration to seek negotiations with the enemy. Contrary to the fulminations of super-patriots like Senator Dodd, antiwar advocates were hardly a significant threat to the administration or to the war effort in October 1965.

Few antiwar actions during the next three weeks attracted more attention than those of two young pacifists who immolated themselves. The first, Norman Morrison, was a thirty-one-year-old Quaker from Baltimore. On November 2, he burned himself to death within forty feet of McNamara's window at the Pentagon. He left a wife and three young children. A week later, Roger LaPorte, a twenty-two-year-old student and member of the Catholic Worker movement, set himself afire outside UN headquarters in New York City. Still alive, he gasped, "I'm a Catholic worker. I'm against war, all wars. I did this as a religious action." LaPorte clung to life through the night of the blackout but died the next day.

Sacrifices such as these, however, did not seem to move the population at large. Many Americans, swept up in Cold War fears, continued to insist that the United States fight against communist aggression. Four days after Morrison's death, counterdemonstrators showed up to heckle antiwar protestors in New York City's Union Square. "Do not weep for Norman Morrison and his family," they called out. "Let us weep instead for the lethargy of this nation." They raised a rhythmic cry, "Give us joy! Bomb Hanoi!" When a few pacifists, pelted with flying objects and doused with water, nonetheless managed to burn their draft cards, the crowd chanted, "Burn your-selves! Not your cards!" Police, after arresting four protestors for burn-ing their cards, escorted the leaders away for their own protection. Roving bands attacked button-wearing activists as they dispersed.[36]

The biggest nationwide protests of the fall, organized by the Com-mittee for a Sane Nuclear Policy (SANE), took place on November 27. As in October, Berkeley-area protestors marched to Oakland, where a recently formed rock band, Country Joe and the Fish, played what later became a popular antiwar song, "I-Feel-Like-I'm-Fixin'-to-Die Rag."[37] The largest turnout was in Washington, where many of the fif-teen thousand to twenty-five thousand demonstrators who had come to the city gathered in front of the White House. (LBJ was away at his ranch.) Some chanted, "Hey, hey, LBJ! How many kids have you killed today?" The demonstrators then rallied at the Washington Monument.

Though stories and photographs in the media left an impression that irresponsible young radicals controlled the scene in Washington, this was not in fact the case. The demonstrators were peaceful. Some of the major speakers—Coretta Scott King, Benjamin Spock, and the aged socialist-pacifist Norman Thomas—had met before the rally with LBJ at the White House. Most of the speakers refrained from demand-ing the immediate removal of American troops from Vietnam.

An exception was Carl Oglesby, a thirty-year-old father of three who was the newly elected president of SDS. In a closing speech that SDS members then and later hailed as a masterfully coherent explica-tion of the socioeconomic sources of American militarism, Oglesby, identifying himself as a radical, linked the Vietnam War to the baneful influences of materialism, corruption, and corporate liberalism. In tracing America's involvement in wars from the Truman era to the present, he identified many leaders—Bundy, McNamara, Lodge, Rusk, President Johnson—as people "who study the maps, give the commands, push the buttons, and tally the dead."

"We have become a nation of young, bright-eyed, hard-hearted, slim-waisted, bullet-headed make-out artists," Oglesby declared. " . . . A nation, may I say it?—of beardless liberals."[38] His speech received sustained applause, but little attention in the press.

JOHNSON DID NOT NEED TO BE AT THE WHITE HOUSE THAT DAY TO understand the obvious: the war was rousing popular alarm. SDS, though still small, had quadrupled in size in 1965, acquiring a membership of forty-three hundred by December.[39] Moreover, the credibility gap Johnson had opened up in the spring remained wide. Though polls continued to show substantial support for the president's policies, they did not measure the extent of popular unease that had been growing over the course of the fall. "The polls give the President high marks on Vietnam," a National Security Committee staff member observed in December, "but I have a vague feeling that this support may be more superficial than it is deep and committed (many people probably do not even understand what it is that they are supporting)."[40]

McNamara, meanwhile, had for the first time developed serious doubts about the escalation that he had recommended in July. During his visit to Vietnam, Westmoreland told him that the United States would need to station up to four hundred thousand troops in Vietnam by the end of 1966 and six hundred thousand by the end of 1967. This would be more than a tripling of American forces that were there at the time. Even these, Westmoreland believed, would not guarantee victory: at best, massive escalation of that sort might prevent a communist takeover of South Vietnam.

Shaken, McNamara gave thought on return to a proposal by John McNaughton, his top civilian adviser, to call for a temporary cessation of all American military operations in Vietnam. Such a move, he thought, might cause Hanoi to consider negotiations and avert massive escalation in the future. Circulating the idea among top administration advisers, he succeeded in gaining the interest of Bundy. But Bundy, reflecting, then changed his mind. Other presidential advisers worried that such a move would further endanger South Vietnam, much of which was falling under the control of the Vietcong.

McNamara nonetheless brought up the idea at a White House meeting on December 17, the same day that LBJ expressed his yearning for peace while lighting the National Christmas Tree. But no one—not even George Ball—stepped up to back it, and the proposal was cast aside. McNamara then switched gears to urge a less dramatic gesture that had also been circulating at high governmental levels: a bombing halt.[41]

Johnson, bolstered by the Joint Chiefs, at first resisted such advice. But as he had made clear at the tree-lighting ceremony, he wished to seem eager for peace, and after further meetings, the Chiefs relented. On December 19 he announced that a one-week bombing halt would start on Christmas morning. He also dispatched emissaries—Vice President Humphrey, UN representative Arthur Goldberg, Ambassador at Large W. Averell Harriman—on highly touted missions all over the world aimed at gathering international support for negotiations with North Vietnam.

As the year came to a close, however, the bloody warfare on the ground continued, and it seemed highly unlikely that the bombing halt would bring Hanoi to the bargaining table. By then, American troop strength in Vietnam had risen from 23,000 (dubbed "military advisers") in late 1964 to 184,000 soldiers, many of whom were regularly engaging in combat. The number of Americans killed in action by the end of 1965 was later estimated to be 1,863, with another 7,337 wounded.[42] Vietnamese casualties, on both sides, were considerably higher.

This was a grimly unsatisfying end to nearly eleven months of American military escalation that had started in early February in response to the Vietcong attack at Pleiku.

EPILOGUE

1966 and the Later Sixties

JANUARY 1, 1966, WAS A TRAUMATIC MORNING FOR PEOPLE WHO lived in and around New York City: a strike of transit workers, which had started at midnight, idled subway trains that ordinarily carried 4.6 million people a day. Choked by more than eight hundred thousand cars, the city was paralyzed for twelve days before its liberal new mayor, John Lindsay, capitulated by granting wage increases of 6.3 percent to the union.

Lyndon Johnson, too, had a stressful New Year's Day. On December 31, Bethlehem Steel suddenly announced a hike of $5 per ton in the price of its structural steel. When LBJ heard the news at his ranch, he was furious. Phoning Califano in Washington, he snapped, "They probably thought we would all be out partying somewhere. I want to call these bastards war profiteers. That's exactly what they are."[1] For the next three days he bombarded Califano and others with messages aimed at forcing steel executives to back down.

Presidential jawboning succeeded. But as Califano later observed, this would be the "last major wage settlement within the [administration's] guideposts."[2] Inflation began to mount, by 3 percent as of the end of the year. Investors soon grew bearish: the Dow, which briefly reached a high of 1,000 in mid-January, fell thereafter and finished the year at 785.59.

Johnson, meanwhile, maintained that in 1966 he would continue to deliver butter as well as guns. "This Nation," he proclaimed in his State of the Union address on January 12, "is mighty enough, its society is healthy enough, its people are strong enough, to pursue our goals in the rest of the world while still building a Great Society here at home." He called on Congress to authorize a new cabinet-level Department of Transportation (DOT), widen consumer protections, strengthen clean air and water laws, improve mine and highway safety, expand education and health policies, continue the War on Poverty, provide money for rent subsidies, enact a civil rights law that would prevent racial discrimination in the sale or rental of private properties, and fund a new urban program. To be run by HUD, this effort, later known as Model Cities, would employ comprehensive planning to promote urban rehabilitation, delivery of better social services, and enhanced citizen participation.

As for guns, LBJ left no one in doubt. "The days may become months and the months may become years," he said, "but we will carry on as long as aggression commands us to battle."[3]

Many legislators, hearing of Johnson's agenda, grumbled that he had presented a totally unrealistic wish list. Indeed he had. Though it was expected that Vietnam War costs would skyrocket during the coming fiscal year, he estimated that the deficit would be only $1.8 billion. "Are we really going to do this?" one congressman wondered. Trying to digest LBJ's urban proposals, another asked Califano, "Joe, you can't be serious. How can you push this program? Where are we going to get the money?"[4]

These were good questions, for though many of Johnson's top economic advisers were urging him to seek a tax increase to pay for the war, LBJ knew that a hike in taxes was politically out of the question in a congressional election year.[5] It soon became obvious that revenue for domestic programs, sucked away as the Vietnam War escalated, was simply not there. Liberals, realizing that the president would not fight hard to expand Great Society programs, grew restive. When Johnson failed to ask for an increase in ESEA spending, Representative Hugh

Carey, a Democrat, exclaimed unhappily, "We are forced to make a choice here between books and bullets."[6]

As his party was dividing, Johnson's poll ratings began to plunge—from 62 percent in December 1965 to 46 percent by May 1966.[7] Still, he scored some domestic policy victories in 1966. By the end of the session, Congress had passed a truth-in-packaging law to protect consumers and authorized creation of a DOT and a Model Cities initiative. It also approved more funding for higher education as well as the Clean Waters Restoration Act, which required oil companies to remove spills in navigable waters. And it accomplished two presidential goals it had failed to support at the end of the 1965 session: an appropriation for rent subsidies and a minimum-wage law extending coverage to millions of previously unprotected workers. Thanks in part to well-publicized efforts by Cesar Chavez, whose National Farm Workers Union was now recognized as the bargaining agent in contract negotiations with growers, the law included some farm laborers in its coverage.[8]

Passage of these measures indicated that the overwhelmingly Democratic Eighty-Ninth Congress was still willing to back important Great Society programs.[9] But Model Cities, its focus unclear, proved unable to turn around America's problem-ridden inner cities. Congress again refused to repeal Section 14(b) of the Taft-Hartley Act, which authorized so-called right-to-work laws. Reflecting rising alarm about crime and urban unrest—thirty-eight American cities experienced racial disorder during the incendiary summer of 1966—the lawmakers also rejected LBJ's most ambitious request: his controversial measure to combat racial discrimination in housing.

Great Society bureaucracies also continued to provoke controversy. These included not only the Office of Economic Opportunity, which as earlier encountered criticism from the Left as well as the Right, but also the Equal Employment Opportunity Commission. In late June, when Betty Friedan and others called for establishment of what became the National Organization for Women, they complained especially about the EEOC's failure to rule against sex-segregated want ads.[10]

—

BLACK AMERICANS WELCOMED A FEW DEVELOPMENTS EARLY IN 1966. IN January, Johnson named Robert Weaver, chief of the Housing and Home Finance Agency, to head HUD. Weaver thereby became the first black cabinet secretary in American history. In April, an all-black starting five on an unheralded basketball team from Texas Western University upset the Kentucky Wildcats, an all-white power-house from the segregationist Southeastern Conference, and won the NCAA basketball tournament.

In the same month, Bill Russell, still a superstar player (he was the NBA's Most Valuable Player in 1964–1965), was named coach of the Boston Celtics, thus becoming the first black person in American history to lead a major professional sports team. It was nothing less than ironic that Russell, a feisty black man who made no secret of his anger at white racism, represented Boston, the same city in which Louise Day Hicks was rising to fame. For black Americans his new role was understandably a widely celebrated triumph.

Even more gratifying, blacks who had been enabled to register by the Voting Rights Act of 1965 succeeded in making a difference at the polls. Turning out in spring primary elections in the South, they helped defeat a number of segregationist white opponents. One of the losers was an especially inviting target: the infamous Sheriff Jim Clark of Dallas County, Alabama.

Other events of early 1966, however, outraged advocates for civil rights. One of the most infuriating occurred on January 3, when a white service station attendant shot and killed Sammy Younge Jr., a twenty-one-year-old navy veteran and Tuskegee Institute student. Younge, who had demonstrated at Selma in 1965, was helping SNCC with voter registration in Macon County, Alabama. His crime: trying to use the "whites-only" restroom. Younge's killing, protested by more than two thousand marchers in Tuskegee the next day, led SNCC to declare its opposition to the Vietnam War on January 6. SNCC linked the murder to the killing that the United States gov-ernment was sanctioning in Vietnam: "The murder of Samuel Younge of Tuskegee, Ala. is no different than the murder of peasants in Vietnam. . . . We ask: where is the draft for the freedom fight in the United States? We therefore encourage those Americans who prefer to use their energy in building democratic forms within this country . . . knowing full well that it may cost them their lives—as painfully as in Vietnam."[11]

The rage of blacks over the murder of Younge did not stop whites from committing other racist acts. A few days later, white legislators in Georgia voted, 184–12, to deny a seat to Julian Bond, a prominent black leader who had been elected to the state legislature. Bond, director of communications for SNCC, had endorsed the organization's statement opposing the Vietnam War.[12] On the same day, KKK nightriders firebombed the Hattiesburg, Mississippi, house and store of Vernon Dahmer, age fifty-seven, a NAACP organizer who had also been engaged in voter registration efforts. Dahmer died as a result of the blaze.

It was also in January—a year from the time he had opened his campaign in Selma—that Martin Luther King launched his first sustained civil rights drive in the North. Choosing Chicago as his base of action, he moved into an impoverished black neighborhood to undertake what he called a "full-scale assault" on the racist practices of the Windy City. By August, after having encountered violent white opposition (at one rally, a white person threw a rock that hit him in the head and injured him), he secured an agreement with the Chicago Real Estate Board to open up housing opportunities for blacks in the metropolitan area. But white hostility in the Windy City staggered King, who exclaimed, "I have never seen anything like it in my life." He added, "The people of Mississippi ought to come to Chicago to learn how to hate."[13]

The agreement with the board, moreover, did not satisfy militants for civil rights or make a dent in the city's segregated housing. De facto segregation in Chicago schools, having evaded Keppel's attempt in 1965 to curb it, also persisted. King's venture made it more obvious than ever that the quest for racial equality in the North, stymied by unbending white opposition, would continue to be long and perilous.[14] This was indeed the case—some forty-five years later, Chicago's schools had the dubious distinction of being ranked as the most racially segregated of any city in the United States.[15]

Events like these further embittered already rebellious activists within civil rights organizations. In May, SNCC elected Stokely Carmichael, an outspoken militant, as its new leader over John Lewis.

In June, joining James Meredith's March Against Fear in Mississippi, Carmichael called for a strategy based on "Black Power," a vague but combative slogan that signaled his rejection of significant interracial cooperation. By the end of the year, activists in Oakland had founded the Black Panther Party, and SNCC had expelled its white staff members.

All these developments reflected an escalation of militancy among black activists that had surfaced significantly in 1965. They also alienated many liberal white allies and deprived SNCC of funding. Well before the end of the year the organization was bankrupt. Though the black freedom struggle went on, the interracial, nonviolent civil rights movement, which had peaked in early 1965, had fallen apart.

The world of popular rock 'n' roll and folk-rock music, which had featured significant racial integration in the early 1960s, also began to split along racial lines in 1966: rock was becoming a largely white genre, while many black performers were leading a trend toward a style that *Billboard* was soon to label "soul." This was not a "separate but equal" division: white rockers tended to draw far larger audiences and to sell far more records. And as the split widened, many black artists began to feel unappreciated. All sixteen musicians who received Grammy nominations in three "contemporary (rock and roll)" performance categories in 1966 were white.[16]

―――

THE VIETNAM WAR WENT ESPECIALLY BADLY FOR THE UNITED States in 1966. Though Johnson extended the Christmastime bombing halt to January 31, Hanoi denounced the moratorium as a fraud and a cover for further escalation. Efforts for negotiation with North Vietnam went nowhere, and America's bombing resumed with even greater ferocity than earlier. Robert Kennedy, reflecting widespread dismay with the bombing, publicly assailed LBJ for ending the halt. Resumption of bombing, he exclaimed, "may become the first in a series of steps on a road from which there is no turning back—a road that leads to catastrophe for all mankind."[17]

In early February, William Fulbright opened nationally televised Senate Foreign Relations Committee hearings on Vietnam, at which luminaries such as veteran diplomat George Kennan sniped at Johnson's conduct of the war and antiwar senators grilled top administration officials. "Halfbright," as LBJ called him in private, helped to expose a wider public—an estimated thirty million people watched some of the hearings—to the follies of "Johnson's War." And New Left opposition to his policies continued to grow: SDS, focusing primarily by that time on antiwar activity, did not experience anything like the rapid growth that occurred in the later 1960s, but it had 5,500 members as of late March—1,200 more than in December.[18] Recognizing the widening restlessness of young people, *Time* later named the "Twenty-Five and Under" generation as its Man of the Year for 1966.

LBJ, aware that the Fulbright hearings would harm his cause, once again wondered if conspirators were to blame. He called on the FBI to discover whether communists or other subversive ideas were influencing his critics in the Senate. He also tried to divert popular attention from the hearings by organizing a high-level and well-publicized conference in Honolulu. Using the occasion not only to feed the ego of Prime Minister Ky, who attended, but also to exhort American and South Vietnamese officials to smash the enemy, he told his listeners, Texas-style, that he wanted "coonskins on the wall."[19]

Meanwhile, American escalation on the ground, now featuring offensive search-and-destroy missions, became even more widespread than in 1965. And more expensive: it was later estimated that government spending on the war cost $6 billion in fiscal 1966 (ending on June 30, 1966) and $20.6 billion in fiscal 1967.[20] The federal deficit, moderate at $1.6 billion in fiscal 1965, rose to $3.8 billion in fiscal 1966 and to $8.7 billion in fiscal 1967.[21] The impact of the war on American troops was also heavy in 1966. A total of 1,361 American soldiers were killed in the first ninety-nine days of 1966 alone.[22] By December, draft calls had risen to 45,000 per month, and more than 200,000 additional American troops—the largest number in any year of the war—had landed in Vietnam. They raised the total to some 400,000. During the year, 6,143 Americans lost their lives as a result of the fighting, for a total since January 1965 of 8,006.[23]

As these troubles mounted, polls indicated that Democrats were rapidly losing ground. Indeed they were, for many voters were deserting the party. A Gallup poll in late July revealed that only 33 percent of Americans expressed confidence in Johnson's handling of the war.[24] This was his low for the year. More ominously for defenders of liberalism, polls indicated that Americans were losing faith in government. In early 1965, more than three-fourths of people polled had agreed that government could be trusted "to do right most of the time." Thereafter, these percentages fell, to 64 percent in 1968, 56 percent in 1970, and 38 percent in 1974. A scholarly account described the decline as a "virtual explosion of anti-government feeling."[25]

Reflecting such developments, Republicans gained 3 seats in the Senate and 47 in the House in the November elections, thereby securing 10 more seats in the lower chamber (187) than they had had in 1963–1964.[26] They also fared well in gubernatorial races, gaining 8 governorships and earning a split nationwide of 25 to 25. Not all of the newly seated Republicans were conservatives. Successful moderates, who still occupied a significant place within the GOP in 1966, included George H. W. Bush, who won a House seat from Houston. Mark Hatfield of Oregon and Charles Percy of Illinois captured Senate seats. Another new GOP senator was Edward Brooke of Massachusetts, the first African American in United States history to be popularly elected to the upper house. Liberal and moderate Republicans still held governorships: George Romney in Michigan, Nelson Rockefeller in New York, William Scranton in Pennsylvania.

Many newly elected Republicans, however, were conservatives who were on their way to assuming ever-greater power within the GOP. By far the most prominent candidate on the Right was Reagan. A strong campaigner, he overwhelmed Pat Brown, who was the only two-term Democratic governor in California history and who had defeated Richard Nixon in 1962. When Reagan called for "law and order," there was no misunderstanding what he expected voters to remember: troubles at Berkeley and in Watts that had received nationwide attention since the Free Speech Movement had shaken the state in late 1964.[27]

Conservative Democrats also scored triumphs. Among the new Democratic governors were Lester Maddox of Georgia, an outspoken segregationist, and Lurleen Wallace of Alabama, who stood in for her husband, George. (State law had rendered him ineligible to run again in 1966.) All told, political enemies of the administration rejoiced at the result. Nixon, who was eyeing a race for the presidency in 1968, exulted to an aide, "We've beaten hell out of them, and we're going to kill them in '68."[28]

This did not signify that the Democratic Party was collapsing in 1966. Far from it: Democrats continued to enjoy dependable margins in both houses of Congress during the late 1960s and the 1970s. Responding in these years to still ascending demands for rights and entitlements, they enacted legislation to improve the environment, extend rights for people with disabilities, and protect consumers. To safeguard workers they created the Occupational Safety and Health Administration (OSHA) in 1973. They also indexed Social Security and other social benefits, expanded food stamps, and established an Earned Income Tax Credit program (EITC). Approval of these and other initiatives indicated that rights-conscious claimants, overriding popular doubts in the abstract about Big Government, were strong enough to broaden the federal government's reach into domestic policy areas. Thanks in part to the courts, which endorsed various affirmative action plans, the EEOC's enforcement capacity also expanded.

Moreover, landmark legislation of 1965—the Elementary and Secondary Education Act, Medicare and Medicaid, the Voting Rights Act, immigration reform, the Higher Education Act, the National Endowments for the Arts and Humanities, and many others—remained on the books. These significant laws, the most important liberal legacies of Johnson's unprecedented successes as congressional leader, were reminders that 1965 had been transformational in the realm of domestic policies.[29]

It is therefore an oversimplification to conclude, as some historians have tended to do, that an Age of Conservatism arrived as of the election of 1966. Though more and more Americans after 1965 voiced distrust of Big Government, the federal establishment expanded thereafter, thriving even during the deficit-ridden presidential administrations of Nixon and Reagan and on into the twenty-first century. The Supreme Court, which continued to issue important liberal decisions—*Miranda v. Arizona* (1966), which expanded the rights of alleged criminal offenders, and *Roe v. Wade* (1973) were among the most significant—also proved to be a reliable defender of liberal programs and ideas until the mid-1970s.

Still, the 1966 elections demonstrated that the once powerful political clout of liberalism was no more. Fallout from the pivotal events that had started to weaken it in mid and late 1965—above all, escalation in Vietnam and the disturbances at Watts—had seriously afflicted it, ushering in the more contentious political world that followed. The earliest of these more polarized years, extending from late 1965 into the early 1970s, are what should be remembered as the Sixties.

—

AT THE SAME TIME, CONSERVATIVES WERE STARTING TO LOSE WHAT later became known as the Culture Wars. This was not the case with television, where familiar prime-time favorites—*Bonanza, The Andy Griffith Show, Bewitched*—continued to draw large audiences. Risk-averse new shows like *The Monkees* joined them in 1966. On Broadway, noncontroversial musicals such as *Man of La Mancha, Cabaret,* and *Sweet Charity* were box-office hits. It was not until early 1968 that a more venturesome musical began to break cultural ground on the big-time Broadway stage. This was *Hair,* which featured rock music, profanity, antiwar lyrics, drug use, and—most talked-about—a nude scene involving male as well as female actors.

Nor was a turning of the cultural tide consistently apparent in the boisterous and unpredictable world of popular music, where continuities in 1966 accompanied changes. Performers who had achieved stardom by early 1965 again scored number 1 hits in 1966—Petula Clark ("My Love"), Frank Sinatra (his album *Strangers in the Night*), the Supremes ("You Can't Hurry Love"). Most startling to people who were opposing the Vietnam War was the extraordinary appeal early in the year of "The Ballad of the Green Berets," a song that celebrated the machismo of American soldiers. It was written and sung by Staff Sergeant Barry Sadler, a Green Beret who had served as a medic and been wounded in Vietnam. Robin Moore, whose novel *The Green Berets* had attracted a large readership in late 1965, helped him write it.

"The Ballad of the Green Berets," a catchy tune, leapt quickly to the top of the singles charts and as of March 5 stayed there for five weeks, a long time for a popular song. Moore's publisher produced a paperback edition of his novel that depicted Sadler, with a green beret on his head, on the cover. It ultimately sold more than 1.5 million copies.[30] The popular appeal of the song and the book suggested that while increasing numbers of Americans were opposing the course of the war, many others not only admired the bravery of the men who were fighting there but also (perhaps) were looking for reasons to explain or to defend what the United States was doing in Southeast Asia.

A significant sign of continuing change in American popular music, however, occurred in August 1966, when the Beatles released their seventh studio album, *Revolver*. It indicated, as had *Rubber Soul* in December, that the Fab Four would no longer present themselves as happy mop-tops singing upbeat and bouncy ballads. "Taxman," the opening track, delivered an acerbic message. "Eleanor Rigby" (which employed violins to back up the singing) addressed death, desolation, and loneliness. The lyrics for the album's final song, John Lennon's "Tomorrow Never Knows," drew on LSD guru Timothy Leary's *The Psychedelic Experience*, thereby becoming an early contribution to the genre of psychedelic rock. *Revolver*, drawing the cultural battle lines more tightly, rose to number 1 on the album charts and stayed there for six weeks.

—

THE POLITICAL AND CULTURAL CHANGES THAT FIRST GAINED strength in 1965 and sharpened ideological conflict in 1966 further advanced in the late 1960s, during which time still powerful popular expectations continued to transform America's familiar culture of rules into a more hotly contested culture of rights and benefits. Advocates for women's rights were slowly gaining visibility and influence. Hippies and countercultural communes, though involving fairly small numbers of young people, were beginning to attract reams of publicity. So were miniskirts, which—like the hippies—shocked traditionalists. "Acid rock," as performed by the Doors and other musical groups, was flourishing by 1967. Movies such as *Bonnie and Clyde* and *The Graduate*—both appeared in 1967—broke with the hitherto sacrosanct conventions of Hollywood, thereby rendering Hollywood's puritanical Production Code unenforceable. In November 1968, a film-rating system replaced it. Dramatic changes in sexual behavior and family life—more demands for sexual freedom, more premarital sex, more cohabitation, more fatherless children, more divorce—began to shake American society and culture in ways that could scarcely have been imagined before 1965.[31]

Urban disorders, which worsened in 1967 and 1968, revealed the intensity of rage that had gripped many black people by 1965 and further inflamed popular fears of black violence and racial polarization. Campus protests—against university rules and regulations as well as the war—demonstrated the ever-burgeoning rights-consciousness of many in the large and often demonstrative boomer generation. In early 1968, the Tet offensive in Vietnam ended in military defeat for North Vietnam's armed forces but shocked the American people and contributed to LBJ's decision in March not to run again for president. In the spring, Martin Luther King and Robert Kennedy were assassinated. In November, Richard Nixon beat Hubert Humphrey to win the presidential election. By the end of 1968, SDS membership had swelled to roughly 80,000—its all-time high. In the fighting in Vietnam that year, 14,594 Americans were killed and 87,388 wounded. It remained the bloodiest year in the history of America's long involvement in the war. In 1969, as the US began a policy of "Vietnamization" of the war, American casualties began to drop. Restlessness, however, continued to rise on the domestic front. In June, gays and lesbians protested angrily against a police raid on the Stonewall Inn, a gay bar in Greenwich Village. A Weatherman faction calling for violent revolution broke off from SDS, which soon splintered into disarray. In August, some 500,000 people, most of them young, many of them stoned, cavorted in the rain and mud while attending a star-studded rock concert at the Woodstock Music Festival at a farm in New York State. Many of the performers, having adopted radical political stances, railed against American racism and imperialism.

The long-term impact of the Stonewall protest, which by capturing considerable media attention helped to advance the modern gay rights movement, was positive. No such satisfaction, however, is generated by memories of the Weathermen or of an awful event that closed the final year of the '60s. In December, more than three hundred thousand fans thronged to a rock concert organized and headlined by the Rolling Stones at the Altamont Speedway in California. Many in the crowd anticipated experiencing the happy spirit of Woodstock. As the concert progressed, however, drugs and drink took a toll. Fights erupted, causing many injuries. Some of the scuffling, close to the stage, unnerved and disrupted the Stones as they were trying to perform. Members of the Hell's Angels, a motorcycle gang hired as security, stabbed and stomped to death a menacing and drug-addled eighteen-year-old black man. Cameras caught the killing. The Stones, who witnessed the scuffling—but not the stabbing—played on.

—

AMERICANS WHO THINK ABOUT THE SIXTIES OFTEN HIGHLIGHT the dramatic events of 1968 and 1969. This is hardly surprising, for the volatile mixture of restlessness, rights-consciousness, and discord that had first become clearly evident in 1965 peaked in those extraordinarily tumultuous years. By 1970, many once stable institutions of American culture, society, and politics were struggling against powerful pressures for change. While some of these forces enhanced rights, choices, and life chances for previously disadvantaged people, ultimately producing a more just and tolerant society, they also sparked angry controversy and fragmentation.

In 1966, as later in these Sixties, the triumphalism that had energized LBJ while lighting the National Christmas Tree in December 1964 would have seemed absurd. After 1965, for better and for worse, many aspects of life in the United States would never be the same again.

ACKNOWLEDGMENTS

Many people have helped me think about this book or reviewed portions of it in draft forms. They include my daughter, Marnie Cochran, an editor; John Wright, my agent; Lalor Burdick, my brother-in-law; Edward Berkowitz, a historian with expert knowledge of public policy formation; Steven Lawson, a historian of civil rights and of the Voting Rights Act; and George Herring, a historian of the Vietnam War and US foreign relations.

Cherrie Guerzon, Julissa Bautista, and especially Mary Beth Bryson—staff at the Brown University history department—dealt expertly with my many problems involving computers and preparation of drafts. Pembroke Herbert of Picture Research Consultants, Topsfield, MA, and Jane Martin/The Photo Editor, Washington, DC, did a fine job locating and securing relevant photographs. At Basic Books, Katy O'Donnell was a knowledgeable guide throughout the process of bringing the book into print. Sandra Beris, senior project editor at Basic Books, and Beth Wright, copyeditor, were skilled at their tasks.

I am especially indebted to the following scholars, all of whom read and criticized the entire manuscript in draft form: John Dittmer of De Pauw University, Steven Gillon of the University of Oklahoma and the History Channel, Gareth Davies of Oxford University, and Lara

Heimert, my editor at Basic Books. The independent editor David Groff offered a host of useful suggestions to improve my final draft.

My friends Luther Spoehr of the history and education departments of Brown University, Tom Roberts of the Rhode Island School of Design, and David Hilliard of New York City, a former editor, spent a good deal of time talking to me about the book and bettering my drafts. Their comments on a near-final draft were especially helpful concerning cultural matters.

James T. Patterson
Providence, Rhode Island
August 2012

NOTES

Preface: 1965

1. *Newsweek*, Jan. 4, 1965, 10; American Presidency Project, www
.presidency.ucsb/.

2. For the quotation from Burns, see Rick Perlstein, *Before the Storm: Barry Goldwater and the Unmaking of the American Consensus* (New York: Hill and Wang, 2001), xi; James Reston, *New York Times*, Jan. 1, 1965; "On the Fringe of a Golden Era," *Time*, Jan. 29, 1965, 56–59.

3. Richard N. Goodwin, *Remembering America: A Voice from the Sixties* (Boston: Little, Brown, 1988), 343, 349; Nicholas Lemann, *The Promised Land: The Great Black Migration and How It Changed America* (New York: Vintage, 1991), 171–172; George Will, "Eventful 1995," *Public Interest* (Fall 1995): 3–15.

4. Luc Sante, *New York Times Book Review*, June 25, 2006, 4.

5. Stephen E. Ambrose, *Eisenhower: Soldier and President* (New York: Simon & Schuster, 1990), 563–564.

6. Newt Gingrich, *To Renew America* (New York: HarperCollins, 1995), 7.

7. At Indiana University campus unrest peaked most famously in October 1967, when some thirty-five antiwar students staged a sit-in at interview rooms set aside for recruiters from Dow Chemical, makers of napalm used by the American military in the war. Police arrested the

protestors, beating some of them severely. The next day, some two hundred students wearing "Peace" armbands shouted "Liar!" and "Murderer!" at Secretary of State Dean Rusk, who was struggling to give a speech. I was present at this occasion, which deeply divided the audience.

8. For an account that offers the notion of a very long 1960s, see Tom Hayden, *The Long Sixties: From 1960 to Barack Obama* (Boulder: Paradigm Publishers, 2009).

9. These books are: Fred Kaplan, *1959: The Year Everything Changed* (Hoboken, NJ: J. Wiley & Sons, 2009); Jon Margolis, *The Last Innocent Year: America in 1964: The Beginning of the "Sixties"* (New York: William Morrow, 1999); Rob Kirkpatrick, *1969: The Year Everything Changed* (New York: Skyhorse, 2009); Mark Kurlansky, *1968: The Year That Rocked the World* (New York: Ballantine Books, 2004); and Jules Witcover, *The Year the Dream Died: Revisiting 1968 in America* (New York: Warner Books, 1997).

10. For thoughtful interpretations of the immensely varied literature on the 1960s in America, see M. J. Heale, "The Sixties as History: A Review of the Political Historiography," *Reviews in American History* 33 (March 2005): 133–152; and Rick Perlstein, "Who Owns the Sixties? The Opening of a Scholarly Generation Gap," in *Quick Studies: The Best of Lingua Franca*, ed. Alexander Star (New York: Farrar, Straus and Giroux, 2002), 234–246.

11. Theodore White, "For President Kennedy: An Epilogue," *Life*, Dec. 3, 1963. See also James Piereson, *Camelot and the Cultural Revolution: How the Assassination of John F. Kennedy Shattered American Liberalism* (New York: Encounter Books, 2007).

12. To learn what Johnson *did* say in December 1965, read on.

Chapter 1: High Expectations

1. Charles Lindbergh won the first Man of the Year award in 1927. The only women to receive this award have been Wallis Simpson in 1936, Mme Chiang Kai-shek (together with her husband, Generalissimo Chiang Kai-shek) in 1937, Queen Elizabeth II in 1952, and Corazon Aquino, president of the Philippines in 1986. In 1999, *Time* renamed the award Person of the Year (and awarded it to Jeff Bezos, founder of Amazon).

2. Jon Margolis, *The Last Innocent Year: America in 1964: The Beginning of the "Sixties"* (New York: William Morrow, 1999), 364; Robert Cohen, *Mario Savio and the Radical Legacy of the 1960s* (New York: Oxford University Press, 2009).

3. Ethan Rarick, *California Rising: The Life and Times of Pat Brown* (Berkeley: University of California Press, 2005), 292–310; *Time,* Dec. 18, 1964, 68–69; Margolis, *The Last Innocent Year,* 339–344, 355, 363–364.

4. Kirkpatrick Sale, *SDS* (New York: Vintage Books, 1974), 165–166.

5. Students at some other campuses, including public universities such as Penn State, Michigan State, and Kent State, had already been forming antiwar groups in 1963–1964. See Kenneth J. Heineman, *Campus Wars: The Peace Movement at American State Universities in the Vietnam Era* (New York: New York University Press, 1993), 124–125.

6. See John Dittmer, *Local People: The Struggle for Civil Rights in Mississippi* (Urbana: University of Illinois Press, 1994), 215–271.

7. Ibid., 424–445; Robert Weisbrot, *Freedom Bound: A History of America's Civil Rights Movement* (New York: W. W. Norton, 1990), 94–95, 110–114; Todd Gitlin, *The Sixties: Years of Hope, Days of Rage* (New York: Bantam Books, 1987), 149–161.

8. In September, a grand jury cleared the policeman, who said the boy was slashing at him with a knife.

9. Manning Marable, *Malcolm X: A Life of Reinvention* (New York: Viking, 2011).

10. Joseph A. Califano Jr., *The Triumph and Tragedy of Lyndon Johnson: The White House Years* (New York: Simon & Schuster, 1991), 56.

11. Robert Dallek, *Flawed Giant: Lyndon Johnson and His Times, 1961–1973* (New York: Oxford University Press, 1998), 164. The NAACP, founded in 1909, is formally known as the National Association for the Advancement of Colored People.

12. James T. Patterson, *Grand Expectations: America, 1945–1974* (New York: Oxford University Press, 1996), 554–557; Dittmer, *Local People,* 272–294, 302; Margolis, *The Last Innocent Year,* 311–320; Gitlin, *The Sixties,* 151–161.

13. Dittmer, *Local People,* 302.

14. "On the Fringe of a Golden Era," *Time,* Jan. 29, 1965, 56–59. See also Arlene Skolnick, *Embattled Paradise: The American Family in an Age of Uncertainty* (New York: Basic Books, 1991), 82–84.

15. See essays by Wolfe, written in 1964–1965, in *The Kandy-Kolored Tangerine-Flake Streamline Baby* (New York: Noonday Press, 1965). Young rebels such as these, Wolfe wrote, inhabited a "teenage netherworld," 91.

16. *Newsweek,* Oct. 18, 1965, 29, in a story reporting that *Seventeen* would not always continue to do so in the future.

17. *North Hill High School Hand Book, 1964–65,* compliments of my Brown University colleague Luther Spoehr (a student there at that time.)

18. *New York Times,* Jan. 1, 1965.

19. In April 1965, Vidal Sassoon, already the rage of London, opened a salon in New York City. Within a few years, Sassoon-style "wash and wear" haircuts—bobs and other more natural styles—had become popular.

20. *The Gallup Poll: Public Opinion,* vol. 3: 1955–1971 (New York: Random House, 1972), Dec. 27, 1964, 1912. Henceforth cited in notes as *Gallup Poll.*

21. Morris Dickstein, *Gates of Eden: American Culture in the Sixties* (New York: Basic Books, 1977), 185–186.

22. For trends in popular music, see Elijah Wald, *How the Beatles Destroyed Rock 'n' Roll: An Alternative History of American Popular Music* (New York: Oxford University Press, 2009), 213–229; Robert Shelton, *No Direction Home: The Life and Music of Bob Dylan* (New York: William Morrow,'1986), 239–283; Glenn C. Altschuler, *All Shook Up: How Rock 'n' Roll Changed America* (New York: Oxford University Press, 2003); and Fred Bronson, *The Billboard Book of Number One Hits, 1955–1987* (New York: Billboard Publications, 1988).

23. For coverage of TV, see Mary Ann Watson, *Defining Visions: Television and the American Experience Since 1945* (Ft. Worth: Harcourt Brace, 1998); Ronald L. Smith, *Sweethearts of 60s TV* (New York: St. Martin's Press, 1989), 4, 331; Steven D. Stark, *Glued to the Set: The 60 Television Shows and Events That Made Us Who We Are* (New York: Free Press, 1997), 107–111; and Margolis, *The Last Innocent Year,* 104, 106–109.

24. For discussion of films, see James Baughman, *The Republic of Mass Culture: Journalism, Filmmaking, and Broadcasting in America Since 1941* (Baltimore: Johns Hopkins University Press, 1992); Peter Biskind, *Easy Riders, Raging Bulls: How the Sex-Drugs-and-Rock-'n'-Roll Generation Saved Hollywood* (New York: Simon & Schuster, 1998), 18–20; Ronald L. Davis, *Celluloid Mirrors: Hollywood and American Society Since 1945* (Orlando: Harcourt Brace, 1997), 99–104; and Mark Harris, *Pictures at a Revolution: Five Movies and the Birth of the New Hollywood* (New York: Penguin, 2008), 236.

25. Helen Gurley Brown, *Sex and the Single Girl* (New York: Bernard Geis Associates, 1962), 89, 94. See also John D'Emilio and Estelle B. Freedman, *Intimate Matters: A History of Sexuality* (New York: Harper & Row, 1988), 304. It was reported that Brown's book sold two million copies.

26. Noting the existence of a homosexual "subculture" in San Francisco, one issue of *Life* referred to it as a "sad and sordid world."

27. For trends in sexual behavior, see David Allyn, *Make Love, Not War: The Sexual Revolution, An Unfettered History* (Boston: Little, Brown,

2000), 95–97, 117–118; John Modell, *Into One's Own: From Youth to Adulthood in the United States, 1920–1975* (Berkeley: University of California Press, 1989), 305–314; Ann Fessler, *The Girls Who Went Away: The Hidden History of Women Who Surrendered Children for Adoption in the Decades Before* Roe v. Wade (New York: Penguin, 2006); and Leslie Reagan, *When Abortion Was a Crime: Women, Medicine, and Law in the United States, 1867–1973* (Berkeley: University of California Press, 1997), 221–222.

28. *Gallup Poll,* 1917.

29. In 1968, Pope Paul VI issued *Humanae Vitae* ("Of Human Life") reaffirming the Catholic church's ban on all artificial means of birth control.

30. Allyn, *Make Love, Not War,* 177–178.

31. For Johnson, *Time,* Oct. 8, 1965, 81; *Newsweek,* Oct. 11, 1965, 92; *New York Times,* Sept. 25, 1965. Also Elaine Tyler May, *America and the Pill: A History of Promise, Peril, and Liberation* (New York: Basic Books, 2010), 2, 16, 79–80; Gail Collins, *When Everything Changed: The Amazing Journey of American Women from 1960 to the Present* (New York: Little, Brown, 2009), 101–102.

32. For Johnson, *Time,* Oct. 8, 1965, 81; *Newsweek,* Oct. 11, 1965, 92; *New York Times,* Sept. 25, 1965.

33. For an account of United States involvement in Vietnam in late 1964, see the next chapter.

34. In 1965, men received 11,596 law degrees, women, 404; men 6,869 medical degrees, women, 476; men 76,000 master's degrees, women, 36,000. Men received 320,000 bachelor's degrees, women 219,000. Starting mainly in the 1970s, when feminism gained strength, change accelerated. By 1996, more women than men were graduating from four-year colleges and universities. By 2010, more than two-thirds of women over the age of sixteen were in the work force. Women by then received two-thirds of bachelor's and master's degrees, half of law and medical degrees, and 43 percent of MBAs. Lisa Berkin, "Calling Me Mom?," *New York Times Magazine,* Oct. 24, 2010, 12–13.

35. Margolis, *The Last Innocent Year,* 320, 354; William H. Chafe, *The Unfinished Journey: America Since World War II* (New York: Oxford University Press, 1986), 334.

36. Sale, *SDS,* 161, 170–172; Todd Gitlin, *The Whole World Is Watching: Mass Media in the Making and Unmaking of the New Left* (1980; rept., Berkeley: University of California Press, 2003), 21–34.

37. See Andrew L. Yarrow, *Measuring America: How Economic Growth Came to Define American Greatness in the Late Twentieth Century* (Amherst: University of Massachusetts Press, 2010).

38. This figure of $3,130 measured gross, pretax, cash income. It did not include the value of noncash benefits (as, for example, food stamps in later years). The official poverty line for a family of four in 2011, using the same guidelines and taking into account the rising cost of living as measured by the government, was $23,050. At that time, a recessionary year, 15 percent of Americans were identified as living in poverty.

39. Timothy Noah, *The Great Divergence: America's Growing Inequality Crisis and What We Can Do About It* (New York: Bloomsbury, 2012); *New York Times*, Jan. 5, 2012.

40. The low number of foreign-born (who tend to be relatively poor) was yet another reason for the relatively egalitarian nature of America in the post–World War II years.

41. See Nathan Glazer and Daniel Patrick Moynihan, *Beyond the Melting Pot: The Negroes, Puerto Ricans, Jews, Italians and Irish of New York City* (Cambridge, MA: MIT Press, 1963).

Chapter 2: Gathering Storms

1. For Reagan and "The Speech," see Matthew Dallek, *The Right Moment: Ronald Reagan's First Victory and the Decisive Turning Point in American Politics* (New York: Oxford University Press, 2004), 67–68.

2. For conservatism and the 1964 campaign, see John Andrew, *The Other Side of the Sixties: Young Americans for Freedom and the Rise of Conservative Politics* (New Brunswick, NJ: Rutgers University Press, 1997), 209–212; and Rick Perlstein, *Before the Storm: Barry Goldwater and the Unmaking of the American Consensus* (New York: Hill & Wang, 2001), 493–514.

3. John Blum, *Years of Discord: American Politics and Society, 1961–1974* (New York: W. W. Norton, 1991), 161.

4. William E. Leuchtenburg, "A Visit with LBJ," *American Heritage* 41, no. 4 (May–June 1990): 47–64.

5. See Jon Margolis, *The Last Innocent Year: America in 1964: The Beginning of the "Sixties"* (New York: William Morrow, 1999), 327; and Robert Dallek, *Flawed Giant: Lyndon Johnson and His Times, 1961–1973* (New York: Oxford University Press, 1998), 175–176.

6. Quotes from William H. Chafe, *The Unfinished Journey: America Since World War II* (New York: Oxford University Press, 1986), 273; and George C. Herring, *America's Longest War: The United States and Vietnam, 1950–1975*, 2nd ed. (Philadelphia: Temple University Press, 1986), 16–17.

7. *Public Papers of the Presidents of the United States: Lyndon B. Johnson, 1963–64* (Washington, DC: Government Printing Office, 1965), 875.

8. Dallek, *Flawed Giant*, 145.

9. Stanley Karnow, *Vietnam: A History*, rev. and updated ed. (New York: Viking, 1991), 337.

10. Ibid., 399: Karnow estimated that American aid totaled more than half a billion dollars in 1964.

11. "Vietcong" (or "Viet Cong") was a derisive version of "Vietnam Communist."

12. Karnow, *Vietnam*, 34–37, 346–360, 365, 416–419.

13. This was on the evening of August 4, Vietnam time, which was twelve hours ahead of Washington, DC, time.

14. The captain explained that his earlier message had been based on reports by "overeager sonarmen" who had misread "freak weather effects" (it was a dark and stormy night). Most scholarly accounts have concluded that no enemy attacks took place on August 4. Johnson later told Undersecretary of State George Ball, "those dumb, stupid sailors were just shooting at flying fish." See Dallek, *Flawed Giant*, 155, and Margolis, *The Last Innocent Year*, 296. For accounts of the events surrounding the Tonkin Gulf incident, see also John Prados, *Vietnam: The History of an Unwinnable War, 1945–1975* (Lawrence: University Press of Kansas, 2009), 93–102; Fredrik Logevall, *Choosing War: The Lost Chance for Peace and the Escalation of War in Vietnam* (Berkeley: University of California Press, 1999), 196–203; Dallek, *Flawed Giant*, 147–156; Herring, *America's Longest War*, 119–23; and Karnow, *Vietnam*, 376–392.

15. Karnow, *Vietnam*, 391. J. William Fulbright of Arkansas, chair of the Senate Foreign Relations Committee and a later foe of the war, led the chamber in backing the resolution.

16. Todd Gitlin, *The Whole World Is Watching: Mass Media in the Making and Unmaking of the New Left* (1980; rept., Berkeley: University of California Press, 2003), 143; Margolis, *The Last Innocent Year*, 296.

17. Robert Collins, *More: The Politics of Economic Growth in Postwar America* (New York: Oxford University Press, 2000), 21–23.

18. Fredrik Logevall, *The Origins of the Vietnam War* (Harlow, UK: Longman, 2001), 66–67.

19. Charles Peters, *Lyndon B. Johnson* (New York: Times Books, 2010), 92–96.

20. Perlstein, *Before the Storm*, 497.

21. Karnow, *Vietnam*, 341.

22. Michael Beschloss, ed., *Reaching for Glory: Lyndon Johnson's Secret White House Tapes, 1964–1965* (New York: Simon & Schuster, 2001), 132–133.

23. Perlstein, *Before the Storm*, xi; Dallek, *The Right Moment*, 69; Philip Converse, "Electoral Myth and Reality: The 1964 Election," *American Political Science Review* 59 (June 1965): 321–336.

24. For LBJ and Vietnam in late 1964, see Prados, *Vietnam*, 104–114, and Karnow, *Vietnam*, 417–425.

25. In 1963, Ball had complained to Kennedy, "Some day we might have as many as 300,000 troops in Vietnam." JFK, laughing, replied, "Well, George, you're supposed to be one of the smartest guys in town, but you're crazier than hell. . . . That will never happen." Karnow, *Vietnam*, 266.

26. Tim Weiner, *Legacy of Ashes: The History of the CIA* (New York: Doubleday, 2007), 233, 246–247.

27. John Lewis Gaddis, *Strategies of Containment: A Critical Appraisal of Postwar American National Security Policy* (New York: Oxford University Press, 1982), 258; Logevall, *Choosing War*, 375–413.

28. Michael Beschloss, ed., *Taking Charge: The Johnson White House Tapes, 1963–1964* (New York: Simon & Schuster, 1997), 136–137.

29. Dallek, *Flawed Giant*, 87–90. For the description of Bundy, see *Time*, May 7, 1965, 24.

30. Richard Goodwin, *Remembering America: A Voice from the Sixties* (Boston: Little, Brown, 1988), 374.

31. Margolis, *The Last Innocent Year*, 58; Dallek, *Flawed Giant*, 238–246.

32. Herring, *America's Longest War*, 46–48.

33. *Time*, Dec. 4, 1964, 21–22; Herring, *America's Longest War*, 126–128.

34. Gitlin, *The Whole World Is Watching*, 74; Karnow, *Vietnam*, 423–425.

Chapter 3: LBJ

1. *New York Times*, Jan. 2, 1965.

2. See Chapter 5.

3. *New York Times*, Dec. 30, 1964, Jan. 3, 1965.

4. *New York Times*, Jan. 2, 1965.

5. *Life*, Jan. 7, 1965, 4.

6. *New York Times*, Dec. 28–30, 1964; Jan. 3, 1965; Stanley Karnow, *Vietnam: A History*, rev. and updated ed. (New York: Viking, 1991), 423.

7. *New York Times*, Dec. 28, 1964.

8. "To L.B.J.: What *Is* Our Aim in Vietnam?," *Life*, Jan. 8, 1965, 4; C. L. Sulzberger, *New York Times*, Jan. 11, 1965. For Henry Luce's views concerning Vietnam, see Alan Brinkley, *The Publisher: Henry Luce and His American Century* (New York: Alfred A. Knopf, 2010), 445–447.

9. Texas upset Alabama, 21–17.

10. James Reston, *New York Times,* Jan. 20, 1956; "Boom Without Bust?," *Time,* Feb. 5, 1965.

11. By 2010, average NFL player salaries had reached $4.1 million.

12. Seymour Martin Lipset and William Schneider, *The Confidence Gap: Business, Labor, and Government in the Public Mind* (New York: Free Press, 1983), 17.

13. Section 14(b) of the act, which was passed in 1947, authorized states to prohibit union shops, which were workplaces requiring employees to join unions within a short time following initial hiring. States were then free to pass "right-to-work" laws that would pose severe obstacles to union organizing. Unions had long struggled to get 14(b) repealed.

14. *New York Times,* Jan. 26, 1965. He estimated that the deficit for the 1966 fiscal year, which would begin on July 1, 1965, would be $5.3 billion, a significant though not dangerously high sum by the standards of that time. The "administrative" budget did not include government expenditures—from trust funds—for Social Security or federal highway construction.

15. Gareth Davies, *From Opportunity to Entitlement: The Transformation and Decline of Great Society Liberalism* (Lawrence: University Press of Kansas, 1996), 36–53.

16. Daniel Patrick Moynihan, "The Professionalization of Reform," *Public Interest* (Fall 1965): 6–16.

17. *Life,* Jan. 15, 1965, 4; *Newsweek,* Jan. 11, 1965, 16–19.

18. *New York Times,* Jan. 21, 24, 1965; *Newsweek,* Feb. 1, 1965, 10–12.

19. For Johnson as Senate leader, see Robert Caro, *Master of the Senate: The Years of Lyndon Johnson* (New York: Alfred A. Knopf, 2002); and Rowland Evans and Robert Novak, *Lyndon B. Johnson: The Exercise of Power: A Political Biography* (New York: New American Library, 1966).

20. Evans and Novak, *Lyndon B. Johnson,* 104.

21. William O'Neill, *Coming Apart: An Informal History of America in the 1960s* (Chicago: Quadrangle Books, 1971), 195; Joseph A. Califano Jr., *The Triumph and Tragedy of Lyndon Johnson* (New York: Simon & Schuster, 1991), 55.

22. Robert Dallek, "My Search for Lyndon Johnson," *American Heritage* 42, no. 5 (Sept. 1991): 84–88. For the LBJ–Robert Kennedy relationship, see Jeff Shesol, *Mutual Contempt: Lyndon Johnson, Robert Kennedy, and the Feud That Defined a Decade* (New York: W. W. Norton, 1997); and Steven

Gillon, *The Kennedy Assassination—24 Hours After: Lyndon B. Johnson's Pivotal First Day as President* (New York: Basic Books, 2009).

23. Robert Caro, "The Transition: Lyndon Johnson and the Events in Dallas," *New Yorker*, Apr. 2, 2012, 32–49.

24. *Time*, July 30, 1965, 12.

25. Robert Dallek, *Flawed Giant: Lyndon Johnson and His Times, 1961–1973* (New York: Oxford University Press, 1998), 193. The historian was William Leuchtenburg, a well-known authority on the New Deal.

26. Dallek, *Flawed Giant*, 194; *New York Times*, Dec. 28, 1964.

27. For a selection of these, see Michael Beschloss, ed., *Reaching for Glory: Lyndon Johnson's Secret White House Tapes, 1964–65* (New York: Simon & Schuster, 2001).

28. Dallek, *Flawed Giant*, 180.

29. Anecdotes in Califano, *Triumph and Tragedy*, 25–27.

30. Stewart Alsop, "The New President," *Saturday Evening Post*, Dec. 14, 1963.

31. Mark Lytle, *America's Uncivil Wars: The Sixties Era* (New York: Oxford University Press, 2006), 183. LBJ referred to Martha's Vineyard, where many eastern elites congregated, as that "female island." Karnow, *Vietnam*, 338.

32. Dallek, *Flawed Giant*, 186. Dallek explains that the reporter who told this story did not actually observe it but found it to be believable.

33. William E. Leuchtenburg, "A Visit with LBJ," *American Heritage* 41, no. 4 (May–June 1990): 47–64.

34. Charles Peters, *Lyndon B. Johnson* (New York: Times Books, 2010), 140.

35. John A. Andrew, *Lyndon Johnson and the Great Society* (Chicago: Ivan R. Dee, 1998), 9.

36. Peters, *Lyndon B. Johnson*, 138.

37. Cited in Larry Berman, "Lyndon Baines Johnson: Paths Chosen and Opportunities Lost," in *Leadership in the Modern Presidency*, ed. Fred Greenstein (Cambridge, MA: Harvard University Press, 1988), 144–145.

38. Ibid., 167.

39. Robert A. Divine, "The Johnson Literature," in *Exploring the Johnson Years*, ed. Robert Divine (Austin: University of Texas Press, 1981), 11; Edward D. Berkowitz, *Mr. Social Security: The Life of Wilbur J. Cohen* (Lawrence: University Press of Kansas, 1995), 206.

40. Doris Kearns, *Lyndon Johnson and the American Dream* (New York: Harper & Row, 1976), 226; Califano, *Triumph and Tragedy*, 142.

41. Califano, *Triumph and Tragedy*, 94.

42. Dallek, *Flawed Giant*, 195. For a slightly different version, see *Time*, Mar. 12, 1965, 21A.

Chapter 4: Out-Rooseveling Roosevelt

1. Michael Beschloss, ed., *Reaching for Glory: Lyndon Johnson's Secret White House Tapes, 1964–1965* (New York: Simon & Schuster, 2001), 237. In private, LBJ sometimes used the word "Nigro" or "Nigra."

2. Robert Dallek, *Flawed Giant: Lyndon Johnson and His Times, 1961–1973* (New York: Oxford University Press, 1998), 203.

3. For LBJ and Medicare, see Edward D. Berkowitz, *Mr. Social Security: The Life of Wilbur J. Cohen* (Lawrence: University Press of Kansas, 1995), 212–238; John A. Andrew, *Lyndon Johnson and the Great Society* (Chicago: Ivan R. Dee, 1998), 95–102; Charles Peters, *Lyndon B. Johnson* (New York: Times Books, 2010), 104–106; and Dallek, *Flawed Giant*, 203–209.

4. Dallek, *Flawed Giant*, 206.

5. Berkowitz, *Mr. Social Security*, 235.

6. Dallek, *Flawed Giant*, 209.

7. Berkowitz, *Mr. Social Security*, 236–237.

8. Andrew, *Lyndon Johnson and the Great Society*, 97–99.

9. Dallek, *Flawed Giant*, 208–209.

10. *New York Times*, Sept. 20, 2009.

11. See chapter 9 for a discussion of the final bill's passage and its long-range impact.

12. Dallek, *Flawed Giant*, 196.

13. Berkowitz, *Mr. Social Security*, 361.

14. Gareth Davies, *See Government Grow: Education Politics from Johnson to Reagan* (Lawrence: University Press of Kansas, 2007), 9–46; Andrew, *Lyndon Johnson and the Great Society*, 114–115.

15. Davies, *See Government Grow*, 11.

16. Hugh Graham, "The Transformation of Federal Education Policy," in *Exploring the Johnson Years*, ed. Robert A. Divine (Austin: University of Texas Press, 1981), 160–163; Peters, *Lyndon B. Johnson*, 103; Berkowitz, *Mr. Social Security*, 208; Doris Kearns, *Lyndon Johnson and the American Dream* (New York: Harper & Row, 1976), 227; and Andrew, *Lyndon Johnson and the Great Society*, 120–121. A low-income family was defined as one in

which annual earnings were $2,000 a year or less. This was $1,120 lower than the government's official poverty line for a family of four at the time.

17. Stephen Bailey and Edith Mosher, *ESEA: The Office of Education Administers a Law* (Syracuse, NY: Syracuse University Press, 1968), 235–236.

18. Dallek, *Flawed Giant*, 198.

19. Beschloss, ed., *Reaching for Glory*, 197–199.

20. In the meantime, the Appalachia bill was passed and signed by LBJ on March 9.

21. Andrew, *Lyndon Johnson and the Great Society*, 118.

22. Patrick McGuinn, *No Child Left Behind and the Transformation of Federal Education Policy, 1965–2005* (Lawrence: University Press of Kansas, 2005), 13.

23. Peters, *Lyndon B. Johnson*, 103–104; Dallek, *Flawed Giant*, 200–201.

24. Patrick McGuinn and Frederick Hess, "Freedom from Ignorance? The Great Society and the Evolution of the Elementary and Secondary Education Act of 1965," in *The Great Society and the High Tide of Liberalism*, ed. Sidney Milkis and Jerome Mileur (Amherst: University of Massachusetts Press, 2005), 289–319; William E. Leuchtenburg, "A Visit with LBJ," *American Heritage* (May–June 1990): 47–64.

25. McGuinn and Hess, "Freedom from Ignorance?"

26. Davies, *See Government Grow*, 35, 289–290.

27. Dallek, *Flawed Giant*, 200–201.

28. Andrew, *Lyndon Johnson and the Great Society*, 121. The reason why the formula required consideration of a state's per capita spending for elementary and secondary education was that congressmen from Northern states had complained that $2,000—the poverty line for families established in the statute—was lower in real dollars in the North, where the cost of living was relatively high, than it was in the South. Lots of Northern children in families earning more than $2,000, they said, were in fact poor but would not be covered unless the per capita spending multiple was included. Davies, *See Government Grow*, 35.

29. Beschloss, ed., *Reaching for Glory*, 277.

Chapter 5: Bloody Sunday

1. Stanley Karnow, *Vietnam: A History*, rev. and updated ed. (New York: Viking, 1991), 431–432.

2. Ibid., 426–430. This was the afternoon of February 6, Washington time.

3. For this story, see the next chapter.

4. *Newsweek*, Feb. 15, 1965, 23–27.

5. *Gallup Poll*, Jan. 28–Feb. 2, 1965, 1928.

6. Bayard Rustin, "From Protest to Politics: The Future of the Civil Rights Movement," *Commentary* 39 (February 1965): 25–31.

7. Malcolm X canceled shortly before he was assassinated that month. John Dittmer, *Local People: The Struggle For Civil Rights in Mississippi* (Urbana: University of Illinois Press, 1994), 411.

8. See Diana Schaub, "Solve for X," *Claremont Review of Books* 12 (Winter 2011/2012): 22–27.

9. They were early volunteers for the Freedom Summer effort. Two, Michael Schwerner and Andrew Goodman, were whites from the North; the third, James Chaney, was a local black man. See Dittmer, *Local People*, 242–252.

10. *Newsweek*, Jan. 25, 1965, 29; *Time*, Mar. 5, 1965, 25–26. The US Supreme Court in 1966 overruled Judge Cox and reinstated the original felony indictments. Tried in October 1967, seven men (including Deputy Sheriff Cecil Price) were found guilty and sentenced to jail terms of up to ten years. It was the first time that anyone in Mississippi had been convicted on a charge related to the killing of a civil rights worker. Price was released in 1974.

11. These were South Carolina, Georgia, Alabama, Mississippi, and Louisiana.

12. Taylor Branch, *At Canaan's Edge: America in the King Years, 1965–68* (New York: Simon & Schuster, 2006), 20.

13. Nick Kotz, *Judgment Days: Lyndon Baines Johnson, Martin Luther King Jr., and the Laws That Changed America* (Boston: Houghton Mifflin, 2005), 255–256; Hugh Davis Graham, *The Civil Rights Era: Origins and Development of National Policy, 1900–1972* (New York: Oxford University Press, 1990), 164–165.

14. The Twenty-Fourth Amendment to the Constitution, ratified in January 1964, had made poll taxes unconstitutional in federal elections, and in early 1965 only four states—Virginia, Texas, Alabama, and Mississippi—still had poll taxes affecting voters in state and local elections. Literacy tests were then the primary means of discriminating against would-be black voters.

15. Stephen Tuck, "Making the Voting Rights Act," in *The Voting Rights Act: Securing the Ballot*, ed. Richard Valelly (Washington, DC: CQ Press, 2006); David J. Garrow, *Protest at Selma: Martin Luther King Jr., and the Voting*

Rights Act of 1965 (New Haven, CT: Yale University Press, 1978); Steven F. Lawson, *Black Ballots: Voting Rights in the South* (New York: Columbia University Press, 1976), 298–318; Harvard Sitkoff, *The Struggle for Black Equality, 1954–1992*, rev. ed. (New York: Hill and Wang, 1993), 174–183; Kotz, *Judgment Days*, 250–323; and Branch, *At Canaan's Edge*, 6–39.

16. Robert Dallek, *Flawed Giant: Lyndon Johnson and His Times, 1961–1973* (New York: Oxford University Press, 1998), 159.

17. Katzenbach had replaced Robert Kennedy, who had resigned in September 1964 to run for the Senate. Johnson appointed him attorney general on Jan. 28, 1965.

18. Weaver was then head of the Housing and Home Finance Agency.

19. The message, like many of his phone conversations, was taped. See whitehousetapes.net/transcript/johnson/wh6501–046736.

20. Kotz, *Judgment Days*, 258. Much of the following narrative relies on the excellent histories by Kotz, Branch, Graham, Garrow, and Lawson.

21. Kotz, *Judgment Days*, 268–274.

22. *Time*, Feb. 12, 1965, 60.

23. Lawson, *Black Ballots*, 308–309.

24. *Time*, Feb. 19, 1965, 23.

25. Branch, *At Canaan's Edge*, 24–25. In September 1965, a grand jury declined to indict the trooper, James Fowler. More than forty years later, in 2007, he was charged with first-degree and second-degree murder. Pleading guilty to manslaughter, he received a sentence of six months in jail in November 2010.

26. A week earlier, Malcolm X's house in Queens had been fire-bombed in the early hours of the morning. Escaping with his wife and family, he stood outside to watch the house burn down. Though no one was arrested for the arson, it was generally assumed that enemies from the Nation of Islam were responsible for it. Some people, criticizing the failure (as they saw it) of police to investigate threats on Malcolm X's life—and noting the ease with which gunmen were admitted to the Audubon Ballroom—have asserted that a conspiracy involving not only the Nation of Islam but also the police, the FBI, or the CIA lay behind the shootings. No such conspiracy, however, has yet been proven. See Manning Marable, *Malcolm X: A Life of Reinvention* (New York: Viking, 2011). Some people also believe that police investigating the killing bungled the task, failing to arrest the man, also a member of the Nation of Islam, who fired the fatal shot. (In July 2011, this al-

leged shooter was living in Newark, New Jersey.) See *New York Times*, July 23, 2011.

27. Sitkoff, *The Struggle for Black Equality*, 196.

28. *Time*, Mar. 5, 1965, 23; *Newsweek*, Mar. 8, 1965, 24.

29. See William E. Leuchtenburg, "Lyndon Johnson Confronts George Wallace," in *I Wish I'd Been There: Twenty Historians Bring to Life Dramatic Events That Changed America*, ed. Byron Hollinshead (New York: Doubleday, 2006), 317–333; and Kotz, *Judgment Days*, 278–293.

30. *New York Times*, Mar. 8, 1965.

31. John Morton Blum, *Years of Discord: American Politics and Society, 1961–1974* (New York: W. W. Norton, 1991), 166; Doris Kearns, *Lyndon Johnson and the American Dream* (New York: Harper & Row, 1976), 228–230.

32. Branch, *At Canaan's Edge*, 74–77.

33. Kotz, *Judgment Days*, 299–314. Three white men were later indicted for the killing of Reeb but were acquitted by an all-white jury within ninety-seven minutes. See Scott Holmes, "Letter from Selma," *Boston Globe Magazine*, July 17, 2011, 14–21.

34. Charles Peters, *Lyndon B. Johnson* (New York: Times Books, 2010), 108–109; Tuck, "Making the Voting Rights Act," 87.

35. Truman had addressed Congress on May 25, 1946, concerning a threatened national strike by railway workers.

36. Lyndon Johnson, "The Public Promise," *Public Papers of the Presidents of the United States: Lyndon B. Johnson* (Washington, DC: US Government Printing Office, 1966), 281; Kearns, *Lyndon Johnson and the American Dream*, 229.

37. *Gallup Poll*, 1933. The poll also indicated that 72 percent of Republicans and 80 percent of Democrats favored the bill.

38. Robert Weisbrot, *Freedom Bound: A History of America's Civil Rights Movement* (New York: W. W. Norton, 1990), 142.

39. Michael Beschloss, ed., *Reaching for Glory: Lyndon Johnson's Secret White House Tapes, 1964–1965* (New York: Simon & Schuster, 2000), 235.

40. Branch, *At Canaan's Edge*, 164–70; Garrow, *Protest at Selma*, 115–117; Kotz, *Judgment Days*, 320–325.

41. A young black man, Leroy Moton, was also in the car but was miraculously unhurt and managed to grab the wheel and steer the car to a stop along an embankment. The killers were unaware of his presence.

42. Branch, *At Canaan's Edge*, 172–179; Kotz, *Judgment Days*, 246–247.

43. The FBI agent went into a witness protection program. Two of the Klansmen in the car died within the next two years—one in an auto

accident, the other of a heart attack. The third was convicted in 1967 and spent six years in prison.

44. Lee Rainwater and William L. Yancey, *The Moynihan Report and the Politics of Controversy* (Cambridge, MA: MIT Press, 1967), 11–12.

Chapter 6: Fork in the Road

1. The "purge," as it was called, was led by younger military officers, including Air Vice Marshal Nguyen Cao Ky, who was later that year to take over as co-leader of South Vietnam (see Chapter 10). Ambassador Taylor, furious, called the officers together and exclaimed, "Now you have made a real mess. We cannot carry you forever if you do things like this." George C. Herring, *America's Longest War: The United States and Vietnam, 1950–1975*, 2nd ed. (Philadelphia: Temple University Press, 1986), 127.

2. Stephen E. Ambrose, *Nixon*, vol. 2: *The Triumph of a Politician, 1962–1972* (New York: Simon & Schuster, 1987), 61.

3. Alan Brinkley, *The Publisher: Henry Luce and His Century* (New York: Alfred A. Knopf, 2010), 376–379, 445–446. Luce, who was born in China as the son of an American missionary, also dreamed of the overthrow of communist China.

4. See Todd Gitlin, *The Whole World Is Watching: Mass Media in the Making and Unmaking of the New Left* (1980; rept., Berkeley: University of California Press, 2003), esp. 32–77, and Edward Morgan, *What Really Happened to the 1960s: How Mass Media Culture Failed American Democracy* (Lawrence: University Press of Kansas, 2010), esp. 91–115.

5. Robert Dallek, *Flawed Giant: Lyndon Johnson and His Times, 1961–1973* (New York: Oxford University Press, 1998), 289.

6. Fredrik Logevall, *Choosing War: The Lost Chance for Peace and the Escalation of War in Vietnam* (Berkeley: University of California Press, 1999), 136–140.

7. Doris Kearns, *Lyndon Johnson and the American Dream* (New York: Harper & Row, 1976), 252–253.

8. See Fredrik Logevall, "'There Ain't No Daylight': Lyndon Johnson and the Politics of Escalation," in *Making Sense of the Vietnam Wars*, ed. Mark Bradley and Marilyn Young (New York: Oxford University Press, 2008), 90–107.

9. Kearns, *Lyndon Johnson*, 261; Herring, *America's Longest War*, 126–128; *Time*, Feb. 19, 1965, 16–18.

10. Dallek, *Flawed Giant*, 246–258.

11. Stanley Karnow, *Vietnam: A History*, rev. and updated ed. (New York: Viking, 1991), 429.

12. Ibid., 431; Herring, *America's Longest War*, 130.

13. Herring, *America's Longest War*, 149.

14. Karnow, *Vietnam*, 472.

15. *Gallup Poll*, Feb. 16–24, 1925, 1929.

16. *Time*, Feb. 26, 1965, 19.

17. See *Newsweek*, Feb. 22, 1965, 19–20, which printed excerpts from a number of newspaper editorials after February 6.

18. Walter Lippmann, "Toward Peace in Asia," *Newsweek*, Feb. 15, 1965, 19.

19. Kennan was a respected authority concerning international affairs, Morgenthau a political scientist and renowned student of international relations at the University of Chicago. Some contemporaries spoke of the "Kennan-Morgenthau School of American Realpolitik." Niebuhr was the nation's most widely known Protestant theologian.

20. Taylor Branch, *At Canaan's Edge: America in the King Years, 1965–68* (New York: Simon & Schuster, 2006), 23; Simon Hall, *Peace and Freedom: The Civil Rights and Antiwar Movements of the 1960s* (Philadelphia: University of Pennsylvania Press, 2005), 26.

21. *Time*, Feb. 26, 1965, 19; *Newsweek*, Mar. 1, 1965, 19.

22. *Life*'s issue also carried an article by the famed war correspondent Bill Mauldin, who happened to be at Pleiku at the time of the attack.

23. In late 1965, *Time* picked General Westmoreland as its Man of the Year.

24. *Time*, Feb. 19, 1965, 19–20; Feb. 26, 1965, 19. The February 26 issue also ran a story (22–24) about events in Selma featuring a photo of black children being herded on a forced march out of the city. The story's headline read, "Negro Children on Forced March Near Selma."

25. *Newsweek*, Mar. 15, 1965, 26.

26. Nick Kotz, *Judgment Days: Lyndon Baines Johnson, Martin Luther King Jr., and the Laws That Changed America* (Boston: Houghton Mifflin, 2005), 286.

27. Michael Beschloss, ed., *Reaching for Glory: Lyndon Johnson's Secret White House Tapes, 1964–1965* (New York: Simon & Schuster, 2001), 213, 216.

28. Philip Caputo, *A Rumor of War* (1977; rept., New York: Ballantine Books, 1994), xiii, 46, 69–70. Caputo was apparently unaware that

Americans had earlier called the Spanish-American War of 1898 a "splendid little war."

29. Herring, *America's Longest War*, 131.

30. Karnow, *Vietnam*, 432–434.

31. Herring, *America's Longest War*, 39–40.

32. The call, which had been for only seven thousand in February, rose to seventeen thousand by July. Unmarried men age eighteen through twenty-six were subject to the draft, for two-year terms of duty. Until 1969, however, undergraduate and graduate students enjoyed deferments from the draft. Most Americans who served in the military during the Vietnam War years were young men who were not college students and were from blue-collar or poor families.

33. See Chapter 8.

34. *Newsweek*, Mar. 29, 1965, 70.

35. Only twenty-three teams then played for the Division I championship. (By 2011, the total in Division I men's basketball had risen to sixty-eight.) Princeton's Bill Bradley, who eventually starred in the National Basketball Association and later became a senator from New Jersey, was named the tournament's Most Outstanding Player in 1965. For the second straight year, UCLA took the title, beating Michigan in the championship game.

36. Howard Sounes, *Down the Highway: The Life of Bob Dylan* (New York: Grove Press, 2001), 166–170.

37. *Newsweek*, Mar. 15, 1965, 100. He also referred to the movie as "S&M."

38. In inflation-adjusted dollars, the movie was said in the late 1970s to have been the third highest-grossing movie of all time, behind *Gone with the Wind* (1939) and *Star Wars* (1977).

39. *Time*, Mar. 5, 1965, 98–100.

40. *Gallup Poll*, 1933–1935.

41. In December 1964, SDS membership had been estimated to be 1,365. See Chapter 1.

42. Gitlin, *The Whole World Is Watching*, 32–77.

43. Tim Weiner, *Legacy of Ashes: The History of the CIA* (New York: Doubleday, 2007).

44. John Prados, *Vietnam: The History of an Unwinnable War, 1945–1975* (Lawrence: University Press of Kansas, 2009), 127.

45. Karnow, *Vietnam*, 434.

46. *Time*, Apr. 16, 1965, 23. The TVA was the Tennessee Valley Au-

thority, an area development and electrification program established by FDR in 1933. In 1966, LBJ returned to this theme, saying that he hoped to "turn the Mekong into the Tennessee Valley."

47. Kearns, *Lyndon Johnson*, 267; Fredrik Logevall, *The Origins of the Vietnam War* (Harlow, UK: Longman, 2001), 77–78. For Lippmann, see *Newsweek*, Apr. 12, 1965, 25.

48. Beschloss, ed., *Reaching for Glory*, 281.

49. Joseph Alsop, *Time*, Mar. 3, 1965, 38.

Chapter 7: "Maximum Feasible Participation"

1. *Time*, May 21, 1965, 84–88. See also Tony Fletcher, *All Hopped Up and Ready to Go: Music from the Streets of New York, 1927–77* (New York: W. W. Norton, 2009), 222–223, and Tom Wolfe, *The Kandy-Kolored Tangerine-Flake Streamline Baby* (New York: Noonday Press, 1965), ix–xvii, 51–57.

2. Player got even in June, winning the US Open.

3. *New York Times*, May 26, 1965.

4. *Time*, Apr. 9, 1965, 92; *Newsweek*, May 17, 1965, 80. It was also called *Intelstat 1*.

5. *Time*, Apr. 2, 1965, 84–91.

6. Ibid.

7. *New York Times*, Apr. 29, 1965.

8. *New York Times*, May 29, 1965. Sterling Hayden played Jack D. Ripper. The full title of the movie is *Dr. Strangelove or: How I Learned to Stop Worrying and Love the Bomb*.

9. *New York Times*, May 29, 1965. Thereafter, as anthropologists predicted in 1965, the average height of Americans hardly grew at all. In 2011, the average height of native-born American men was five feet nine. Life expectancy at birth in the United States (not the world's leader in this respect) rose from 59.7 years in 1930 to 70.2 in 1965, with women in 1965 living on the average 5 years longer than men. In 1965, white men lived an average of 6.5 years longer than black men, and white women lived an average of 7.3 years longer than black women. *Statistical Abstract of the United States, 1967* (Washington, DC: US Department of Commerce, Bureau of the Census, 1967), 54; and *New York Times*, Apr. 27, 2011.

10. Michael Beschloss, ed., *Reaching for Glory: Lyndon Johnson's Secret White House Tapes, 1964–1965* (New York: Simon & Schuster, 2001), 277.

11. Cited in *Time*, Apr. 2, 1965, 76.

12. *Time*, Mar. 5, 1965, 21.

13. As noted earlier, the official poverty line for a family of four at the time was $3,130.

14. Gareth Davies, *From Opportunity to Entitlement: The Transformation and Decline of Great Society Liberalism* (Lawrence: University Press of Kansas, 1996), 30–53.

15. James T. Patterson, *America's Struggle Against Poverty in the Twentieth Century* (Cambridge, MA: Harvard University Press, 2000), 122–149.

16. Ibid., 136, 138.

17. John A. Andrew, *Lyndon Johnson and the Great Society* (Chicago: Ivan R. Dee, 1998), 73; *Time*, Mar. 5, 1965, 21.

18. Patterson, *America's Struggle*, 140; *Newsweek*, Apr. 26, 1965, 29.

19. See Katherine Newman and Elisabeth Jacobs, *Who Cares? Public Ambivalence and Government Activism from the New Deal to the Second Gilded Age* (Princeton, NJ: Princeton University Press, 2010).

20. *Gallup Poll*, Nov. 20–25, 1964, 1919.

21. Charles Silberman, "The Mixed-Up War on Poverty," *Fortune* 72 (Aug. 1965): 156–158, 218–226.

22. David J. Garrow, *Protest at Selma: Martin Luther King, Jr., and the Voting Rights Act of 1965* (New Haven, CT: Yale University Press, 1978), 127–131.

23. Charles Peters, *Lyndon B. Johnson* (New York: Times Books, 2010), 110.

24. The payment of poll taxes as a requirement for voting in federal elections was banned by the Twenty-Fourth Amendment to the Constitution in 1964.

25. Steven F. Lawson, *Black Ballots: Voting Rights in the South* (New York: Columbia University Press, 1976), 314–318.

26. *Gallup Poll*, Apr. 25–28, 1965, 1941–1942.

27. *New York Times*, Apr. 26, 1965.

28. In 1971–1973, Hicks served a term as a US representative, replacing Speaker McCormack. She also served as a member and chair of Boston's city council.

29. James Reston, *New York Times*, May 26, 1965.

30. *The Negro Family: The Case for National Action* (Washington, DC: US Department of Labor, March 1965), 3, 45, 47. The report did not indicate that Moynihan was the author. In August, it was leaked to the public, at which point it became known as the Moynihan Report and unleashed widespread public controversy. See Chapter 11.

31. Lee Rainwater and William Yancey, *The Moynihan Report and the Politics of Controversy* (Cambridge, MA: MIT Press, 1967), 22–23.

32. *New York Times,* June 5, 7, 1965; *Newsweek,* June 14, 1965, 37–38.

33. James T. Patterson, *Freedom Is Not Enough: The Moynihan Report and America's Struggle over Black Family Life from LBJ to Obama* (New York: Basic Books, 2010), ix–xv. For the text of the speech see Rainwater and Yancey, *The Moynihan Report,* 125–132.

34. Beschloss, ed., *Reaching for Glory,* 389.

Chapter 8: A Credibility Gap

1. George C. Herring, *America's Longest War: The United States and Vietnam, 1950–1975,* 2nd ed. (Philadelphia: Temple University Press, 1986), 130.

2. *Time,* Apr. 16, 1965, 23.

3. Some estimates counted as many as thirty thousand participants.

4. "New Look on the New Left: Solidarity Forever," *Newsweek,* May 24, 1965, 29–32.

5. In the summer of 1965, efforts to coordinate antiwar activities led to the formation of the National Coordinating Committee to End the War, which helped to organize huge rallies in the fall. But it, too, faced internal divisions, disbanding in early 1966.

6. Kirkpatrick Sale, *SDS* (New York: Vintage Books, 1974), 193.

7. Ibid., 479–480.

8. Studies of the antiwar movement include Simon Hall, *Peace and Freedom: The Civil Rights and Antiwar Movements of the 1960s* (Philadelphia: University of Pennsylvania Press, 2005); Kenneth J. Heineman, *Campus Wars: The Peace Movement at American State Universities in the Vietnam Era* (New York: New York University Press, 1993); Todd Gitlin, *The Whole World Is Watching: Mass Media in the Making and Unmaking of the New Left* (1980; rept., Berkeley: University of California Press, 2003), esp. xiii–xxv, 1–77; Todd Gitlin, *The Sixties: Years of Hope, Days of Rage* (New York: Bantam Books, 1987); and Sale, *SDS.*

9. Hall, *Peace and Freedom,* 12.

10. Gitlin, *The Whole World Is Watching,* 29–35.

11. Senator Wayne Morse of Oregon was the other anti–Tonkin Gulf Resolution senator at that time.

12. *New York Times,* Apr. 18, 1965. See also Gitlin, *The Whole World Is Watching,* 45–60, which focuses on media coverage of the demonstrations.

13. Gitlin, *The Whole World Is Watching,* 56.

14. Gitlin, *The Sixties*, 182–183.

15. Doris Kearns, *Lyndon Johnson and the American Dream* (New York: Harper & Row, 1976), 312.

16. Though LBJ did not announce the decision, it became an open secret, thereby arousing widespread commentary, much of it reflecting alarm at the situation in Vietnam.

17. Herring, *America's Longest War*, 132. The figure of forty thousand included not only the seven thousand combat soldiers sent since March 8 but also the twenty-three thousand or so, many of whom were noncombat soldiers, who had been in Vietnam as military advisers in January. Others, authorized previously, were under way.

18. Michael Beschloss, ed., *Reaching for Glory: Lyndon Johnson's Secret White House Tapes* (New York: Simon & Schuster, 2001), 282.

19. Ibid.

20. *Newsweek*, May 10, 1965, 35–38. See also Robert Dallek, *Flawed Giant: Lyndon Johnson and His Times* (New York: Oxford University Press, 1998), 262–268; and George C. Herring, *From Colony to Superpower: U.S. Foreign Relations Since 1776* (New York: Oxford University Press, 2008), 735–736.

21. For telephone conversations between LBJ and others about this rebellion, see Beschloss, ed., *Reaching for Glory*, 284–342.

22. Tim Weiner, *Legacy of Ashes: The History of the CIA* (New York: Doubleday, 2007), 230–231.

23. Herring, *From Colony to Superpower*, 735.

24. Stephen E. Ambrose, *Rise to Globalism: American Foreign Policy, 1938–1980* (New York: Penguin Books, 1980), 219–221.

25. Weiner, *Legacy of Ashes*, 231.

26. Beschloss, ed., *Reaching for Glory*, 308.

27. Herring, *From Colony to Superpower*, 735. Some contemporary news reports estimated the number of American troops there to be as high as thirty-two thousand. See *Newsweek*, May 17, 1965, 27.

28. Beschloss, ed., *Reaching for Glory*, 317.

29. *Gallup Poll*, May 13–18, 1965, 1942–1943.

30. Beschloss, ed., *Reaching for Glory*, 310.

31. Defense Department estimates. *Newsweek*, May 10, 1965, 35–38, estimated the US death toil at that point at around sixty.

32. Herring, *America's Longest War*, 131–132.

33. Fredrik Logevall, *The Origins of the Vietnam War* (Harlow, UK: Longman, 2001), 80–82.

34. Stanley Karnow, *Vietnam: A History*, rev. and updated ed. (New York: Viking, 1991), 437.

35. *Newsweek*, May 24, 1965, 48. At this time, one of the earliest books detailing America's early 1960s blunders in Vietnam, David Halberstam's *The Making of a Quagmire*, appeared. Halberstam had been a *New York Times* reporter in Vietnam.

36. *New York Times*, June 10, 1965, and June 30, 1985.

37. Emmett Hughes, *Newsweek*, May 31, 1965, 17.

38. Dallek, *Flawed Giant*, 280–281.

39. Art Buchwald, *Newsweek*, June 7, 1965, 48.

40. *Gallup Poll*, April 23–28, 1940; *Newsweek*, May 17, 1965, 34.

41. Joseph A. Califano Jr., *The Triumph and Tragedy of Lyndon Johnson: The White House Years* (New York: Simon & Schuster, 1991), 33.

42. Karnow, *Vietnam*, 481.

43. Philip Caputo, *A Rumor of War* (1977; rept., New York: Ballantine Books, 1994), xx, 74, 109.

Chapter 9: "The Times They Are A-Changin'"

1. *Life*, June 18, 1965. It was a four-day journey. James McDivitt, commander of *Gemini IV*, took photos from inside the capsule. White was the second man to "walk" in space, following Soviet cosmonaut Aleksei Leonov, who did so on March 18 of that year. Tragically, White was also to become one of three American astronauts who died in a spacecraft fire during a launch-pad test in January 1967. The others were Gus Grissom and Roger Chaffee.

2. *New York Times*, July 2, 1965. The jobless rate for adult women was 4.8 percent, for blacks as a whole 8 percent, and for whites, 4.3 percent.

3. *New York Times*, July 8, 1965. Critics, however, complained that GM cars in 1966 would not feature dual braking systems or steering wheels that would absorb the impact of a crash. Others demanded that manufacturers add devices to curb exhaust fumes.

4. *New York Times*, July 17, 1965.

5. By then, Salinger had retreated to New Hampshire, where he lived reclusively until his death in 2010.

6. The theme song, "What's New Pussycat?" as sung by Tom Jones, later rose to number 3 on pop music charts.

7. "(I Can't Get No) Satisfaction," Wikipedia, en.wikipedia.org/wiki/%28I_Can%27t_Get_No%29_Satisfaction.

8. Todd Gitlin, *The Sixties: Years of Hope, Days of Rage* (New York: Bantam Books, 1987), 199.

9. Howard Sounes, *Down the Highway: The Life of Bob Dylan* (New York: Grove Press, 2001), 178–179.

10. Tony Fletcher, *All Hopped Up and Ready to Go: Music from the Streets of New York, 1927–77* (New York: W. W. Norton, 2009), 220–221. See also Glenn C. Altschuler, *All Shook Up: How Rock 'n' Roll Changed America* (New York: Oxford University Press, 2003), 184.

11. Morris Dickstein, *Gates of Eden: American Culture in the Sixties* (New York: Basic Books, 1977), 191.

12. Robert Shelton, *No Direction Home: The Life and Music of Bob Dylan* (New York: William Morrow, 1986), 301–304; Sounes, *Down the Highway*, 180–183.

13. "The Children of Bobby Dylan," *Life*, Nov. 5, 1965, 43–50.

14. Tony Fletcher, *All Hopped Up*, 221; *New York Times*, Mar. 15, 2007. For Dylan and Newport, especially in 2002, see Sean Wilentz, *Bob Dylan in America* (New York: Doubleday, 2010), 276–286.

15. Dickstein, *Gates of Eden*, 188.

16. Gitlin, *The Sixties*, 199. See also Dickstein, *Gates of Eden*, 202–204.

17. Dickstein, *Gates of Eden*, 191. "Like a Rolling Stone" appeared in Dylan's next album, *Highway 61 Revisited*, which was released on August 31.

18. Fans paid $5 (plus 65 cents in taxes) for a field-box ticket at Shea. The Beatles' tour ended with hugely successful concerts at the Cow Palace in San Francisco. *Time*, Sept. 10, 1965, 34. The Beatles' movie *Help!* opened in early August and was also a hit.

19. For Sinatra's fame in 1965, see Gay Talese, "Frank Sinatra Has a Cold," *Esquire* (March 1966): 89–98.

20. Joel Whitburn, *The Billboard Book of Top 40 Albums* (New York: Billboard Publications, 1987).

21. *Abernathy v. Alabama* (on April 5, 1965). This decision did not require the Supreme Court to write a new opinion. The Court simply cited an earlier Interstate Commerce Commission ruling that had mandated the desegregation of interstate public travel facilities.

22. The case number is 381 U.S. 479 (1965). See Mark Stein, "The Supreme Court's Sexual Counter-Revolution," *Organization of American History Magazine* (March 2006): 21–25; David Allyn, *Make Love, Not War: The Sexual Revolution, An Unfettered History* (Boston: Little, Brown, 2000), 36–39, 196; Elaine Tyler May, *America and the Pill: A History of Promise, Peril, and Liberation* (New York: Basic Books, 2010), 118; and Gail Collins, *When Everything Changed: The Amazing Journey of American Women from 1960 to the Present* (New York: Little, Brown, 2009), 158–163.

23. *New York Times,* June 2, 1965; *Time,* June 11, 1965. No such trend, however, developed. In 2011, thirty-five states and the federal government authorized the death penalty.

24. *New York Times,* June 17, 21, 1965. In mid-June, Congress also approved excise tax cuts totaling $4.8 billion over the next four years.

25. The Housing and Redevelopment Act was passed in late July. For Medicare and voting rights legislation, see later in this chapter.

26. In 1965, 52 percent of men and 34 percent of women smoked. By 2009, no thanks to this act, the percentages had fallen to 23.5 percent and 17.9 percent.

27. As noted earlier, Section 14(b) permitted states to outlaw "union shops" (in which a worker must join a union to keep his or her job). These were known as "right-to-work" laws and were bitterly opposed by unions. Nineteen states had such laws at the time. See *Time,* Aug. 6, 1965, 22–23. (In 2012, twenty-two states had them.)

28. Robert Dallek, *Flawed Giant: Lyndon Johnson and His Times, 1961–1973* (New York: Oxford University Press, 1998), 209–210.

29. Of the 30 GOP senators who voted on the final version, 13 backed it. In the House, 70 of the 138 Republicans who voted on it approved it.

30. John A. Andrew, *Lyndon Johnson and the Great Society* (Chicago: Ivan R. Dee, 1998), 102.

31. *Time,* July 16, 1965, 16; *Newsweek,* Aug. 2, 1965, 27.

32. Dallek, *Flawed Giant,* 211.

33. Edward Berkowitz, "Medicare: The Great Society's Enduring National Health Program," in *The Great Society and the High Tide of American Liberalism,* ed. Sidney Milkis and Jerome Mileur (Amherst: University of Massachusetts Press, 2005), 320–350.

34. For a careful description of the law, see Steven F. Lawson, *Black Ballots: Voting Rights in the South* (New York: Columbia University Press, 1976), 14–15, 321–322.

35. In 2012, for instance, advocates of a remapping of legislative districts in Texas had to seek the approval of the DC court. See *New York Times,* Jan. 10, 2012.

36. Taylor Branch, *At Canaan's Edge: America in the King Years, 1965–68* (New York: Simon & Schuster, 2006), 277.

37. In March 1966, the Supreme Court declared that poll taxes were unconstitutional requirements for voting in state and local elections. The case was *Harper v. Virginia State Board of Elections.*

38. *New York Times,* Aug. 7, 1965.

39. Lawson, *Black Ballots*, 321–2; *Newsweek*, Aug. 16, 1965, 15.

40. David J. Garrow, *Protest at Selma: Martin Luther King, Jr., and the Voting Rights Act of 1965* (New Haven, CT: Yale University Press, 1978), 189.

41. Steven F. Lawson, *In Pursuit of Power: Southern Blacks and Electoral Politics, 1965–1982* (New York: Columbia University Press, 1985), 296–303. Lewis later estimated that in August 1965 there were only three hundred African Americans holding elective office—a number that the Voting Rights Act, bolstered by later legislation, helped to increase to nine thousand (including forty-three US congressmen) by 2011. Lewis, "A Poll Tax by Another Name," *New York Times*, Aug. 27, 2011.

Chapter 10: Bombshell from Saigon

1. Stanley Karnow, *Vietnam: A History*, rev. and updated ed. (New York: Viking, 1991), 437–441.

2. *Time*, Oct. 22, 1965, 28–40. This was a lengthy cover story on improvements in Vietnam since June.

3. George C. Herring, *America's Longest War: The United States and Vietnam, 1950–1975*, 2nd ed. (Philadelphia: Temple University Press, 1986), 137.

4. Karnow, *Vietnam*, 439.

5. Key sources for this chapter include John Prados, *Vietnam: The History of an Unwinnable War, 1945–1975* (Lawrence: University Press of Kansas, 2009), 128–132; Herring, *America's Longest War*, 137–143; Michael Beschloss, ed., *Reaching for Glory: Lyndon Johnson's Secret White House Tapes, 1964–1965* (New York: Simon & Schuster, 2001), 343–354; Robert Dallek, *Flawed Giant: Lyndon Johnson and His Times, 1961–1973* (New York: Oxford University Press, 1998), 268–284; Joseph A. Califano Jr., *The Triumph and the Tragedy of Lyndon Johnson: The White House Years* (New York: Simon and Schuster, 1991), 32–36; Doris Kearns, *Lyndon Johnson and the American Dream* (New York: Harper & Row, 1976), 280–285; Francis Bator, "No Good Choices: LBJ and the Vietnam/Great Society Connection," *Diplomatic History* 32 (June 2008): 309–340; and Karnow, *Vietnam*, 437–441.

6. *New York Times*, June 10, 1965.

7. Prados, *Vietnam*, 128.

8. For discussion of constitutional issues related to calling up reserve forces, see Rachel Maddow, *Drift: The Unmooring of American Military Power* (New York: Crown, 2012). Maddow sees LBJ's bypassing of Congress in the summer of 1965 as the key step in the subsequent rise of executive monopoly of America's military policies.

9. *New York Times,* June 17, 1965; Bator, "No Good Choices," 315–317.

10. Karnow, *Vietnam,* 438.

11. Beschloss, ed., *Reaching for Glory,* 364–365.

12. Ibid., 346–347.

13. Herring, *America's Longest War,* 138. Emphasis Ball's.

14. Dallek, *Flawed Giant,* 273.

15. Eric Goldman, *The Tragedy of Lyndon Johnson* (New York: Alfred A. Knopf, 1969), 419.

16. *New York Times,* June 12, 1965; Goldman, *Tragedy of Lyndon Johnson,* 427.

17. Goldman, *Tragedy of Lyndon Johnson,* 475.

18. Ibid., 450–451; Dallek, *Flawed Giant,* 281.

19. Larry Berman, *Lyndon Johnson's War: The Road to Stalemate in Vietnam* (New York: W. W. Norton, 1989), 17–18.

20. George C. Herring, "People Quite Apart: Americans, South Vietnamese, and the War in Vietnam," *Diplomatic History* 14 (Winter 1990): 3; Herring, *America's Longest War,* 137.

21. Berman, *Lyndon Johnson's War,* 79.

22. Herring, "People Quite Apart," 3. See also *New York Times,* July 24, 2011 (Ky's obituary, in which he was quoted as having said he liked the jibe about the saxophonist).

23. Cited in *Newsweek,* July 19, 1965, 19. Wicker added, "But when was this strange and unaccountable man anything else?"

24. Dallek, *Flawed Giant,* 281.

25. Ibid., 281–282. Moyers, too, had broken with the president. It is difficult to assess the accuracy and credibility of recollections that repeat, as if from memory, verbatim conversations.

26. Ibid., 282; Beschloss, ed., *Reaching for Glory,* 378.

27. Dallek, *Flawed Giant,* 283. JFK had promised in his inaugural address that the United States would "pay any price, bear any burden . . . to assure the survival and the success of liberty."

28. Beschloss, ed., *Reaching for Glory,* 365.

29. Dallek, *Flawed Giant,* 284.

30. Beschloss, ed., *Reaching for Glory,* 350.

31. Kearns, *Lyndon Johnson,* 282.

32. Ibid., 282–283.

33. *New York Times,* June 25, 1965.

34. *Newsweek,* June 28, 1965, 19–20; *Time,* July 23, 1965, 13.

35. *New York Times,* July 5, 1965.

36. *Time*, July 23, 1965, 16. It did not make clear whether the South Vietnamese numbers were limited to 1965. It estimated that enemy dead or wounded totaled 107,000.

37. *Gallup Poll*, July 16–21, 1965, 1957.

38. *New York Times*, July 21, 1965.

39. Kearns, *Lyndon Johnson*, 280–285; Dallek, *Flawed Giant*, 274–277.

40. Dallek, *Flawed Giant*, 274–275.

41. Ibid., 275.

42. Kearns, *Lyndon Johnson*, 252.

43. Herring, *America's Longest War*, 139–143.

44. Beschloss, ed., *Reaching for Glory*, 412–413.

45. Califano, *Triumph and Tragedy*, 35–36.

46. Bator, "No Good Choices," 317.

47. Karnow, *Vietnam*, 440–441.

48. Ibid., 345.

49. Lou Cannon, *President Reagan* (New York: Public Affairs, 1991), 290.

50. For thoughtful assessments of "might-have-beens" such as these, see Thomas Paterson, "Historical Memory and Illusive Victories: Vietnam and Central America," *Diplomatic History* 12 (Winter 1988): 1–18; and George C. Herring, "The War in Vietnam," in *Exploring the Johnson Years*, ed. Robert A. Divine (Austin: University of Texas Press, 1981), 27–62.

Chapter 11: Violence in the Streets

1. Mary Ann Watson, *Defining Visions: Television and the American Experience Since 1945* (Fort Worth: Harcourt Brace College, 1998), 243–244. For analysis of TV coverage of the war, see Chester Pach, "And That's the Way It Was: The Vietnam War on the Nightly News," in *The Sixties: From Memory to History*, ed. David Farber (Chapel Hill: University of North Carolina Press, 1994), 90–118; and Edward P. Morgan, *What Really Happened to the 1960s: How Mass Media Culture Failed American Democracy* (Lawrence: University Press of Kansas, 2010), 133–134.

2. *Newsweek*, Aug. 16, 1965, 30–31.

3. Mark Lytle, *America's Uncivil Wars: The Sixties Era* (New York: Oxford University Press, 2006), 191; Robert Dallek, *Flawed Giant: Lyndon Johnson and His Times, 1961–1973* (New York: Oxford University Press, 1998), 286.

4. *Newsweek*, Aug. 2, 1965, 17.

5. *Herald Tribune* editorial cited in *Time*, Aug. 6, 1965, 52.

6. *Life*, Aug. 13, 1965, 30.

7. See Ethan Rarick, *California Rising: The Life and Times of Pat Brown* (Berkeley: University of California Press, 2005), 314–340; Robert Conot, *Rivers of Blood, Years of Darkness: The Unforgettable Classic Account of the Watts Riot* (New York: William Morrow, 1968); and Nick Kotz, *Judgment Days: Lyndon Johnson, Martin Luther King Jr., and the Laws That Changed America* (Boston: Houghton Mifflin, 2005), 338–341. (The woman wasn't pregnant but was wearing loose clothing.)

8. For damage estimates, see Kotz, *Judgment Days*, 343.

9. *Newsweek*, Aug. 30, 1965, 17.

10. William E. Leuchtenburg, *A Troubled Feast: American Society Since 1945* (Boston: Little, Brown, 1973), 153.

11. Robert Weisbrot, *Freedom Bound: A History of America's Civil Rights Movement* (New York: W. W. Norton, 1990), 159.

12. As Watts was erupting, reviews appeared of an autobiographical book, *Manchild in the Promised Land*, by Claude Brown, a black man. It graphically described the miseries of ghetto life in Harlem and received widespread attention.

13. *Newsweek*, Aug. 30, 1965, 15.

14. Kotz, *Judgment Days*, 343.

15. Lee Rainwater and William Yancey, *The Moynihan Report and the Politics of Controversy* (Cambridge, MA: MIT Press, 1967), 192.

16. Michael Beschloss, ed., *Reaching for Glory: Lyndon Johnson's Secret White House Tapes, 1964–1965* (New York: Simon & Schuster, 2001), 420.

17. Califano, *Triumph and Tragedy*, 59–63. Reagan did run, blasting white liberals for having been permissive in the face of black violence.

18. Dallek, *Flawed Giant*, 223–224.

19. *New York Times*, Aug. 20, 1965.

20. Taylor Branch, *At Canaan's Edge: America in the King Years, 1965–68* (New York: Simon & Schuster, 2006), 306–307.

21. A total of twenty-six black people were killed by police or guardsmen. In addition, a storeowner shot and killed a looter, a white policeman was killed by another policeman who accidentally discharged his gun, a white firefighter lost his life when a wall collapsed on him, and a white deputy sheriff was accidentally killed by rioters. The causes of the other four deaths, of the total of thirty-four, were unexplained. See Charles Silberman, "Beware the Day When They Change Their Minds," *Fortune* (Nov. 1965): 150–154, 255–267.

22. Rarick, *California Rising*, 333; James T. Patterson, *Freedom Is Not Enough: The Moynihan Report and America's Struggle over Black Family Life from LBJ to Obama* (New York: Basic Books, 2010), 68.

23. Silberman, "Beware the Day They Change Their Minds."

24. Patterson, *Freedom Is Not Enough*, 70.

25. Gareth Davies, *From Opportunity to Entitlement: The Transformation and Decline of Great Society Liberalism* (Lawrence: University Press of Kansas, 1996), 100.

26. *Violence in the City: An End or a Beginning?* (McCone Report); "Violence in the City," *Newsweek*, Dec. 13, 1965, 29–32; *Time*, Dec. 17, 1965, 21.

27. For excellent analysis of Watts and of subsequent reports concerning it, see Michael W. Flamm, *Law and Order: Street Crime, Civil Unrest, and the Crisis of Liberalism in the 1960s* (New York: Columbia University Press, 2005), 62–65.

28. Dallek, *Flawed Giant*, 323.

29. Jonathan Rieder, *Canarsie: The Jews and Italians of Brooklyn Against Liberalism* (Cambridge, MA: Harvard University Press, 1985), 102, 254–255.

30. Harvard Sitkoff, *The Struggle for Black Equality, 1954–1992*, rev. ed. (New York: Hill and Wang, 1993), 190.

31. David Carter, *The Music Has Gone Out of the Movement: Civil Rights and the Johnson Administration, 1965–1968* (Chapel Hill: University of North Carolina Press, 2009), and Davies, *From Opportunity to Entitlement*, 94–104.

32. Patterson, *Freedom Is Not Enough*, 76. The 1966 conference, dominated by Johnson loyalists, failed to accomplish anything of substance.

33. Califano, *Triumph and Tragedy*, 64–69; Branch, *At Canaan's Edge*, 333; and Timothy Thurber, *The Politics of Equality: Hubert H. Humphrey and the African American Freedom Struggle* (New York: Columbia University Press, 1999), 181. LBJ had never been close to Humphrey, who had raised questions about his policies in Vietnam. He also thought that Humphrey talked too much. (In December, he complained to Califano that Humphrey had "running-water disease"—"something in the water" in Minnesota rendered him unable to "keep his mouth shut." Califano, *Triumph and Tragedy*, 113–114.)

34. See "CRIME in the Streets," *Newsweek*, Aug. 16, 1965, 20–29; Flamm, *Law and Order*, 51–53.

35. Daniel Patrick Moynihan, "The President and the Negro: The Moment Lost," *Commentary* (February 1967): 31–45.

36. *Statistical Abstract of the United States, 1967* (Washington, DC: US Department of Commerce, Bureau of the Census, 1967), 338.

37. The power of labor unions, significant in the manufacturing sector during the early 1960s, also faded rapidly in later years.

Chapter 12: Eve of Destruction

1. See Anthony Giardina, "Robert Culp," *New York Times Magazine*, Dec. 26, 2010, 44.

2. Another new group, the Doors, with Jim Morrison as lead singer, became fully formed as a band in Los Angeles in September. Until then they had called themselves the Warlords. But they didn't become famous until 1967.

3. *Time*, Sept. 17, 1965, 102.

4. Ibid.

5. Todd Gitlin, *The Sixties: Years of Hope, Days of Rage* (New York: Bantam Books, 1987), 195.

6. Stephen Nugent and Charlie Gillett, eds., *Rock Almanac: Top Twenty American and British Singles and Albums of the '50s, '60s, and '70s* (Norwell, MA: Anchor Books, 1978), 92, 230.

7. Quotes by Robert Shelton, *The Direction Home: The Life and Music of Bob Dylan* (New York: William Morrow, 1986), 310, and Howard Sounes, *Down the Highway: The Life of Bob Dylan* (New York: Grove Press, 2001), 187.

8. R. Serge Denisoff, "Protest Songs: Muted Music of the Revolution," in *The Discontented Society: Interpretations of Twentieth-Century Protest*, ed. LeRoy Ashby and Bruce Stave (Chicago: Rand McNally, 1972), 258–268; Gitlin, *The Sixties*, 197.

9. Robert Dallek, *Flawed Giant: Lyndon Johnson and His Times, 1961–1973* (New York: Oxford University Press, 1998), 280.

10. Joseph A. Califano Jr., *The Triumph and Tragedy of Lyndon Johnson: The White House Years* (New York: Simon & Schuster, 1991), 86–94; *Newsweek*, Sept. 13, 1965, 20.

11. Chavez's union later became called the United Farm Workers.

12. *Newsweek*, Dec. 27, 1965, 57.

13. *New York Times*, Oct. 19, Dec. 16, 18, 19, 1965; *Time*, Dec. 10, 1965, 96; *Newsweek*, Dec. 27, 1965, 57–58.

14. *Time*, Sept. 24, 1965, 53; Oct. 15, 1965, 110; "What's Wrong with the Press?," *Newsweek*, Nov. 29, 1965, 55–60.

15. *Newsweek*, Aug. 30, 1965, 20–21; Oct. 11, 1965, 36–37. The killing of Daniels was important in sparking the rise at that time, supported by local civil rights advocates and SNCC, of the Lowndes County Freedom Organization, which adopted a black panther as the logo for its political

party. See Hasan Kwame Jeffries, *Bloody Lowndes: Civil Rights and Black Power in Alabama's Black Belt* (New York: New York University Press, 2009).

16. By 1970, one-fourth of American college students were recipients of Higher Education Act money. The United States then had the world's highest rate of college graduates. Dallek, *Flawed Giant*, 202.

17. See *Time*, Sept. 3, 1965, 20–21.

18. *New York Times*, Oct. 4, 1965.

19. See Steven M. Gillon, *That's Not What We Meant to Do: Reform and Its Unintended Consequences in Twentieth-Century America* (New York: W. W. Norton, 2000), 163–199.

20. William E. Leuchtenburg, "Lyndon Johnson in the Shadow of Franklin Roosevelt," in *The Great Society and the High Tide of Liberalism*, ed. Sidney Milkis and Jerome Mileur (Amherst: University of Massachusetts Press, 2005), 205.

21. Tom Wicker, *New York Times*, Oct. 25, 1965.

22. William E. Leuchtenburg, "A Visit with LBJ," *American Heritage* (May/June 1990): 47–74.

23. Steven F. Lawson, "Civil Rights," in *Exploring the Johnson Years*, ed. Robert A. Divine (Austin: University of Texas Press, 1981), 93, 95.

24. James Deakin, "The Dark Side of L.B.J.," in *Smiling Through the Apocalypse: Esquire's History of the Sixties*, ed. Harold Hayes (New York: McCall, 1969), 506–522.

25. See "Levine," Department of Political Science, Wellesley College, www.wellesley.edu/Polisci/wj/Vietimages/Cartoons/levine.htm. The date of the original publication, in the *New York Review of Books*, was May 12, 1966.

26. Dallek, *Flawed Giant*, 522; Eric Goldman, *The Tragedy of Lyndon Johnson* (New York: Alfred A. Knopf, 1969), 337.

27. The Water Quality Act required states to set antipollution standards for interstate waters; the Clean Air Act authorized federal regulation of auto emissions.

28. Califano, *Triumph and Tragedy*, 84–86; Dallek, *Flawed Giant*, 229–230; John A. Andrew, *Lyndon Johnson and the Great Society* (Chicago: Ivan R. Dee, 1998), 173. *Time*, Sept. 24, 1965, 27.

29. Dallek, *Flawed Giant*, 299.

30. Tom Wicker, *New York Times*, Oct. 25, 1965.

31. *Time*, Dec. 17, 1965, 17–20.

32. *Washington Post*, Oct. 21, 1965.

Chapter 13: From Crisis to Crisis

1. Gareth Davies, *From Opportunity to Entitlement: The Transformation and Decline of Great Society Liberalism* (Lawrence: University Press of Kansas, 1996), 101–104.

2. See Chapter 7.

3. "Poverty War Out of Hand?," *US News & World Report*, Aug. 23, 1965, 48–52.

4. *Newsweek*, Sept. 13, 1965, 22–30.

5. *Time*, July 16, 1965, 19; *Newsweek*, Sept. 6, 1965, 18. See also Joseph A. Califano Jr., *The Triumph and Tragedy of Lyndon Johnson* (New York: Simon & Schuster, 1991), 77–80.

6. Italics in the original.

7. Califano, *Triumph and Tragedy*, 77–80.

8. Ibid., 65. See also an editorial in *Life*, revealingly titled "The 'War on Poverty' Needs a Battle Plan," Dec. 3, 1965, 4. It observed that the OEO had set up a "series of surface-scratching pilot projects" and "called them a war."

9. Davies, *From Opportunity to Entitlement*, 229–243.

10. Title VII specified that the EEOC's oversight in its first year would affect businesses and unions with one hundred or more employees. Over the next four years, the EEOC broadened its reach, to include businesses and unions with twenty-five or more employees.

11. Hugh Davis Graham, *The Civil Rights Era: Origins and Development of National Policy, 1960–1972* (New York: Oxford University Press, 1990), 155–162, 177–183; and John Skrentny, *Color Lines: Affirmative Action, Immigration, and Civil Rights Options for America* (Chicago: University of Chicago Press, 2001), are excellent on the many issues surrounding the creation and development of the EEOC. In August, Congress authorized $2.7 million to support the EEOC during its first year. This was $450,000 less than the administration had requested. *New York Times*, Aug. 13, 1965.

12. *New York Times*, July 2, 1965.

13. Graham, *Civil Rights Era*, 191.

14. Ibid., 184–190.

15. See Ruth Rosen, *The World Split Open: How the Modern Women's Movement Changed America* (New York: Viking, 2000), 72–73; and Cynthia Harrison, *On Account of Sex: The Politics of Women's Issues, 1945–1968* (Berkeley: University of California Press, 1988), 189.

16. *New York Times*, Aug. 20, 1965.

17. Ibid., July 3, 1965.

18. *New York Times*, Aug. 19, 1965.

19. Gail Collins, *When Everything Changed: The Amazing Journey of American Women from 1960 to the Present* (New York: Little, Brown, 2009), 82–85.

20. James T. Patterson, *Brown v. Board of Education: A Civil Rights Milestone and Its Troubled Legacy* (New York: Oxford University Press, 2000).

21. Thomas J. Sugrue, *The Origins of the Urban Crisis: Race and Inequality in Postwar Detroit* (Princeton, NJ: Princeton University Press, 1996).

22. See Davies, *From Opportunity to Entitlement*, 92–93.

23. *Newsweek*, July 12, 1965, 31.

24. Nicholas Lemann, *The Promised Land: The Great Migration and How It Changed America* (New York: Vintage Books, 1991), 183.

25. *Time*, Aug. 27, 1965, 56.

26. Ibid.

27. *Time*, Sept. 25, 1965, 70; Nov. 12, 1965, 33–35; *Newsweek*, Oct. 4, 1965, 36.

28. *Newsweek*, Sept. 20, 1965, 56–57.

29. John A. Andrew, *Lyndon Johnson and the Great Society* (Chicago: Ivan R. Dee, 1998), 120–125.

30. *Newsweek*, Oct. 11, 1965, 94; Oct. 18, 1965, 98; *Time*, Oct. 15, 1965, 67.

31. *Time*, Oct. 15, 1965.

32. Edward D. Berkowitz, *Mr. Social Security: The Life of Wilbur J. Cohen* (Lawrence: University Press of Kansas, 1995), 248; Califano, *Triumph and Tragedy*, 71–74.

33. *Newsweek*, Oct. 18, 1965, 98.

34. Leo Litwak, "The Ronald Reagan Story; Or How Tom Sawyer Enters Politics," *New York Times Magazine*, Nov. 14, 1965; *Time*, Dec. 24, 1965, 12–13.

35. *Time*, Nov. 1, 1965, 90.

Chapter 14: America at the End of 1965

1. *New York Times*, Dec. 6, 1965.

2. *Time*, Jan. 14, 1966, 20.

3. *New York Times*, Dec. 17, 1965.

4. "The Longest Night," *Newsweek*, Nov. 22, 1965, 27–33. See also *Time*, Nov. 19, 1965, 36–43.

5. Lincoln had been Kennedy's long-time personal secretary.

6. Taylor Branch, *At Canaan's Edge: America in the King Years, 1965–68* (New York: Simon & Schuster, 2006), 373–374.

7. Sometimes known in the singular, "The Sound of Silence."

8. David Browne, *Fire and Rain: The Beatles, Simon & Garfunkel, James Taylor, CSNY, and the Lost Story of 1970* (New York: Da Capo Press, 2011), 35.

9. See Lyndon B. Johnson, "Remarks at the Lighting of the Nation's Christmas Tree," Dec. 17, 1965, *The American Presidency Project*, www .presidency.ucsb.edu/ws/?pid=27411, and *Washington Post*, Dec. 18, 1965.

10. Branch, *At Canaan's Edge*, 390.

11. *Newsweek*, Nov. 8, 1965, 33–34; Branch, *At Canaan's Edge*, 382. By the end of 1965, a total of 229,000 African Americans had been registered in thirty-two Southern counties in Alabama, Mississippi, Louisiana, and South Carolina. Steven F. Lawson, *In Pursuit of Power: Southern Blacks and Electoral Power, 1965–1982* (New York: Columbia University Press, 1985), 18–19.

12. Lawson, *In Pursuit of Power*, 24–25.

13. See Chapter 7.

14. Lee Rainwater and William Yancey, *The Moynihan Report and the Politics of Controversy* (Cambridge, MA: MIT Press, 1967), 254–258. Also James T. Patterson, *Freedom Is Not Enough: The Moynihan Report and America's Struggle over Black Family Life from LBJ to Obama* (New York: Basic Books, 2010), 83–85.

15. Branch, *At Canaan's Edge*, 384.

16. Ibid., 391–393; *Newsweek*, Dec. 13, 1965, 34 (summarizing the *New York Times* article).

17. Charles Silberman, "Beware the Day They Change Their Minds," *Fortune* (Nov. 1965): 150–154, 255–267.

18. *Newsweek*, Sept. 13, 1965, 82.

19. *Gallup Poll*, 1969–1971.

20. Ibid., 1964, 1968, 1972, 1977; *Newsweek*, Nov. 1, 1965, 25.

21. *Life*, Nov. 15, 1965, 36–41; *Time*, Oct. 1, 1965, 38; *Newsweek*, Oct. 25, 1965, 41.

22. *Time*, Oct. 22, 1965, 28–40.

23. *Time* also noted the contributions of allies, including nearly 600,000 ARVN troops, 6,500 from South Korea, and 1,550 from Australia and New Zealand.

24. *Newsweek*, Dec. 6, 1965, 42–43. Between 1965 and 1973, some seventy-two hundred black Americans were killed in Vietnam. This was roughly 12.5 percent of America's more than fifty-eight thousand deaths during that time.

25. Philip Caputo, *A Rumor of War* (1977; rept., New York: Ballantine Books, 1994), xiv–v, 216–217, 230–231.

26. See *New York Times*, Nov. 20, 1965. This story further estimated that 678 Americans had been killed in the seven weeks prior to the Ia Drang battles. See also Stanley Karnow, *Vietnam: A History*, rev. and updated ed. (New York: Viking, 1991), 493–495.

27. For late 1965 activities of SDS and other antiwar groups, see Todd Gitlin, *The Whole World Is Watching: Mass Media in the Making and Unmaking of the New Left* (1980; rept., Berkeley: University of California Press, 2003), 78–123.

28. Ibid., 81–83.

29. "The Demonstrators: Why? How Many," *Newsweek*, Nov. 1, 1965, 25–34.

30. Matthew Dallek, *The Right Moment: Ronald Reagan's First Victory and the Decisive Turning Point in American Politics* (New York: Oxford University Press, 2000), 190.

31. Gitlin, *The Whole World Is Watching*, 76–77.

32. "Vietniks: Self-Defeating Dissent," *Time*, Oct. 29, 1965, 44–45. *Time* soon named General Westmoreland as its Man of the Year. LBJ, it will be recalled, had been *Time*'s choice for 1964.

33. "The Demonstrators," 25–34.

34. Ibid.; *Time*, Oct. 29, 1965, 44–45.

35. "The Demonstrators," 25–34; Branch, *At Canaan's Edge*, 357.

36. Branch, *At Canaan's Edge*, 361.

37. The band featured Country Joe McDonald, lead vocalist, and Barry Melton, lead guitarist. The song was a hit at the Woodstock music festival in 1969.

38. Gitlin, *The Whole World Is Watching*, 117–119; Branch, *At Canaan's Edge*, 385–387.

39. Kirkpatrick Sale, *SDS* (New York: Vintage Books, 1974), 246–248.

40. Robert Dallek, *Flawed Giant: Lyndon Johnson and His Times, 1961–1973* (New York: Oxford University Press, 1998), 290–291.

41. See Benjamin Harrison and Christopher Mosher, "The Secret Diary of McNamara's Dove: The Long-Lost Story of John T. McNaughton's Opposition to the Vietnam War," *Diplomatic History* 35 (June 2011): 505–534; Larry Berman, *Lyndon Johnson's War: The Road to Stalemate in Vietnam* (New York: W. W. Norton, 1989), 12; Dallek, *Flawed Giant*, 340–51; and Karnow, *Vietnam*, 495.

42. Ray Smith, "Casualties—US vs NVA/VC," *Ray's Web Server*, www .rjsmith.com/kia_tbl.html.

Epilogue: 1966 and the Later Sixties

1. Joseph A. Califano Jr., *The Triumph and Tragedy of Lyndon Johnson* (New York: Simon & Schuster, 1991), 102–103.

2. Ibid., 105.

3. *New York Times*, Jan. 13, 1966; Stanley Karnow, *Vietnam: A History*, rev. and updated ed. (New York: Viking, 1991), 497.

4. Robert Dallek, *Flawed Giant: Lyndon Johnson and His Times, 1961–1973* (New York: Oxford University Press, 1998), 299–302.

5. Top advisers in favor of a tax hike included Budget Director Charles Schultze and Council of Economic Advisers chair Gardner Ackley.

6. Gareth Davies, *From Opportunity to Entitlement: The Transformation and Decline of Great Society Liberalism* (Lawrence: University Press of Kansas, 1996), 107–112.

7. Ibid., 105.

8. For the 1966 Congress, see Dallek, *Flawed Giant*, 325–334.

9. See Califano, *Triumph and Tragedy*, 149–164 (a chapter titled "The Great 89th").

10. NOW was formally organized at a meeting in Washington in October 1966.

11. Taylor Branch, *At Canaan's Edge: America in the King Years, 1965–68* (New York: Simon & Schuster, 2006), 406–407, and *Time*, Jan. 14, 1966, 29. In December 1966, an all-white jury found the attendant, sixty-seven-year-old Marvin Segrest, not guilty of second-degree murder.

12. Thanks to the Supreme Court, which declared the legislature's action unconstitutional, Bond was able to take his seat in January 1967.

13. *New York Times*, Aug. 6, 1966.

14. See Branch, *At Canaan's Edge*, 427–445.

15. *New York Times*, May 13, 2012. This lengthy survey emphasized that the public schools in many other large American cities in the 2009–2010 school year were almost as segregated as Chicago's. (Dallas, New York City, and Philadelphia were close behind.) In Chicago, the survey showed, 80 percent of students would have to move to different schools to enable integration to become a reality.

16. Elijah Wald, *How the Beatles Destroyed Rock 'n' Roll: An Alternative History of American Popular Music* (New York: Oxford University Press, 2009), 244–254. The Beatles gave their last concert at Candlestick Park in San Francisco on August 29, 1966. Thereafter, they recorded in studios.

17. Karnow, *Vietnam*, 499.

18. Kirkpatrick Sale, *SDS* (New York: Vintage Books, 1974), 246, 271.

19. Dallek, *Flawed Giant*, 352; Karnow, *Vietnam*, 459.

20. Davies, *From Opportunity to Entitlement*, 133.

21. US Bureau of the Census, *Historical Statistics of the United States* (New York: Basic Books, 1976), 1105. The deficit soared in fiscal 1968 to $25.2 billion.

22. *New York Times*, Apr. 16, 1966.

23. Ray Smith, "Casualties—US vs NVA/VC," *Ray's Web Server*, www .rjsmith.com/kia_tbl.html. The number wounded in 1966 was 29,992, compared to 7,337 in 1965.

24. Davies, *From Opportunity to Entitlement*, 131.

25. Seymour Martin Lipset and William Schneider, *The Confidence Gap: Business, Labor, and Government in the Public Mind* (New York: Free Press, 1983), 16–17.

26. Democratic margins in 1967 were 248–187 in the House and 64–36 in the Senate.

27. Matthew Dallek, *The Right Moment: Ronald Reagan's First Victory and the Decisive Turning Point in American Politics* (New York: Oxford University Press, 2004), 238–239.

28. Stephen E. Ambrose, *Nixon*, vol. 2: *The Triumph of a Politician, 1962–1972* (New York: Simon & Schuster, 1989), 100.

29. See Sidney Milkis and Jerome Mileur, eds., *The Great Society and the High Tide of Liberalism* (Amherst: University of Massachusetts Press, 2005).

30. See Fred Bronson, *The Billboard Book of Number One Hits* (New York: Billboard Publications, 1988), 195. In 1968, John Wayne starred in the movie *The Green Berets*.

31. In early 1966, Virginia Masters and William Johnson published *Human Sexual Response*, which asserted among other things that women possessed at least as much sexual energy as men and enjoyed a variety of sexual responses, including multiple orgasms. Based on observation of men and women engaging in sexual activities, it received great coverage in the media.

A NOTE ON SOURCES

ALTHOUGH THIS BOOK INCLUDES ENDNOTES, I ADD THIS NOTE ON Sources directing readers to books I found to be especially useful. I do not list reports of the Gallup Poll, which I cite throughout the book, or articles from sources such as *Time, Life, Newsweek,* and the *New York Times.* As readers will recognize, I often rely on these and other contemporary sources to give readers a firsthand feel for developments in 1965.

The listing of books here is topical and alphabetical by author within each category.

Interpretations and Surveys of the 1960s

David Farber, Beth Bailey, et al., *The Columbia Guide to America in the 1960s* (New York: Columbia University Press, 2001); David Farber, ed., *The Sixties: From Memory to History* (Chapel Hill: University of North Carolina Press, 1994); Todd Gitlin, *The Sixties: Years of Hope, Days of Rage* (New York: Bantam Brooks, 1987); Harold Hayes, ed., *Smiling Through the Apocalypse: Esquire's History of the Sixties* (New York: McCall, 1969); Rita Lang Kleinfelder, *When We Were Young: A Baby Boomer Yearbook* (New York: Hall, 1993); Jon Margolis, *The Last Innocent Year: America in 1964: The Beginning of the "Sixties"* (New York: William Morrow, 1999); Allen J. Matusow, *The Unraveling of America: A History of Liberalism in the 1960s* (New York: Harper & Row, 1984); and (a collection of contemporary essays) Tom

Wolfe, *The Kandy-Kolored Tangerine-Flake Streamline Baby* (New York: Noonday Press, 1965).

Lyndon Johnson

John A. Andrew, *Lyndon Johnson and the Great Society* (Chicago: Ivan R. Dee, 1998); Michael Beschloss, ed., *Reaching for Glory: Lyndon Johnson's Secret White House Tapes, 1964–1965* (New York: Simon & Schuster, 2001); Joseph A. Califano Jr., *The Triumph and Tragedy of Lyndon Johnson: The White House Years* (New York: Simon & Schuster, 1991); Robert Dallek, *Flawed Giant: Lyndon Johnson and His Times, 1961–1973* (New York: Oxford University Press, 1998); and Robert A. Divine, ed., *Exploring the Johnson Years* (Austin: University of Texas Press, 1981).

Also Eric F. Goldman, *The Tragedy of Lyndon Johnson* (New York: Alfred A. Knopf, 1969); Richard N. Goodwin, *Remembering America: A Voice from the Sixties* (Boston: Little, Brown, 1988); Doris Kearns, *Lyndon Johnson and the American Dream* (New York: Harper & Row, 1976); William E. Leuchtenburg, *The White House Looks South: Franklin D. Roosevelt, Harry S. Truman, Lyndon B. Johnson* (Baton Rouge: Louisiana State University Press, 2005); Charles Peters, *Lyndon B. Johnson* (New York: Times Books, 2010); and Jeff Shesol, *Mutual Contempt: Lyndon Johnson, Robert Kennedy, and the Feud That Defined a Decade* (New York: W. W. Norton, 1997).

Great Society Programs

Edward D. Berkowitz, *Mr. Social Security: The Life of Wilbur J. Cohen* (Lawrence: University Press of Kansas, 1995), especially on Social Security, Medicare, and Medicaid; Gareth Davies, *From Opportunity to Entitlement: The Transformation and Decline of Great Society Liberalism* (Lawrence: University Press of Kansas, 1996); Gareth Davies, *See Government Grow: Education Politics from Johnson to Reagan* (Lawrence: University Press of Kansas, 2007); and Steven M. Gillon, *That's Not What We Meant to Do: Reform and Its Unintended Consequences in Twentieth-Century America* (New York: W. W. Norton, 2000), especially on immigration reform.

Also Steven F. Lawson, *Black Ballots: Voting Rights in the South, 1944–1969* (New York: Columbia University Press, 1976); Steven F. Lawson, *In Pursuit of Power: Southern Blacks and Electoral Politics, 1965–1982* (New York: Columbia University Press, 1985); Patrick J. McGuinn, *No Child Left Behind and the Transformation of Federal Education Policy, 1965–2005* (Lawrence: University Press of Kansas, 2005); Sidney M. Milkis and Jerome M. Mileur, eds., *The Great Society and the High Tide of Liberalism* (Amherst: University of

Massachusetts Press, 2005); James T. Patterson, *America's Struggle Against Poverty in the Twentieth Century* (Cambridge, MA: Harvard University Press, 2000); and Richard M. Valelly, ed., *The Voting Rights Act: Securing the Ballot* (Washington, DC: CQ Press, 2006).

National Politics

Matthew Dallek, *The Right Moment: Ronald Reagan's First Victory and the Decisive Turning Point in American Politics* (New York: Oxford University Press, 2004); Rick Perlstein, *Before the Storm: Barry Goldwater and the Unmaking of the American Consensus* (New York: Hill and Wang, 2001); and James Piereson, *Camelot and the Cultural Revolution: How the Assassination of John F. Kennedy Shattered American Liberalism* (New York: Encounter Books, 2007).

Civil Rights and Race Relations

Taylor Branch, *At Canaan's Edge: America in the King Years, 1965–68* (New York: Simon & Schuster, 2006); John Dittmer, *Local People: The Struggle for Civil Rights in Mississippi* (Urbana: University of Illinois Press, 1994); Michael W. Flamm, *Law and Order: Street Crime, Civil Unrest, and the Crisis of Liberalism in the 1960s* (New York: Columbia University Press, 2005); and David J. Garrow, *Protest at Selma: Martin Luther King, Jr., and the Voting Rights Act of 1965* (New Haven, CT: Yale University Press, 1978).

Also Hugh Davis Graham, *The Civil Rights Era: Origins and Development of National Policy, 1960–1972* (New York: Oxford University Press, 1990); Nick Kotz, *Judgment Days: Lyndon Baines Johnson, Martin Luther King, Jr., and the Laws That Changed America* (Boston: Houghton Mifflin, 2005); Nicholas Lemann, *The Promised Land: The Great Black Migration and How It Changed America* (New York: Vintage, 1991); Manning Marable, *Malcolm X: A Life of Reinvention* (New York: Viking, 2011); Lee Rainwater and William L. Yancey, *The Moynihan Report and the Politics of Controversy* (Cambridge, MA: MIT Press, 1967); Harvard Sitkoff, *The Struggle for Black Equality, 1954–1992*, rev. ed. (New York: Hill and Wang, 1993); and Robert Weisbrot, *Freedom Bound: A History of America's Civil Rights Movement* (New York: W. W. Norton, 1990).

Socioeconomic and Cultural Trends

David Allyn, *Make Love, Not War: The Sexual Revolution, An Unfettered History* (Boston: Little, Brown, 2000); Robert M. Collins, *More: The Politics of Economic Growth in Postwar America* (New York: Oxford University

Press, 2000); Morris Dickstein, *Gates of Eden: American Culture in the Sixties* (New York: Basic Books, 1977); Miriam Pawel, *The Union of Their Dreams: Power, Hope, and Struggle in Cesar Chavez's Farm Worker Movement* (New York: Bloomsbury Press, 2009); and Arlene Skolnick, *Embattled Paradise: The American Family in an Age of Uncertainty* (New York: Basic Books, 1991).

Women and Feminism

Gail Collins, *When Everything Changed: The Amazing Journey of American Women from 1960 to the Present* (New York: Little, Brown, 2009); Cynthia Harrison, *On Account of Sex: The Politics of Women's Issues, 1945–1968* (Berkeley: University of California Press, 1988); Elaine Tyler May, *America and the Pill: A History of Promise, Peril, and Liberation* (New York: Basic Books, 2010); and Ruth Rosen, *The World Split Open: How the Modern Women's Movement Changed America* (New York: Viking, 2000).

Youth, Protest, and the Media

Terry H. Anderson, *The Movement and the Sixties: Protest in America from Greensboro to Wounded Knee* (New York: Oxford University Press, 1995); John A. Andrew III, *The Other Side of the Sixties: Young Americans for Freedom and the Rise of Conservative Politics* (New Brunswick, NJ: Rutgers University Press, 1997); Alan Brinkley, *The Publisher: Henry Luce and His American Century* (New York: Alfred A. Knopf, 2010); Todd Gitlin, *The Whole World Is Watching: Mass Media in the Making and Unmaking of the New Left* (1980; rept., Berkeley: University of California Press, 2003); Simon Hall, *Peace and Freedom: The Civil Rights and Antiwar Movements in the 1960s* (Philadelphia: University of Pennsylvania Press, 2005); Kenneth J. Heineman, *Campus Wars: The Peace Movement at American State Universities in the Vietnam Era* (New York: New York University Press, 1993); and Kirkpatrick Sale, *SDS* (New York: Vintage Books, 1974).

Foreign Policy and Vietnam

Larry Berman, *Lyndon Johnson's War: The Road to Stalemate in Vietnam* (New York: W. W. Norton, 1989); Philip Caputo, *A Rumor of War* (1977; rept., New York: Ballantine Books, 1994); George C. Herring, *America's Longest War: The United States and Vietnam, 1950–1975*, 2nd ed. (Philadelphia: Temple University Press, 1986); Stanley Karnow, *Vietnam: A History*, rev. and updated ed. (New York: Viking, 1991); Fredrik Logevall, *Choosing War: The Lost Chance for Peace and the Escalation of War in Vietnam* (Berkeley: University of California Press, 1999); John Prados, *Vietnam: The History of an Unwinnable War, 1945–1975* (Lawrence: University Press of Kansas, 2009); and Tim Weiner, *Legacy of Ashes: The History of the CIA* (New York: Doubleday, 2007).

Art and Film

James L. Baughman, *The Republic of Mass Culture: Journalism, Film-making, and Broadcasting in America Since 1941* (Baltimore: Johns Hopkins University Press, 1992); Peter Biskind, *Easy Riders, Raging Bulls: How the Sex-Drugs-and-Rock-'n'-Roll Generation Saved Hollywood* (New York: Simon & Schuster, 1998); Ronald L. Davis, *Celluloid Mirrors: Hollywood and American Society Since 1945* (Orlando: Harcourt Brace, 1997); Mark Harris, *Pictures at a Revolution: Five Movies and the Birth of the New Hollywood* (New York: Penguin, 2008); and Paul Wood et al., *Modernism in Dispute: Art Since the Forties* (New Haven, CT: Yale University Press, 1993).

Television and Radio

Tim Brooks and Earle Marsh, *The Complete Directory to Prime Time Network and Cable TV, 1946–Present* (New York: Bedford Books, 1999); Ronald L. Smith, *Sweethearts of 60s TV* (New York: St. Martin's Press, 1989); Christopher H. Sterling and John M. Kittross, *Stay Tuned: A Concise History of American Broadcasting* (Belmont, CA: Wadsworth, 1978); and Mary Ann Watson, *Defining Visions: Television and the American Experience Since 1945* (Fort Worth: Harcourt Brace College, 1998).

Popular Music

Glenn C. Altschuler, *All Shook Up: How Rock 'n' Roll Changed America* (New York: Oxford University Press, 2003); Fred Bronson, *The Billboard Book of Number One Hits* (New York: Billboard Publications, 1988); Tony Fletcher, *All Hopped Up and Ready to Go: Music from the Streets of New York, 1927–77* (New York: W. W. Norton, 2009); Robert Shelton, *No Direction Home: The Life and Music of Bob Dylan* (New York: William Morrow, 1986); Howard Sounes, *Down the Highway: The Life of Bob Dylan* (New York: Grove Press, 2001); Elijah Wald, *How the Beatles Destroyed Rock 'n' Roll: An Alternative History of American Popular Music* (New York: Oxford University Press, 2009); and Sean Wilentz, *Bob Dylan in America* (New York: Doubleday, 2010).

Reference/Statistics

Useful reference books include *The Gallup Poll: Public Opinion, 1935–1971*, vol. 3 (New York: Random House, 1972); Susan Carter et al., eds., *Historical Statistics of the United States: Earlier Times to the Present*, 5 vols. (New York: Cambridge University Press, 2006); US Census Bureau, *Statistical History of the United States* (New York: Basic Books, 1976); and annual editions of the US Census Bureau, *Statistical Abstract of the United States* (Washington, DC: US Government Printing Office).

INDEX